THE NEW GOLD MOUNTAIN
THE SUCCESS OF CHINESE AMERICANS IN GREATER CHINA

... And What You Need To Know To Get There

by Larry Wang

ANDIREMAR PUBLICATIONS

Published in Hong Kong by:
ANDIREMAR PUBLICATIONS
4/F Hang Shun Building
10-12 Wyndham Street
Central, Hong Kong

ISBN 962-85270-1-0

Design/Cover: George Ngan/New Strategy
Illustrations: Henry Wong
Layout: Polly Yu Production Ltd

Printed and bound in Hong Kong

To my Mom and Dad

for their unconditional support of my life in Asia

and

to my Grandma for her inspiration,

the reason why I'm here

Author's Notes

. . . Some Important Clarifications

Before you begin, I'd like to define the term Greater China, or the Greater China region. Greater China encompasses Hong Kong, Mainland China, and Taiwan. What links connects these countries is that they are all places where a Chinese dialect is the dominant language. Therefore, when I use the term "the region" or "here," I'm referring mainly to the Greater China region, where I'm based.

When I use the term Chinese American, I am referring to both American-born Chinese (also known as ABCs) and Asian-born returnees (ABRs, or Greater China-born Chinese who have lived in North America and decided to later return). It's these Chinese Americans, with bilingual and bicultural Asian and western backgrounds, who will benefit most from this book. Later, I elaborate on the main characteristics of both groups.

Finally, the anecdotes and stories that follow are drawn from the experiences of Chinese Americans in Greater China. I believe, however, the viewpoints also apply to the situations of other Asian and Southeast Asian Americans looking to return to their home countries. Furthermore, the job-seeking advice is highly applicable to Canadian, European and Australian Chinese, as well as Asiaphiles and any others with the background and skills to achieve results in Greater China's localized business environment.

Acknowledgments

The entire process of putting together this book has been an enjoyable one, particularly the opportunity to meet and speak in depth with so many interesting and inspiring people about their experiences in Greater China. In addition to those included in the book, I'd like to thank the following people who may not have been mentioned, but who's comments and insights were essential in researching and developing the content I have shared: Crystal Chan, Vaughn Chang, Andrea Chen, David Chen, Curtis Chin, Danny Chiu, Greg Eng, Virginia Fang, Steve Hale, Brad Holt, Julie Chang Holt, Calvin Hsu, Leonard Kim, Frank Lee, Susan Lin, Sandi Mao, Renee So, Yvonne So, Pui-Wing Tam, David Townsend, Ronica Wang, Lily Wu, Earl Yen, and Joanne-Lee Young.

I'd also like to thank the readers who helped provide invaluable feedback on some very unpolished, early manuscript drafts: Francis Chen, Connie Hsu, Lily Lai, Victor Li, Virginia Li, Judi Moi, Betty Wong and Caroline Wang. Thanks in particular to Lilian Yip for her willingness to painstakingly review and edit several such draft versions of the book. I'd also like to thank Henry Wong for the deft sense of humor he has incorporated into the book's illustrations, and George Ngan for the book layout and cover design.

Finally, I'd like to especially thank all my colleagues at Wang & Li who contributed considerable time and energy in reviewing and researching the book and gave their full support to this project: Carmen Koon, Chui Lau, Carol Lee, Simone Leung, Luci Li, Judy Muramoto, Jennifer Sun, Catherine Wang, Sondra WuDunn and Sandra Yuan. And my utmost appreciation to Vivian Tsai and Christine Hsu who helped in the writing of several key sections for the book.

Contents

Part V: The Wrap-up

Introduction

"Our time is now!" That's what the Chinese American woman emphasized while being interviewed for this book. "Nowhere else in the world and at no other time has there existed such opportunities for Chinese Americans," she added. At age 31, she was based in Hong Kong as an Asia Pacific regional marketing manager, covering nine countries for a major U.S. consumer products company. Her brief statement came before I even had a chance to reveal to her my theme for *The New Gold Mountain,* or my insights about Chinese Americans in Greater China. Talk about someone stealing your thunder.

But I was glad she said it. Her assessment was exactly right. Chinese Americans are taking off in their careers throughout the region. Look around and you'll find countless numbers of bilingual and bicultural Chinese Americans using their blend of Asian and western backgrounds and abilities to achieve fast-track professional success and pursue exceptional opportunities before them.

It's no secret that Greater China is flourishing. Its surging economy is creating tremendous, long-awaited chances for multinationals bold and smart enough to meet the demands of rapidly developing markets. Yet another exciting, under-recognized story has emerged beneath the macroeconomic picture. To grow and succeed, these multinationals are in dire need of qualified staff. They're hungry for professionals with a foot in both the East and the West. They want people who possess the best of both worlds in terms of culture, language, education, and professional training, and who can effectively implement western corporate business strategies within local markets. In response, bilingual and bicultural Chinese Americans are fitting the bill. They are a key group providing the capabilities needed to support the region's unquestioned drive to develop and modernize.

I've written this book to share the exciting story of Chinese Americans who are excelling in Greater China. As a Chinese American myself, I've always identified closely with the professional and personal aspirations of other Chinese Americans who desire to be here. I even started a cross-border recruiting firm, Wang & Li Asia Resources, to support the presence, interests, and opportunities of the Chinese American community in the region. Wang & Li specializes in bridging the gap between bilingual and bicultural professionals from the U.S. and Greater China-based multinational firms seeking each other out. Since our inception in January 1994, we've advised and placed hundreds who have become part of Greater China's growing professional workforce. Increasingly, many find themselves playing significant roles in the success of both multinational firms and the region's overall emergence. I believe their story may be a real eye-opener for many in the U.S. who are unaware of the widespread achievements of Chinese Americans out here.

My other reason for writing this book is to provide practical advice on how to find a job in Greater China. I'd like to make the prospect of living and working in the region more accessible to those with such an interest. Although outstanding career opportunities await, getting here is no easy task. If you've ever tried to search for a job here from the States, you'll know how true this is. In my own case, the step from first thinking about coming out to actually finding a suitable opportunity was a giant one. It took me nearly five years! Having grown up in North Carolina and Maryland, I possessed few skills to function, let alone do business, in Greater China. I couldn't speak Mandarin (how would a kid raised in the South know that speaking Chinese would be important someday). I had limited exposure to Chinese people (other than family gatherings and Chinese restaurants), had never lived before in Asia (only visited once with my grandma), and had little knowledge of the region's business environment.

It wasn't by chance that I arrived. I chose to come and actively pursued it. Over the years, my efforts included obtaining an MBA focused on international business, an intensive study Chinese program at Middlebury College's summer language school, a summer internship working in Taipei, and numerous Mandarin tutors. Ultimately, there were few resources to turn to that were helpful in my job search quest. Even getting useful Greater China job market information was difficult. In the end, it was an unanticipated connection that led to my relocation to Asia. The Chinese never underestimate the power of *guanxi*, or connections. I'm telling you, out here it really works!

Fortunately, getting to Greater China is much easier today. There are far more footsteps to follow and resources to draw upon compared to just a few years ago. This book shares the experiences and perspectives of Chinese Americans who have successfully taken the plunge to live and work here. They've either done it the smart way or learned it the hard way.

This book also addresses basic, but difficult to answer issues that hold back many from coming to the region. It identifies key skills that multinational managers are seeking. It provides a realistic job search approach to help you connect with the many openings out here. It also presents the other side of the picture. Living and working in Greater China is not for everyone. Drawbacks include long working hours, grueling business travel, cultural adjustments, burnout, transience, and a less diverse lifestyle. By anticipating these trade-offs, disappointment from unrealistic expectations can be avoided and the risk of relocating unprepared minimized.

Finally, this book highlights some of the deeper, personal aspirations that Greater China is fulfilling for Chinese Americans. For instance, since coming here I've learned to speak Mandarin (admittedly with a heavy western accent). I've come to understand a tremendous amount about Chinese people, culture, and society. I've also been able to develop my Asian interests and express my bicultural persona more completely than I ever could in the U.S. I believe the realization of such personal goals are extremely relevant to many Chinese Americans who move out here and helps make Greater China a very meaningful experience.

It may be somewhat ironic that there is such a strong desire to return to Asia among so many Chinese Americans who make up the current generation of young professionals. For our parents and grandparents, the dream was to head West. During their day, countless families and individuals from Greater China went to extraordinary lengths to make the trip across the Pacific Ocean and reach for what was considered the land of opportunity. In America, they would arrive in San Francisco, also referred to by these new immigrants as *Jiu Jin Shan*, or simply *The Gold Mountain*.

My own grandparents came to the U.S. from Mainland China almost 50 years ago, leaving behind virtually everything they owned. As an immigrant family, they embarked on a journey over the next several decades, which may represent a somewhat familiar one for many Chinese American households. My maternal grandparents started a series of Chinese restaurants. The first was a modest chop suey and chow mein restaurant in New York City's Washington Heights in uptown Manhattan. Within a few years, they opened one of the first and most successful Chinese restaurants, introducing traditional, gourmet Chinese cuisine to the U.S. In its day, "it was the place to be seen among New York's social circle," according to my aunt. I can still remember the celebrity pictures of Sandy Koufax, Kirk Douglas, Ed McMahon, and Barbara Feldon (remember Agent 99 from *Get Smart*?) on the walls.

Meanwhile, their children — my parents, aunts, and uncles — studied hard for the chance to attend the best schools and to pursue worthy vocations. Over the years, the masters and doctoral degrees accumulated and the achievements as academics, doctors, lawyers, and civil servants mounted. In turn, their hard work and perseverance resulted in a comfortable life and privileged opportunities for their children — my brother, sister, cousins, and me.

Certainly, many others have succeeded and found a life much better in America than they would have ever seen in Greater China. As a community, Chinese Americans have achieved an impressive level of success. Yet, the reasons why many Chinese Americans are returning to the region today are unmistakable. Greater China is proving to be a place where the potential for Chinese Americans to excel can be even greater and more of a reality than what the U.S. can offer. It's a place where Chinese Americans are finding opportunities to be exceptional and to do exceptional things, where they are able to obtain gratifying professional and personal rewards far above what they might achieve elsewhere.

Although it may sound like it, I did not write this book to sell Greater China. There are numerous others more qualified than I who can talk about the region's phenomenal development and economic outlook. Instead, this book tries to highlight a simple truth: Greater China is *the* place to be for bilingual, bicultural Chinese Americans. It is *The New Gold Mountain* for many of today's generation of Chinese Americans. Through this book, I hope many others will come to experience the riches that the region can bring to life.

Part I

Chinese Americans In Greater China

Chapter 1 An Exceptional Time

Everyone I know who moves to Greater China remembers the exact date they arrived. Mine was September 23, 1990. When I landed in Taipei, I felt like I was *the* one, the original Chinese American pioneering Asia. I was 30 years old, coming from a place (the United States) where I was comfortable with my life and at a point in my career where I was beginning to feel established. Yet, here I was moving to a place I was relatively unfamiliar with and totally unestablished in. What was I thinking?!?

The move wouldn't have seemed so monumental if I knew what to expect. Unfortunately, I found no role models to follow. Rarely did I run into anyone whose situation was similar to my own. Other Chinese Americans I knew of out here were typically of two types. They were either senior-level expat managers or fresh college graduates who were studying Chinese and teaching English. I was neither. I was a mid-career professional, who was trying to apply in Greater China the several years of work experience I had gained in the States.

Of course, there were a few others scattered about with backgrounds and ambitions similar to mine. Like myself, they were also paving their own roads. But I wasn't running into many of them. As a result, I often felt isolated. I even dramatized my situation. Without other examples to follow, nor fellow brethren to accompany me through this unexplored region, I envisioned myself as the lone person blazing a trail for my kind. In my mind, I was like *The Last of the Mohicans* (or actually, the first in my case).

Back then, I also had a recurring feeling of being an oddity to those around me. With few previous encounters with Chinese Americans to draw from, local Taiwanese just didn't know what to make of me. Their inquiries were constant and remarkably similar. Why are you here? Did you come to Taiwan to have fun? Wasn't your life successful in the U.S.? Their puzzlement with my background was best reflected in my frequent conversations with Taipei's cab drivers. Upon hearing my heavily accented "take me to ..." instructions in Mandarin, a repeated dialogue would inevitably unfold.

Taipei cab driver:	Ni bu shi Taiwan ren.	(You aren't Taiwanese)
Me:	*Mei cuo.*	*(That's right)*
Taipei cab driver	Ni cong nali lai de?	(Where are you from?)
Me:	*Ni cai.*	*(You guess)*
Taipei cab driver:	Ni shi Riben ren.	(You're Japanese)
Me:	*Wo bu shi.*	*(No, I'm not)*
Taipei cab driver:	Ni shi Hanguo ren.	(You're Korean)
Me:	*Wo bu shi.*	*(Nope)*
Taipei cab driver:	Ni shi Philippine ren ma?	(Are you Filipino?)
Me:	*Wo bu shi.*	*(Wrong again)*
Taipei cab driver:	Ni shi nali ren?	(What the hell are you then???)
Me:	*Wo shi Meiguo huaqiao.*	*(I'm Chinese American)*
Taipei cab driver:	Zhen de, ... keshi, wei shenme ni de Guoyu zenme name lan?	(Get out of town!, ... then why is your Chinese so bad?)

This usually led to an unsolicited debate in which the cab driver would then want to know whether I thought I was Chinese or American. No matter how I responded, neither answer ever seemed to be the right one. If I claimed Chinese, the driver would say, "yes, you have a Chinese face, but everything else about you is American." If I said American, they would say, "but your face is not white like other Americans. Your parents are from Asia. You're Chinese people!"

Normally, I didn't mind the discussions. Chatting it up with cab drivers was good practice for my Mandarin (unfortunately they were right, it needed a lot of work). But sometimes I was too tired and just not in the mood to explain or justify who I was. Was it possible to go somewhere without getting in a heated debate with a total stranger? By the end of some rides, I'd be almost screaming in my head in an Elephantman-like way, "I am a Chinese American! I am a Chinese American!"

When I first arrived in Greater China, that's the way it was. Chinese Americans were a huge unknown. Overall, few people viewed us as an asset of any kind. If there was a prevailing opinion, the most common one seemed to be that we were the worst of both worlds. With accented Chinese, non-native demeanors, and poor understanding of Chinese culture, we weren't really Chinese. At the same time, because of our Asian faces, somehow we were less American or western than our Caucasian peers. In effect, we were a kind of undesirable mutant! Sometimes, it was difficult not to feel that way.

How things have changed in a few short years. During that entire first year in Taipei, I could count on two hands the number of Chinese Americans I encountered. Recently, I went to a party at a club in Lan Kwai Fong, Hong Kong's popular nightlife area. There were easily over 100 Chinese Americans at just this one gathering. After exchanging business cards with several others (also known as the Asian handshake), I quickly collected a stack that identified a virtual *Who's Who* of Fortune 1000 firms. Morgan Stanley, Nike, Microsoft, AT Kearney, Walt Disney, Andersen Consulting, and Merrill Lynch were among the companies represented.

It was an inspiring sight. But it was only a reflection of what's happening in Greater China right now. These days you can run into Chinese Americans everywhere you go in Taiwan, Hong Kong, and China. Rather than being an oddity, our presence is now widespread. In so many instances, Chinese Americans are leading major business initiatives, defining corporate strategies, and managing growing operations for multinational firms. Our success has significantly elevated our visibility and confidence level in the region. In Greater China, we have found a place for ourselves, and we are thriving.

Chinese Americans In The United States

Glass Ceiling

The unhindered, upwardly mobile career tracks for Chinese Americans in Greater China are in many ways the antithesis of what many Chinese Americans in the U.S. experience. Whenever I speak at Asian American business conferences or professional forums in the U.S., the glass ceiling topic is often touched upon. Unfortunately, it's an issue many Chinese Americans are still dealing with to some degree.

Statistics indicate that there exists a significant disproportion of Chinese American management staff in "Corporate America," in spite of the fact that Chinese Americans are among the best educated and trained demographic groups in the U.S. A survey of Fortune 1500 companies conducted by Korn/Ferry International in 1989 found that 97 percent of senior level male managers were Caucasian, while only 0.3 percent were Asian American. This despite that Asian Americans made up 3 percent of the U.S. population and were more than one and a half times as likely to have a bachelor's degree than Caucasian Americans, according to 1994 national statistics. Asian Americans also consistently received a lower earnings return on education at almost every education level. For example, in a 1990 California survey, Asian American per capita income was 27.8 percent below that of the Caucasian American population for comparable professionals who were 35 years old.

Many believe the inequalities persist because, to a large extent, career success in the U.S. is influenced by how well one can fit into a traditional Caucasian American, old boys network, particularly when moving up through management levels. Whatever the reasons, it is not my intention to make any controversial statements about the U.S. or its overall corporate culture, or to go into the social aspects of why the glass ceiling exists. I merely wish to highlight the frustrations many Chinese Americans feel with regard to their career-track experience in the U.S.

One Chinese American investment banker described how he felt while working in "Corporate America," when he was a financial analyst on Wall Street. "I had a black colleague who was well liked and on a fast track for promotion. I don't mean this in a detrimental way, but he was the whitest black person I'd ever met. When I looked at myself, I began to wonder if this was how I was, too. For my own fast-track career, did I have to 'out-white' everyone else just to fit in? There were certain aspects of my Asian personality I was always hiding. I never felt entirely comfortable about that."

Under-utilization Of Who We Are

Beyond the glass ceiling issue, there is another factor that does not necessarily work against the career advancement of Chinese Americans in the U.S., but certainly contributes little towards it. That is, for the most part, our dual language and cultural backgrounds add negligible value towards our ability to perform and advance in the U.S. business world.

Admittedly, this is not entirely the case for all Chinese American professionals. Many corporations have recognized the need for multilingual and multicultural capabilities in order to target and serve ethnic markets and consumers in the U.S. more effectively. As part of one of the most affluent and free-spending minority groups in the country, some Chinese Americans are able to apply their Chinese language and cultural backgrounds in jobs that are aimed at developing business within the Chinese American community. Others are also able to find positions within U.S. headquarters where job responsibilities involve regular interaction and communications with operations and customers in Asia.

Overall, however, these types of positions provide opportunities for relatively few to leverage their ethnic Chinese backgrounds. For Chinese Americans in the U.S., how much benefit does being bilingual and bicultural have in our job on a daily basis? How often does our "Asianness" come into play in what we do or how we do things? Unfortunately, most bilingual and bicultural Chinese Americans significantly under-utilize the abilities they possess. Although many I meet have comfortable, successful careers in the States, they feel they're capable of much more beyond what they're currently doing.

Chinese Americans in Greater China

Above The Glass Ceiling

For Chinese Americans in Greater China, it's a different story. In my seven years here, I've never even heard the term "glass ceiling" used. Instead, career goals are pursued with significantly fewer limitations or restrictions. Career advancement is based entirely on performance and ability. And rather than being a non-factor, bilingual and bicultural abilities have a premium value. As part of its rapid development, the region is acquiring many of the best new products, services, technologies, and management approaches that the West can offer. As multinationals deliver these to Greater China, they require well-trained employees with western business skills and expertise, who also have strong Chinese language skills and an understanding of local people, culture, and society.

Competitive Advantage

In many ways, Greater China is evolving into a mix of the best of two worlds, the East and the West, which reflects the exact make up and abilities that many Chinese Americans possess. Increasingly, business in the region encompasses a broad spectrum of scenarios, from the entirely Asian to the entirely western and everything in between. Chinese Americans are finding themselves among those capable of adapting to the range of situations that are encountered.

The implication is clear. Bilingual and bicultural Chinese Americans are finding themselves with a distinct competitive advantage. It's not about having either Asian abilities or western professional training alone, but the combination of both that's at a premium. Whereas in the States, you may be just "an average Joe" among thousands of other highly qualified professionals, in Greater China you are able to use everything you possess to their fullest extent. "For the first time I feel that my Asian upbringing works to my advantage," describes the same investment banker in Hong Kong today, who previously felt he had to suppress his Chinese background. "Out here, there's no need to camouflage it. I can express myself more and be who I am."

Better Equipped To Play The Game

Frank Chen was one of the first Chinese Americans I met in Asia. When he was five, Frank moved to the U.S. from Taipei. Although he spent most of his upbringing in L.A., his parents spoke Mandarin with him at home. In 1989, at 28, he returned to Taipei with the goal of attaining success in Asia as a marketing professional. Today, he lives in Shanghai where he's the marketing director for a major consumer goods multinational, responsible for developing and implementing his company's marketing strategy in Mainland China.

Frank is more specific about what Chinese Americans can provide. He refers to his ability to oversee key customer and business relationships. "What we can offer is a greater sensitivity to local situations, as well as a knowledge of what the game out here is all about and how to play it," he says. "For instance, in China, building a relationship is extremely important in doing business. There are so many instances where my Chinese background has helped me establish a connection much faster. Because I speak Mandarin, the Chinese parties I deal with have a greater level of comfort talking about the consumer market or just shooting the breeze with me. At the same time, my western education and experience give me a lot of credibility with them."

"There are so many instances where my Chinese background has helped me establish a connection much faster."

Frank also highlights his ability to communicate more openly and effectively with local staff. "Within my company, co-workers tend to come to me when they want to discuss something either sensitive or personal. To non-Asian managers, they'll always give a polite face, but usually won't go deeper into what they're thinking. With me, I'm treated as someone who is more like them. They'll tell me what's really on their mind. Management knows I can understand the nuances of what's going on with the local staff and can help bridge the gap to handle a lot of situations better. That's viewed as an important contribution to the company."

Eye Catching Success

For Chinese Americans in Greater China today, the professional opportunities are real and happening. Success stories can be found everywhere.

Running The Show

When Celia Chong came to Hong Kong in early 1991, her timing was just right. She joined Star TV (the region's largest satellite TV station today) as they were about to launch their network. Although her previous work experience in the U.S. was in selling public television programming to overseas stations, at Star TV she helped launch and run a TV channel. Over the next three years she learned everything from television operations and marketing to how to cater to Asian viewing tastes.

In January 1994, she joined Turner Broadcasting Systems as the general manager for their regional satellite cable channel, TNT & Cartoon Network. She was 33 years old. Celia was the first person to be hired by TNT in the region. She has since built an office of over 100 staff that broadcasts cartoons and movies all over the Asia Pacific. "If I was in the States, I might be running a small station in a small market at this point in my career," she confesses. "It's highly unlikely I'd have the same opportunity to be in this position with such a major international media network."

In The Money

Ivy Tai came to Hong Kong in 1991 hoping to find an environment with better opportunities to apply her technical background. She never would have guessed back then that she'd be doing what she is today. "It's not a career path I would have envisioned in a million years," says Ivy, describing the transition to her current job as an executive director of private banking for a major U.S. investment bank in Hong Kong.

Ivy graduated from Coopers Union, a small engineering college in New York City. When IBM called to see if she wanted to join their Hong Kong consulting practice, she thought she had found the right job for herself. She did extremely well there, gaining salary increases that were three times what she was previously receiving in the States.

When Asia's financial markets began heating up in 1993, she was approached by several major financial institutions. She realized the once-in-a-lifetime opportunity to make a significant career change. "I chose private banking because of the tremendous amount of wealth that individuals were accumulating in Asia," explains Ivy, age 25 at the time. "I didn't think I was the prototypical private banker though. I had a limited finance background, was not a proven marketer, and did not have a high flying client base."

Ivy quickly learned that although those experiences helped, most important in succeeding as a private banker was the motivation and drive — of which she had plenty — to do well. Particularly attractive to the bank that hired her was her professional acumen, intelligence, and Mandarin language skills. They brought her on board to cover the Taiwan market. Today, Ivy finds herself dealing with clients whose net worth exceeds US$1 billion in some cases. "Anything is possible out here. You just have to be focused," she says modestly.

Leading the Charge

James Yao was a product manager at Oracle in San Francisco, where he managed the research, development, and sales of a hot new product. With a well-rounded technical and marketing background, his career prospects at the home office appeared excellent.

In 1990, Oracle's presence in Asia was still in its infancy, with start-up operations in Hong Kong and China. Management saw the need for an office in Taiwan as well, and called on James for the job. He was 24 years old. Within two years, James grew the operation from zero to 25 employees and US$6 million in revenues annually. Having done such an outstanding job, management next assigned him to Oracle China in Beijing.

"My timing was good when I went to China. Economic reform was just taking off," he recalls. He was sent as the deputy managing director, responsible for overseeing business in the southern half of the country. He was also given responsibilities as the technical director for China. James' involvement was instrumental in growing Oracle's China business from US$3 million to US$40 million in annual revenues and from 10 to 120 employees in two years.

"If I had stayed in the States, I'd probably be a vice president for product development somewhere," James speculates. "I certainly wouldn't have received the general management experience, the opportunity to take on mission critical responsibilities, or the chance to deal with the types of influential people I have out here."

Similar situations are happening to Chinese Americans in other industries as well. There are Chinese American regional marketing directors for major consumer products companies, partners at consulting and accounting firms, and managing directors for major advertising and public relations agencies. The widespread career achievements send a promising message to other Chinese Americans. "Here, you can aspire to be the general manager or managing director of the Asia practice of a major multinational," says Neil Tan, regional business development manager for Avery Dennison in Hong Kong. "It's encouraging to look around and see examples of Chinese Americans reaching the top positions in every industry. We may not all achieve that level of success, but at least the goal is realistic."

Fulfilling Personal Aspirations

Without a doubt, the exceptional professional opportunities and corresponding financial rewards are leading many Chinese Americans to Greater China during this particular period of time. But career and money are not the only reasons. Chinese Americans are coming in pursuit of significant and meaningful personal goals as well. These are aspirations tied to a Chinese heritage that runs deep within many of us.

Exploring Roots

Some come to get more in touch with the region and its culture or to better explore their Asian side. One woman went to China for the first time to study Ching Dynasty history at Beijing University. She had won a scholarship after graduating from college to study abroad. Her stay in China was intended as a one year diversion to pursue this special interest of hers before embarking on her career. She did not expect the trip to affect her the way it did. "My life definitely took a turn after my stay in Beijing. The entire experience was so positive," she recalls. "I met relatives I never knew I had and felt a personal connection with the people and the country."

After returning to San Francisco for a year and a half, she moved back to China to spend more time there. It's where she's been working for the past eight years now. "There's no place else I'd rather be," she says. "It's a great feeling to be Chinese and to be in China at this time. The culture and language I pick up everyday help me develop a great balance in my life."

Kathy Chen: 11 Years Abroad

Personal History: *Born and raised in Washington D.C. Living in Greater China since 1987.*

Parents: *Mom and Dad from Fujian province. Mom grew up in Taipei. Dad grew up in Sichuan province.*

Education: *B.A. in English Literature and M.A. in English from the University of Chicago.*

Languages: *Native English speaker. Fluent Mandarin learned through classroom study and daily use in Taipei and Beijing.*

From a look at her early upbringing, Kathy Chen would be one of the last people you'd expect to have spent the past 11 years living in Taipei, Hong Kong, and Beijing. "I grew up in an upper middle class, white neighborhood," Kathy says. "I didn't have any Chinese or Chinese American friends back then. There weren't any others. Nor did I have any interest in Asia or Asian things. As far as I was concerned, I was an American who happened to look Chinese."

Kathy's interest in Asia began gradually while learning Mandarin in college. She discovered that she liked studying the language and became intent on

Kathy Chen with a local Mosuo tribe official on a mountainside in Yunnan province, during an ASWJ reporting trip in Mainland China (September 1995)

improving her Chinese. After graduation, she decided to move to Taipei to enroll at The Stanford Center, one of the world's most recognized Mandarin language programs. Soon after completing her studies, an opportunity appeared to write for *The China Post,* Taiwan's largest English language daily newspaper. Initially, it was just a chance for Kathy to gain some work experience and earn extra cash.

Unknown to Kathy at the time, it was the start of something big. Friends told her she had a real talent as a reporter. Other reporting jobs began to present themselves. Her career has been in full swing ever since. Beyond *The China Post*, she has also worked for United Press International in Taiwan and for Reuters in Hong Kong. Since 1993, she has been the Beijing correspondent for *The Wall Street Journal* and *The Asian Wall Street Journal*.

Kathy looks upon her years in Greater China with satisfaction. "Each city I've lived in has been a tremendous experience. Taipei is where I became fluent in Mandarin. The country was also going through major changes then, and people were very open to and interested in interacting with westerners. As a journalist, Hong Kong's energy for business was both unique and exciting. But I've liked being in Beijing the most. China is so vast and complex. The country is a fascinating story to cover. As a reporter, I've been able to witness and write about all sorts of things. In the process, I've also made a lot of close Chinese friends."

At a personal level, Kathy believes she has gained a great deal in understanding both herself and her Chinese American background. "Being here has helped me understand my parents and grandparents better. I'm more appreciative of the differences and more aware of the similarities between us," she says. "It's also allowed me to clarify my values and become comfortable with myself as a Chinese American. At the same time, it's helped me to recognize the freedom and individuality I enjoy as someone who is an American."

Improving On Language Skills

Others come to develop Chinese language abilities by spending a semester or a year abroad studying Mandarin at universities or language programs in Taiwan or China. They may enroll in one of the many *bu shi ban* (language cram centers) or do a language exchange, where you swap equal amounts of time with a local partner by teaching them English in return for being tutored in Chinese.

For some, the interest in learning Mandarin doesn't necessarily come early on. One woman took a trip to Hangzhou one summer while in college to spend time with relatives she had never met before. During her visit, she felt embarrassed and frustrated that she couldn't communicate well with them. When she returned to the U.S., she began taking Mandarin classes at school. Just two years later she moved to Beijing to work and continue her Mandarin studies. She now speaks fluently after having spent five years in China.

Making A Difference

There are also those who want to be in a place where they believe they are having an impact. They want to play a role in the development of not only the Greater China region, but of the society and its people as well. "I feel like I'm helping to lead those around me on the right path," says a Chinese American woman working in Shanghai. "Mainlanders have seen so many disappointments in the past. I try to encourage them not to think in the short term. Aside from just training them, I also help them invest time and effort in their skills and plan for their future. I do think that China will become great on its current track. When that happens, I'll feel proud as someone Chinese who was a part of that."

An Irresistible Attraction

Others are simply drawn by a desire or fascination. Another woman came to Taipei for the first time on the *Jian Tan* tour (popularly known as *The Love Boat)* after graduating from college. She planned to spend the six weeks that summer sightseeing and partying in Taipei with the 1000 or so other Chinese Americans her age who were also on the trip sponsored by the Taiwan government's Overseas Chinese Affairs Commission. Afterwards, she would return to Chicago to look for a full time job.

Personal Travelogue

My first trip to Asia was in September of 1985. I was 25 years old. My brother and I accompanied our grandmother back to Mainland China for a seven city tour. It was only her second visit back in almost 40 years. She was 72 at the time.

Although we came along to take care of her, it quickly became apparent during the trip that she had far more stamina and energy than we did. She was the one who ended up taking care of us! There's a picture I have of her and me sitting on the back of a camel. The picture was taken on a sand dune in Dunhuang, one of the western-most cities in inner China. I'm sitting in front looking a bit off-balanced and unnerved. My grandmother is sitting behind me, peering off into the distance with a look of anticipation. In a nutshell, that's my grandma.

The trip was highly memorable for many other reasons. China was just opening up at the time. There was an early spattering of blue jeans, colorful fashions, and western consumer goods. For the most part, however, the flavor of everything we saw was distinctly Chinese. Blue and gray straight-legged suits were the standard dress. The people we met were rustic and weathered. The overall tempo of life was relaxed and lazy, as pedestrians and bicyclers set the pace within the cities and villages we visited. The entire country was very much as underdeveloped and poor as I had imagined.

Throughout the tour, I remember feeling completely humbled. I sensed real admiration from the people I met over the fact that I was a Chinese person who also happened to be an American. My grandparents and parents were able to immigrate to the U.S. For that reason alone, through no doing of my own, I had unlimited opportunities and dreams to pursue. These people did not. That made a deep impression on me. From that point on, I knew I would someday return to Asia. I hoped to participate in some way in the modernization of the region. Five years later I moved to Taipei.

Unexpectedly, she found herself completely taken in by the excitement and energy of the region. "It was a whole new world that I could never have imagined before coming out," she recalled. Although she hadn't thought of working in the region before, she decided to look for a job in Taipei. She did not to return to the States that summer. Over the past six years she has worked in both Taipei and Hong Kong. She's now contemplating her next move to the Mainland.

ALL You Can Be

Finally, for Chinese Americans who try to balance out the influences and attractions of two distinct cultural identities, Greater China offers a unique chance to fully express and apply your Asian and western backgrounds. As Chinese Americans, we each have our personal view as to what degree we are Chinese or American. Depending on our upbringing and influences, our bicultural make-up varies widely for each of us. Some feel they are 100 percent American, others nearly 100 percent Chinese. Most of us find ourselves somewhere in between.

In my own case, I've lived in the U.S. almost my entire life. I admit, I'm extremely westernized. I project that strongly on the surface. If pressed, I'd even define myself as 90 percent American. But that much smaller 10 percent that I identify as Chinese deeply influences key areas of my persona, including my overall values, interests, and viewpoints on many things. It determines a great deal of who I am.

Wherever you fall on the spectrum, in Greater China your bicultural identity can come to light in its truest and most complete form. I believe the gratification this brings is a major reason why many Chinese Americans not only come to the region, but choose to remain as long as they do.

Intertwined Objectives

No matter your reasons or inspirations for coming out, there is no shortage of opportunities to both give and receive in satisfying ways. I can relate well to how one Chinese American, who works for a U.S. media company in Taipei, describes what he finds rewarding about being in Asia. "Out here, I wear many hats," he said. "In almost every encounter, I'm a teacher, facilitator, or ambassador. At the same time, I'm also a student. I like having the chance to step into all those roles."

The pursuit and attainment of professional and personal aspirations are tightly bound together. In fact, they are inseparable. When I first arrived, my intent was to ultimately play a role in Greater China's economic resurgence, perhaps by helping to bridge two cultures and two regions highly interested in each other. The personal growth I've experienced, the development of my Mandarin language skills and understanding of Chinese people, culture, and society has not only been rewarding, it has also led to my ability to pursue the career goals I've set.

Chapter 2 Outstanding Career Opportunities

Although my personal reasons for coming to Greater China were significant, very clearly, I came in pursuit of career goals as well. Professionally, I wanted to learn, be challenged, and see opportunities. The region has not disappointed in any of these areas. There's a dangling carrot enticing those of us out here. People drive themselves because that carrot isn't merely teasing the pursuant. It is attainable. Hard work does pay off.

Chinese Americans are finding chances to take on responsibilities they would not normally have to the same degree, and certainly not at the same stage in their careers, if in the U.S. It's not as if those here feel they can't be successful in the States. In fact, many were on fast tracks before moving out. In Greater China, however, career opportunities occur at an entirely different level. Advancement is quicker and reaches higher than in the U.S. Whereas the U.S. economy has lingered in a steady state, in Asia, the pie keeps getting bigger and bigger. And whereas you're expected to wait your turn in the States, that's not the case in Greater China. There is not an oversupply of quality managers at the middle to senior levels in the region. Management bottlenecks are not found. Add to that the exceptional demand for Asian and western backgrounds and it becomes clear why many Chinese Americans are moving quickly up the career ladder. If you want to see just how good you are and how high you can go, Greater China is the place to test yourself.

Greater Exposure And Responsibility

Go to any happy hour or weekend house party in Hong Kong and you'll meet throngs of young professionals working in the region. Without fail, conversations soon turn to work. You'll hear a slew of stories about major deals and projects being worked on, jet-set travel schedules, and ridiculously demanding work hours. (Yes, these conversations can get tiresome. But don't worry, you'll soon pipe in as well with your own work-related escapades).

Albert Wang: Carrying The Ball

Personal History: *Born and raised in upstate New York. Living in Hong Kong since September 1993.*

Parents: *Mom and Dad born in the Shanghai area. Raised in Taipei.*

Education: *B.A. in Political Science from Colgate University. Law degree from George Washington University.*

Languages: *Native English speaker. Grew up speaking Mandarin at home and attending Chinese school once a week.*

During the first year at his law firm in Hong Kong, Albert Wang was assigned to a large joint venture project in China where his firm represented a multinational beverage client. He played the lead role in the negotiations and due diligence on behalf of the client. When the time came to close the deal, the partner decided that Albert understood the project better than anyone else. Rather than go himself, he sent Albert to Hebei province, outside of Beijing, to attend the signing and close the US$80 million deal on his own. Albert was 25 years old. It was at this point when he was sure he had made the right decision in coming to Asia.

Albert's initial move to Hong Kong after law school was solely based on a feeling that there were tremendous opportunities to be found here. He did not have a job lined up though. In addition, both his exposure to the territory and contacts were limited. He gave himself three months to come up with something.

Albert Wang (far left) and friends during a night out at a karaoke lounge in Seoul, Korea (October 1997)

After two and a half months, just under his self-established deadline, he landed a position at a major U.S. law firm. He was hired as part of the China practice.

Albert began a six-month trial period, after which his performance was to be evaluated. Initially, he spent a great deal of time improving his Chinese language skills, particularly for legal vocabulary. It was a tough time. "Although I spoke Mandarin growing up, I couldn't really read or write it well," he says. "Getting comfortable reviewing Chinese legal contracts, as well as negotiating in Chinese was an important step." His persistence paid off. After six months, he was made a permanent employee with the same package as the other expatriate attorneys sent from the New York head office.

The career benefits he has seen since coming to Hong Kong are clear to Albert. "One rewarding aspect is the impact I feel from my efforts. For instance, I often deal with corporate counsel from major multinationals with up to 20 years of legal experience. But it may be their first China deal. Although I may have much less overall experience, I'm able to advise them on aspects of Chinese law they know little about. It's gratifying knowing that you're adding value on major deals, even though you're at a relatively junior level."

Albert attributes his involvement in large transactions to his ability to review both the English and Chinese documentation and to his willingness to take on responsibility. "There isn't the glossified corporate structure here that you find in the States. There are all sorts of chances to show your stuff and distinguish yourself. To use a football analogy, Asia is for broken field runners. In my case, I'm able to work on high-profile projects and interact with high-level client contacts. But more importantly, I'm given the opportunity to take the point or lead position on transactions a lot sooner. That means exercising the independence and judgment to make things happen at a much earlier stage in my career."

The point is, the average person's involvement in their company's initiatives in the region is substantial. There's a sense of urgency among firms to win business, capture market share, and expand operations. For professionals at all levels, you're given as much responsibility as you can handle. The results are a steep learning curve and the chance to perform.

Business operations in Greater China are also less mature and less structured compared to U.S. ones. Operations tend to run leaner, until the business growth can justify additional resources. Even large multinationals tend to function in a very entrepreneurial, hands-on manner. Most ramp up so fast that many key job functions are not developed or even established.

In addition, companies are not always able to fill a position with the ideal person they have in mind. One line manager summarizes the challenge he has in finding new staff in this way: "There's tremendous pressure to grow the business and enter new markets. To do that you need to increase headcount. With few specialists out here though, it's not always the case that you're hiring the best person for a position. Frequently, you're just hiring the best you can find."

This is why you'll find people doing just about anything and everything. In many situations, you quickly discover that "you da' man" (or da' wo-man) when it comes to handling a job for your company. Suddenly, you're the appointed "expert," despite your lack of expertise in what you're asked to do. This may include setting up new areas of business operations, introducing new products or services, or researching new markets.

Lynne Chen's first job out of UCLA was as a tax consultant at Arthur Andersen in Los Angeles. After completing her MBA at Berkeley's Haas School of Business in 1995, she moved to Shanghai as a manager for Coopers & Lybrand's China Consulting Practice. Today, Lynne is the senior manager for finance and planning for Bacardi-Martini Asia Pacific in Hong Kong. Although her primary responsibilities revolve around strategic planning and finance issues, Lynne has also found herself overseeing the implementation of her company's information technology plans throughout the region. "I'm gaining experience in areas I never thought I'd want to get involved in," she confesses. "I'm learning a lot about different operating areas that are critical to running a business. They're general management type skills that will benefit my career no matter where I am later on."

It's not only the broader scope of work you see, but the regional diversity and Asia-wide perspective as well. "I cover ten countries that span from Japan to Indonesia," says Lynne. "The chance to deal with drastically different markets and cultures is fascinating. I'm always learning something new."

In The Spotlight

If you're the type of person who wants to make a mark, Greater China allows you every chance to do it. Given the flatter corporate structures of multinationals, people in power positions are more accessible. Younger professionals often work closely with senior managers. With the chances to interact with top management, you have more opportunities to both learn and have your contributions recognized. If you're at all good at what you do, you'll stand out.

When she came out of business school, Christine Chow worked as a brand manager in China for Procter & Gamble, at a time when the company was beginning to aggressively expand its China market. Over a three- year period, she launched several major product lines and helped define and establish distribution channels in the mainland. "My career has accelerated," according to Christine. "Here, you can really make an impact. Your efforts are magnified, and that makes everything you do much more exciting. In my case, I worked as a key member of P&G's pioneering team assigned by the company to break into the China market."

"Here, you can really make an impact. Your efforts are magnified, and that makes everything you do much more exciting."

"One of my key roles is to keep U.S. headquarters tuned in to what's happening in Asia," says C.K. Tsang, senior manager in Hong Kong of Asia/Pacific business planning & development for Imagineering, Walt Disney's theme park and attractions division. "It gives me the chance to have significant involvement with major regional projects at the highest levels. For example, I've been pulled into meetings with our Chief Executive Officer, Michael Eisner. And it's not just to attend, but to participate. If I was working in the U.S. office, I don't think I'd even be known to people at the vice president level."

I Can't Believe I'm Doing This At My Age

The opportunities in the region for many Chinese Americans are occurring at very early stages in their career, when such chances would not normally happen. I've met many young professionals, in their mid-twenties to early thirties, who are in critical positions or running significant areas of their firm's business. "That's the challenging and fun part of being out here," says Tom Tsao. "There are so many start-up opportunities you can be a part of."

After graduating from Harvard, Tom joined Merrill Lynch as a corporate finance analyst in New York. He moved to Hong Kong after his third year. In Hong Kong, he was soon promoted to associate and was on a promising career track in one of the bank's fastest growing markets. Then, unexpectedly, he was approached by a start-up Hong Kong investment firm that wanted Tom to help them build their asset management department from scratch. The bank was backed by Chinese money from the mainland, Hong Kong, and Indonesia and had ambitions of becoming the premier Chinese-owned investment bank in the region. After deliberating to size up the opportunity, risk, and company's senior management team, Tom decided to join the new bank.

"Currently, there is no dominant Chinese bank in the region. There's a flat out foot-race going on to become number one." says Tom. "The opportunity is incredibly exciting. I feel like I'm in the center of the action. There's risk of course, but it's a fantastic chance to work side by side with my bank's top management. It's almost inconceivable that what I'm doing now could be happening at this stage of my career back in New York. If things go well, there's the chance for me to become an owner of a major business." In its first year, Tom's group was the top performing small capital fund in Hong Kong. Tom is 27 years old.

Chance To Make Career Changes

I'm constantly amazed at what some people are doing out here, particularly given what they were doing back in the U.S. With a lack of qualified professionals in many areas, Greater China offers outstanding chances to enter new functions and industries. I've heard so many say that, quite frankly, if they didn't come out to the region, it's unlikely they would be working in their current industry or position. Where they found the attainment of career opportunities in the U.S. to be structured, institutionalized (i.e. the necessity of an MBA), and fiercely competitive, those same opportunities in Greater China were much more achievable.

When I first met Rosa Li three years ago, she had just arrived in Hong Kong. With a B.S. degree in computer science and an M.S. degree in electrical engineering, she was looking for a new job. Her resume read: "Five years experience at TRW as a digital signal processing hardware and software engineer, … a key designer of the world's fastest floating-point Fourier transform processor." Now, I'm a mechanical engineer by training, but even I could hardly figure out what she did for a living.

In coming to Greater China, however, she wasn't interested in finding an engineering job. Her intent was to pursue a career in television or movie production. She began by spending the first four months contacting and meeting people in the entertainment industry. On a Hong Kong harbor boat trip, she happened to strike up a conversation with the general manager of a TV broadcasting and production company. Their discussion led to a further meeting, which eventually led to an offer for Rosa to join his company as a business development manager. Over the next two years, she became involved in the planning and development of various television distribution, production, and broadcasting projects. These included the initiation of new media opportunities in Southeast Asia and co-productions with major broadcasters in China, Taiwan, Hong Kong, and South Korea.

Today, Rosa is the acting general manager in Taiwan for a major international media company, responsible for launching a new cable channel in Taipei. She is building it up from the ground floor and managing every aspect of the business from production and programming to marketing and promotions. "My job is to fine tune this channel for the Taiwan market," explains Rosa. "Although I don't have extensive experience in areas such as programming or ad sales, I'm working closely with exceptionally high caliber people from our Los Angeles headquarters who are helping me learn quickly. For instance, each week I'm discussing strategy and deal developments in conference calls with our company's worldwide president."

Rosa's opportunity did not come by accident. Although her timing was good, she was also focused, knowledgeable, and persistent enough to seize her chance when it was presented. Would her chance have happened in the U.S.? Perhaps it would have. But the relatively new businesses, products, and services now being introduced to the region greatly increase the likelihood of entering a career track different from what you may have previously pursued.

Career Advancement

It's Performance That Counts

Perhaps the most attractive aspect that Greater China offers to professionals is its performance-driven environment. It's not like the U.S., where corporate environments can be more hierarchical and political. Out here, the bottom line is, if you can develop a track record and prove yourself, advancement opportunities will come.

Shorter Time To Advance

Chew Swee Chiang, director of human resources at MTV Asia, describes the key hiring challenge she faces. Although she has to identify candidates for positions that must be immediately filled, she must also evaluate these hires for one or two positions down the road. "There's a strong chance a person may move up within 12 to 24 months," she points out. "Because of our ambitious expansion plans, we're always lacking managers at the upper levels. We're not afraid to promote good people."

"Because of our ambitious expansion plans, we're always lacking managers at the upper levels. We're not afraid to promote good people."

Greater China's high job turnover also contributes to fast-track career advancement. Many expat middle and senior managers work in the region on limited two or three-year assignments. As assignments end, companies must refill these key positions. Increasingly, they look to replace these roles with someone already in the region, rather than with more costly expats relocated from abroad.

If Your Company Doesn't Value You, Others Will

What ensures advancement for strong performers in Greater China is the extremely aggressive nature of the hiring market itself. My firm is part of the executive search industry, more commonly referred to as the "headhunting" industry. The practice of "headhunting," or the hiring away or "poaching" of a candidate from one company to another, has taken on new heights in Asia. With a high demand for (and insufficient pool of) qualified professionals, it's a hot field that will remain so as long as multinationals continue their rate of growth in the region.

For those considering a Greater China career, the hiring market is in your favor. If your company does not recognize your contributions and value, another company certainly will. Your assurance is the active poaching practices of Greater China headhunters.

No Comparison

I often ask Chinese Americans I meet to compare their careers in Greater China with what they'd be doing had they stayed in the U.S. over the same period. In nearly every case, the response is that, without a doubt, their careers are advancing much quicker out here. Sometimes I just get a sideways look that conveys the thought: "Are you kidding me?" Many are able to put their careers on fast forward.

For instance, in the U.S., you may typically expect to get promoted every two to four years. In Greater China, advancements can happen within every 18 months. Salary increases also tend to come more often. And where increases may average single digits in the States, double-digit raises are normal in Greater China, with 20 to 30 percent increases not uncommon.

Helen Limm began working for CNBC in 1994, when the station was just beginning to start up its cable production operations in Hong Kong. She came straight from her masters program in communications. Although she had no media experience before arriving, within two years she was producing daily programs. Today, Helen can be seen on channel TVB in Hong Kong. As a producer/reporter for a weekly program called *Money Magazine*, she presents news and public affairs stories from around the region. "In the U.S., it would have been considerably more difficult and taken much longer," she says of her career development. "Here, it's not unusual to reach a certain level in half the time. In fact, that's more the rule rather than the exception."

One comment that seemed to summarize the exceptional career opportunities in Greater China relative to those in the U.S. came from an investment banking associate in his third year working in Hong Kong. When I posed the comparison question to him, it seemed to catch him off-guard. He pondered it for a moment. Then he said, "you know, I don't think about it much when I'm here. The times I notice are when I'm back in the States and talking to friends. They're all doing very well in their jobs. But I can tell that what I'm getting the chance to do here professionally, in terms of regional exposure, level of responsibility, and types of projects blows away what they're doing back there."

Welcome Entrepreneurs

For those with an entrepreneurial bent, Greater China is the promised land. With the region still at a fairly early development stage, you'll find many businesses and services that are either not being done well or not being done at all. A great many niches are unoccupied, offering start-up opportunities for just about anyone inspired by a strong business concept.

My own company is as good an example as any. We began Wang & Li Asia Resources with absolutely no recruiting industry experience. Although there were many established executive search firms in the market already, we believed that multinationals were still having difficulty finding enough well-qualified candidates. Partners in search firms we spoke with emphasized senior executive contacts from which to solicit business as the most important criteria to competing in the recruiting business. However, we felt the emphasis was the other way around. Having a pool of quality candidates to offer was the key.

In addition, many managers and human resources personnel we spoke with were dissatisfied with the service and the value they were getting for the large sums of money they were paying. They were all open to new approaches. Our business concept was simple: a flexible contingency or "success" fee approach; responsive, professional service; and most importantly, top-notch candidates to offer.

We began without a database of candidates, established list of clients, or job placement track record. However, we quickly gained credibility with Fortune 1000 clients by focusing on what hiring managers cared about most: identifying professionals with strong Chinese language and cultural backgrounds and solid western training. Our candidate strategy targeted relationships with Chinese and Chinese American professionals in both North America and Asia, who possessed this highly sought combination. Qualified job seekers came to us because we provided what they cared about most: up-to-date Greater China job market information and help in finding positions within leading multinational firms.

The funny thing is, I never once considered starting or running my own company before coming to Greater China. In fact, I believe it shocked people who knew me back in the U.S. I'm not an entrepreneur by nature. I'm actually kind of easy going and enjoy my free time. The urge to do my own thing didn't even come about until the moment the idea popped into my head. But that's how it happens out here.

Lejen Chen: Bagels For Beijing

Personal History: *Born in Tainan, Taiwan. Moved to the U.S. at age eight. Raised in Brooklyn, New York. Living in Mainland China since 1989.*

Parents: *Mom and Dad originally from Shantou in Guangdong province.*

Education: *B.A. in English from Tufts University, 1984.*

Languages: *Native English speaker. Spoke Shantou dialect with parents while growing up. Fluent in Mandarin from one year of college classroom study, one year of study in Taipei at the Guoyu Ribao (the Mandarin Daily News), and years of daily usage in China.*

Lejen and husband, Shan, in Beijing in front of their bagel company, Mrs. Shanen's

In a hot little bakery off a dusty road 30 minutes outside of Beijing, hidden behind The Double Dragon Metals Company, you'll find Mrs. Shanen's Bagels and Cream Cheese, Mainland China's first authentic New York style bagel company. Mrs. Shanen ends up being Lejen Chen, along with her husband Shan En. Together, they run the fast-growing, family-owned and operated business. Their story has a classic entrepreneurial beginning, which they describe as a complete "accident of timing."

Lejen's extraordinary venture in the most unlikely of places is a far cry from what she was doing during her first few years in China. While attending a worldwide kite-flying event in Beijing, she took up work on a short-term, freelance documentary assignment with CBS. The job led to other film projects that allowed her to remain in the mainland, such as *Secrets of the Wild Panda*, which Lejen produced for *National Geographic*.

Lejen's interest in bagels, however, is not entirely recent. She's a self-professed bagel lover, who was "always collecting bagel material." One of the first videos she ever produced was even on a bagel factory. She remembers her first encounter with a bagel in China, at the Holiday Inn, Guilin. "The salmon was great, the capers and cream cheese were perfect," Lejen recounts. "And then there was this hamburger bun with a hole in the middle." Upon returning from a trip to New York with a bag of bagels, she offered one, a cinnamon raisin bagel, to her good friend Shan En. Shan En thought the product would be a "hit" in Beijing.

On that simple premise, Lejen began experimenting with product development and production out of a friend's kitchen. "We could only make five bagels at a time from this tiny oven," says Lejen. That was in March 1996. Their sole customer was the U.S. Embassy Shop in Beijing. Today, Mrs. Shanen's factory produces over 10,000 bagels a week for customers, such as the China World Hotel, the Kempinski, and the Capital Club. Twice a week, product is even air shipped to Shanghai.

Lejen admits to being a "perfectionist" when it comes to bagels. Her product control is strict. All ingredients, except salt, are imported, including high-quality Canadian wheat. Jalapeno pepper, blueberry, and sun-dried tomato bagels are available, in addition to standards such as sesame, garlic, onion, and the fateful cinnamon raisin. "She's sitting on a gold mine," says *Restaurants Asia* magazine publisher, Frank Rocco, who flew to Beijing to sample Lejen's product. "These are real New York Style bagels. Her product is awesome!"

Lejen and Shan En have since married each other. They are trying to decide how to expand their operations, including the possible opening of a retail bagel shop in Beijing. Although they've received a number of investor inquiries, Lejen and Shan En are reluctant to run the risk of losing the "family business" flavor of their operations. "I would have never considered doing this business in the States. But out here, the same objective has a unique meaningfulness. The Chinese have a real curiosity about trying western things, from Big Macs to pizza. Our ultimate goal is a simple one. We'd like to give Chinese people here a chance to taste bagels."

Opportunities arise that are just too good to pass up. Before you know it, you're moving ahead faster than you ever thought you would to bring your idea to life.

For myself, starting my own business would not have happened in the U.S. But in Greater China, you feel more able to cut the cord to corporate life. Whereas the U.S. is more developed, there are fewer entry barriers and less competition out here.

Right Time, Right Place

Simply put, a better situation could not have been created for Chinese Americans. The supply of qualified bilingual, bicultural staff in Greater China is not meeting the demand. The shortage is offering an unprecedented level of opportunities for Chinese Americans to fill professional and management ranks within leading multinationals in the region.

Openings are even presenting themselves despite the lack of readiness by some to fill the roles. Christine Hsu came to Taipei in April 1995. After studying Mandarin for ten months, she was hired as an assistant manager at Citibank Taiwan. It was a brand new industry and position for her. Within her first month, she was approached by Bank of America to head their electronic commerce initiatives. "It was during my first baby steps into the world of banking," recalls Christine. "Banks in Taiwan are beginning to rely more heavily on non-teller services like the Internet, PC Banking, and ATMs. Unfortunately, there is a serious shortage of professionals with banking and IT backgrounds. The result is a severe inbreeding of banking staff to and from Citibank, Bank of America, and American Express.

"At the time, I knew nothing about electronic commerce. I distinctly remember telling them very politely, but clearly, how terrifically unqualified I was for the position. Their response was, 'it's okay! You understand Chinese, and you speak English well. We can teach you whatever you don't know!' I know my limitations and whether I'm ready to take on something new. Therefore, I turned down the offer. But after hanging up the phone I couldn't help but smile to myself over how marketable I suddenly was!"

Part II

The Employment Situation

Chapter 3 The Situation: A Rapidly Changing Business Environment

It is referred to by several different names; the Pacific Century, the Asia Century, or the Asia Miracle to mention a few. They all allude to the unique period of economic emergence that the Asia Pacific region has been undergoing. It is a period of growth on a scale the world has never seen. In his #1 international best-selling book, *Megatrends Asia*, world-renowned trends forecaster John Naisbitt writes:

> *Globalization is the phenomenon of the 21st century and the dominant region will be Asia. What is happening in Asia is by far the most important development in the world today. Nothing else comes close. Not only for Asians but the entire planet. The economic growth in Asia will drive the global economy to the benefit of us all as we move through the balance of this century. The modernization of Asia will forever re-shape the world as we move towards the next millennium.*

The striking numbers from *Megatrends Asia* tell the story of the region's recent performance and future prospects:

- From 1980–94, Asia increased its share of the world's economic output from 17 to 26 percent. Its growth was nearly twice that of the rest of the world economy during the same period.

- Economies across Asia have been growing at an annual 6-10% rate over the past decade. If this trend continues, the region's middle class will double or triple in the next decade.

- It is estimated that by the year 2012 the Asian middle class could have between US$8 to US$10 trillion in spending power, nearly 50% more than today's U.S. economy.

Within the Asia Pacific region's unprecedented growth, Greater China's fast-paced economies are leading the charge. Take a trip out and just listen to the conversations people are having. Expansion, development, new markets, deals, joint ventures, investment, and opportunity are buzzwords you'll hear repeatedly. These discussions all highlight one fact. Greater China's time has arrived.

It begins with Mainland China. With economic growth that has averaged nearly 10 percent for the past fifteen years, the mainland's standard of living is improving faster and for more people than anywhere in the world. Although it occurs with stops and starts, the long-anticipated consumer market of 1.2 billion people is becoming more accessible to multinational product and service firms with each passing day. Even if growth were to slow to 7 percent per year, within ten years, China's total economy would have the same purchasing power as the U.S. economy had in 1994.

China's investment market is also drawing billions of dollars from abroad at a staggering rate. Since the early 1990's, the mainland has become the world's second leading destination, behind the United States, for international investment. In addition, Taiwan's economy continues to grow steadily. After more than 20 years of 7–8 percent annual growth, the country's standard of living now equals those of many European countries. In 1995, it was the world's 18th largest economy.

In the middle of it all sits Hong Kong. It's per capita GDP was the fourth highest in the world on a purchasing power per capita basis in 1994. More significantly, despite its small physical size, it acts as an Asia Pacific regional center, financial center, and gateway to China. Hong Kong is the world's eighth largest trading economy and the tenth leading exporter of commercial services. In a recent study by the U.S.-based Heritage Foundation, it was rated as the freest economy in the world. Although the Greater China region may experience up and down cycles, its overall trend is unmistakably continued growth.

It may be easy to understand why Greater China's rapid economic advancement is causing professional manpower needs to far outpace supply. But why is the current shortage for qualified professionals and managers so severe? Talk to many multinational managers and they'll tell you they are understaffed and constantly stretching resources. When speaking of new hires, the frequent lament is: "We could have hired that person yesterday."

The professional labor challenges are a result of significant changes that have occurred in recent years within the overall business environment. Over a short time frame, Greater China has become a prime focus for many industries and companies all relatively new to the region. This has in turn generated a sudden, tremendous demand for new business skills and expertise that are hard to come by locally. Compounding the situation are the more aggressive and mature regional business approaches by international firms.

New Industries, Companies, And Skill Sets

Suddenly Services

As recently as ten years ago, consulting was not much of a concept, let alone a business practice, within the region. Investment banking and corporate finance had a limited presence in Greater China until the early 1990s, when the mainland announced its first ever listings of local companies for international investment markets. Similarly, the usage of information technology only began to grow substantially in the region over the past few years. The explosion in media and entertainment has happened only over the past three or four years as well.

It is these relatively new service and service-related industries that are expanding the fastest in Greater China and playing a major role in elevating regional economies. In 1995, Hong Kong was ranked as having the second most highly developed service sector in the world, behind only the U.S. That year, the service sector accounted for an astounding 83.4 percent of Hong Kong's GDP and employed 72 percent of its workforce. Over half of Taiwan's workforce was employed in its service sector at the end of 1996, which is projected to become the main source of Taiwan's economic growth this year.

In 1995, the service sector accounted for an astounding 83.4 percent of the Hong Kong's GDP and employed 72 percent of its workforce.

The catalyst for these rising service industries has been the dramatic increase in both the purchasing power of consumers and the investment spending of companies and governments in the region. Where Asian countries were primarily producers and exporters of goods for many years, today they are major importers. In so many instances, untapped consumer markets are opening up as fast as new products and services can be introduced.

The primary focus, of course, is Mainland China households that are hungry for items ranging from ice cream, CD players, and athletic shoes to mobile phones, soft drinks, and cosmetics. Increasing income levels have also placed a greater emphasis on quality of life and leisure, creating a yearning among consumers for entertainment, media, travel, and sports. The dash by companies to win the country's consumer market has brought on an influx of marketing, communications, advertising, and public relations firms in response. As companies establish new operations or expand existing ones, the demand for consulting and information technology services to support them has skyrocketed as well.

At the same time, large amounts of money are being invested in China infrastructure projects, manufacturing facilities, and business operations. Financial services has emerged as a significant sector providing the capital that is making much of the expansion possible. Meanwhile, legal and accountancy services are needed to help protect the interests and measure the results of foreign participants investing in the mainland.

Multinationals On The Move

Common among these service industries are their western origins. They are industries that have evolved and matured in the U.S. or Europe. Their emergence in Greater China has been paralleled by the recent entrance of numerous multinationals who are committing to the region in a major way. Many have defined the standards of excellence in their industry and established themselves in the West as worldwide leaders for years. The newness of their presence in Greater China, however, may surprise you. Take Microsoft for example. It is arguably the company most associated with leading information technology into the next century. Yet, Microsoft only established its operations in Greater China as recently as 1990. Dell Computer, a company that generates US$12 billion in sales a year, set up its regional headquarters and business operations in 1994.

Similarly, Nike and Walt Disney are global, household names. Yet, it was only in the early 1990s that they began making a concerted effort to grow their Greater China consumer products business. Look at Goldman Sachs, a firm identified as one of the industry's top investment banks. It was in 1992 when it aggressively expanded its regional presence in Hong Kong. McKinsey & Company and the Boston Consulting Group, two leading names in consulting, established their Greater China practices in Hong Kong in 1989. Some of the largest international broadcasting companies are outright newcomers. CNN and ESPN began production operations in the region in 1995. In essence, these and hundreds of other international firms have all been ramping up their efforts in Greater China in unison.

Kentucky Fried Chicken opened its first store in Beijing in 1994. Today, over 200 stores serve the Chinese population.

* * * * * * *

In 1995, Nike opened its first retail store in Shanghai. Now, the city has close to 25 stores.

New Skills

The result of these fast growing industries and multinationals has been the increased demand for western-based professional skills. Consumer product companies are launching new products and entering markets as quickly as they can identify people to manage those businesses. These companies must understand customer needs, send product messages that relate to local consumers, and establish retail and distribution channels. To do this, they require managers with marketing, brand management, product development, sales management, and channel management capabilities.

The rapid expansion of regional operations has made timely and reliable information increasingly critical. Branch offices and headquarters require immediate information access that respond to the region's dynamic and spontaneous business activity. Not only are information systems management skills needed, but so are value-added systems integration, IT consulting, and applications development expertise. Technology firms are on the lookout for project managers, pre- and post-sales support staff, and systems analysts who can design, implement, and oversee information systems.

To attract and manage the investments of global institutional and individual investors, international financial institutions require staff with corporate finance, project finance, capital markets, credit, asset management, risk management, sales and trading, and direct investment experience. Lawyers with international legal backgrounds are needed to assist multinationals expanding through partnerships and joint ventures. Tracking the financial health of such joint ventures and regional operations and determining the viability of existing and potential projects requires finance managers, controllers, and auditors. And to assist multinationals with market entry and business initiatives, as well as governments that are tackling large projects, a range of consultants with strategic planning, market research, general management, and process improvement backgrounds are in demand.

Unfortunately, as with the industries they support, these professional skills are not innate to the region. Rather, they have been developed over decades in the West, nurtured and practiced within the best U.S. business school programs and Fortune 1000 corporate cultures. Within Greater China, however, such capabilities and expertise have had a limited presence.

New Way Of Doing Business

In running their Greater China operations today, it's hardly business as usual for multinationals. For many, earlier approaches to developing business in the region have not produced the expected results. These might include an over reliance on inside connections to win deals or a lack of commitment to develop local internal resources and skills. Today, multinationals are more experienced with regard to what it takes to be successful in the region. There is too much at stake not to be smarter and tougher in their approach and execution.

It Takes More Than Who You Know, It's Also What You Know

You'll encounter many people claiming to know someone who is the key to delivering the China market. Although China is a place where you can never have too many connections, enough companies have learned costly lessons by counting on relationships alone. Beyond just having an inside track, what makes a partnership or venture fruitful is the ability to implement business plans and effectively manage projects.

As a result, multinationals are instilling in the region their western-oriented business expertise. As new kids on the block, without an established name presence to leverage, they are winning business and market share through tried and true techniques that encompass strong customer service, product quality, marketing, project management, and strategic planning activities. The increased presence of multinationals in Greater China is raising the region's standards for professional skills and experience.

Local Skills Needed

In the past, multinationals regularly transferred managers to the region from their corporate headquarters. Home offices sent abroad managers whose primary value was their knowledge of the company's business, corporate culture, and products. The emphasis was in choosing someone known by headquarters who could keep the U.S. side abreast of regional developments. The selection of these managers was usually based on their achievements in the States. Local language skills, market knowledge, or cultural understanding were of less consideration, as few managers possessed these capabilities. Assignments were typically short term.

It's a different situation today. Multinationals know that to improve on their performance in the region, they must adopt a more localized approach. They need professionals who can manage key local relationships and implement western business practices and management approaches in a local environment.

Just as with professional skills, the necessity for local capabilities and experience has also increased. Within nearly all industries, this has significantly narrowed the pool of foreigners that multinationals seek to employ. Some companies even tell us bluntly that the person they're looking to hire must be Asian (unlike the U.S., people in Asia are considerably less politically correct).

Speak Chinese? ... Read And Write It?

My company specializes in making placements at the junior to upper middle management levels, positions that usually involve direct interface with local partners, clients, and vendors. When we began in 1994, job descriptions given to us by clients typically included the words "spoken Mandarin preferred". Back then, speaking Mandarin to nearly any degree helped a candidate attract attention from companies.

"If someone can't speak Chinese, you introduce a significant uncertainty factor into the equation. You can't be fully confident going through translators."

Today, for about 85 percent of the job openings we see, the prerequisite requirement is "spoken Mandarin a must (at a business level), and reading and writing preferred!" In increasing numbers of cases, reading and writing of Chinese has even become a standard qualification. Multinationals want employees who can perform research, gain information, negotiate, and communicate at a local level. These tasks all require strong Chinese language skills.

Janet Tan, director of Andersen Consulting's technology consulting practice in Hong Kong, points out the poor effectiveness of non-Chinese language speakers. As someone who spends a good deal of time in recruiting and staff development, Janet places the greatest value on professionals with local language abilities. "I manage a lot of large-scale information systems projects in China," reveals Janet. "If someone can't speak Chinese, you introduce a significant uncertainty factor into the equation. You can't be fully confident going through translators. They can misinterpret and they don't necessarily understand the objectives and nuances of business discussions. There are enough horror stories of projects and deals that fail because of miscommunication. It's essential to be able to understand and reply clearly. You need to know the local language to do that."

Understanding The Local Business Environment

You can't bank on language skills alone to be successful though. Conducting business effectively in Greater China also requires an understanding of the eastern way of doing things. Multinationals also want employees who can evaluate and manage local markets, situations, and business issues and who can make things happen in a complex, local business environment.

For Mainland China in particular, having in-country exposure to local business practices is critical. It's important to have an insight into the situations you encounter and into what is most important to the local parties you are dealing with. For instance, knowing how to build trust and handle issues of face, or understanding the emphasis of the group over the individual can be key to working out problems and getting results.

Keeping Costs Down

Yesterday's Approach: Investing For The Future

The business approach by multinationals towards Asia and towards running their Asia operations has evolved considerably over recent years. When multinationals first began developing their Greater China business, the region was somewhat of a black hole. It was a far away, exotic place. Not much was known about the people, culture, or how to do business here. One thing they did know, the Greater China market had tremendous potential.

Although their strategies were not well-defined, multinationals knew they should be operating in the region in some capacity. Their initial approach was a long-term investment one. Firms needed to first understand local markets better. They began by setting up offices that allowed them to establish a presence and conduct early market entry and business development activities. Although these operations might lose money each year, the emphasis was to establish a foundation so that when the region's market potential became real, they would be ready to participate in the boom.

Today's Approach: Make Some Money!

An interesting development occurred over the past few years. The long-awaited potential of Asian markets began to arrive. In response, multinational operations in

Greater China have blossomed. The region's economic growth has also brought with it a dramatic change in the objective for multinationals. Today, it's no longer good enough to just have a presence. Operations are now expected to be profitable as quickly as possible. The question home offices are asking their Asia offices is, "when are you going to make money?!?"

Expats Need Not Apply

Whenever I'm briefed on a job opening, at some point the client inevitably emphasizes that "this position offers a local package" or "this is not an expat position." Expatriates, or expats, are traditionally defined as hires who are relocated to a foreign country by a company. They are typically well-compensated.

In the past, an assignment in Asia was not necessarily an attractive proposition. In most cases, it was usually the home office proposing the transfer, rather than the manager making the request. To entice people overseas, companies offered attractive expat packages to those willing to relocate. Packages could easily double or triple the amount of a person's compensation in the U.S. On top of base salary, other premium benefits usually included housing allowance, cost of living adjustment, return trips to the States, club memberships, and educational costs for kids. As you can imagine, it's an incredibly expensive way to run a business. Yet, multinationals were doing it this way with regularity in the region.

"The average expatriate at a middle manager level costs a company about US$320,000, says a regional human resources director for a U.S. telecommunications company. "Senior level expats can cost a company anywhere from between US$500,000 and US$1,000,000. There are companies out here employing dozens of expats. That's a frightening amount of expense for an operations to carry."

With the size of their Asia business and scale of their operations considerably larger than what it was just a few years ago, U.S. home offices are now more focused on the bottom-line results they are achieving. Multinationals know they must conduct their regional business more affordably. For most, managing staffing costs is a major factor for operating profitably.

With companies committed to keeping these costs down, expats at all levels have become a dying breed. Given their high expense, many expats stand out like a beacon of light as overpaid hires relative to other talent that could be employed. Today, language skills and local business capabilities outweigh the home office relationship advantages that expats from corporate headquarters bring out. As a result, their value placed against their pay packages is increasingly difficult to justify. Today, the hiring strategy for all multinationals is the same. They want staff with the professional expertise and functional skills they require, but who are also more locally qualified and affordable.

Chapter 4 The Problem: Shortage Of Asian/Western Professional Talent

More Jobs Than Qualified Professionals

Graham Brandt sees Mainland China as his company's next billion dollar market. Graham is managing director of Microsoft's management consulting services in Greater China. However, like many managers who sense the enormous opportunity, he faces a difficult problem. "It's not the market that's the limiting factor for growth," he says. "It's finding the right staff with the sales, people, and process management skills who can deliver service and customer satisfaction. You don't come across those type often out here."

It hardly matters what industry you speak of. They're all in need of well-trained managers and staff able to operate effectively within local markets. "Show me any good candidates you've got," is the mantra-like request I hear from multinational clients. I've encountered many hiring situations where a job listing remained open for months because a suitable candidate simply could not be found.

One company I know desperately needed a marketing communications manager to cover China. The candidate had to have local media contacts, local marketing and management experience, and a strong public relations and advertising background. The firm began looking to fill the position in February. In August, I heard about the position again. Apparently, the company had met several candidates through various sources over the six-month period. However, nobody fulfilled the requirements. The position continued to remain open.

For expanding multinationals, finding personnel with the combination of Asian and western skills is a key factor for their regional growth and competitiveness. In many cases, companies have little choice but to transfer people out from their U.S. offices. It's expensive and the person may lack local experience and capabilities to obtain the type of results sought, but firms must keep their business moving forward until a better solution arises. Ideally, however, they would like to find employees with the following qualities.

What Multinationals Want

Experience Needed

Multinationals require mature, experienced professionals who can grow operations and develop business in Greater China's fast-changing, competitive environment. These employees must be able to take on responsibility and handle new, demanding situations. It's not that people with little or no experience are unemployable here. We see fresh university graduates land entry-level positions all the time. However, for many companies in high-growth, short-handed situations, the expectations and pressures are for each staff to hit the ground running and to contribute as soon as possible.

Western Training

Multinationals also look to hire staff who have received their business training in the West. Companies want employees who have worked in well-run firms and high caliber professional environments. For instance, investment banks in the region are keen on anyone who has worked on Wall Street or with an established Wall Street firm. Technology companies are interested in professionals from Silicon Valley.

Professionals with sales and marketing training from Midwestern consumer goods makers, as well as advertising and public relations backgrounds from New York and Los Angeles, are also sought. In general, multinationals are attracted to candidates with work experience from Fortune 1000 or similarly reputable companies.

... With Local Exposure Too

Having a solid track record in the U.S. does not automatically translate into successful performance in Greater China. It's a different game out here. If you've never played it, there are bound to be surprises and setbacks. Companies prefer candidates with prior exposure to the region, who have some understanding of local business practices and markets. Such local experience significantly reduces a candidate's learning curve and provides for a smoother transition into the local business environment.

Western-oriented Thinking

Going Outside The Box

Doing business in Greater China is like driving someplace new without a road map. There are no directions to guide you and few people to tell you how to get around. Because there is often no precedent to follow, multinationals need staff who can approach situations creatively, resourcefully, and independently. Managers are always asking me for candidates with strong problem solving abilities, communications skills, initiative, teamwork, and an ability to think outside the box. These are highly valued traits that western-trained professionals bring to business challenges regularly encountered here. Unfortunately, these qualities are in short supply among locally educated professionals.

More Middle Managers Please

The hiring shortages we're speaking of are not at senior management levels. Although diminishing in number, attractive expat packages continue to lure enough executives from the home office for many top positions. Instead, the greatest staffing demands are at the hands-on, operating levels. Companies seek junior, middle, and upper middle managers who can execute day-to-day client service, operations management, and business development functions.

According to a recent *Far Eastern Economic Review* Asian Executives Poll, the entire Asia Pacific region is facing a desperate shortage of skilled manpower to service its economies. Over half the respondents say that their respective countries do not have enough business managers to cope with demand over the next ten years.

Over half the respondents say that their respective countries do not have enough business managers to cope with demand over the next 10 years — a recent Far Eastern Economic Review _Asian Executives Poll._

"I can't think of a single country in the region that has a solid base of middle management," says Jonathan Fox, head of Grey Advertising's Asia Pacific operations in Hong Kong. A study by the Pacific Economic Co-operation Council in Singapore revealed that managers account for only 4.82 percent of the workforce in Taiwan and 8.54 percent in Hong Kong. In China, the ratio is even worse. This compares to 13.26 percent of the workforce in the U.S. There is a severe lack of well-trained local managers who are able to communicate effectively, think strategically, and function within a western business context.

Because of the demand for local managers, the poaching for such talent by one firm from another is getting out of hand. "There's a bidding war going on for the relatively few good ones out here," according to Joe Wong, Asia Pacific human resources director for Tricon Restaurants International (formerly Pepsi Restaurants International). "Increasingly, however, companies aren't getting what they're paying for. For comparable spending, there's gotten to be a growing disparity between the level of talent you get in China compared to that found in other countries."

Beyond A Two Year Stint

In the past, a typical foreigner working in the region might stick it out for a two to four-year assignment before returning home. Companies accepted this natural turnover. Today, multinationals are aiming to build more stable operations. They want to minimize cases where employees come to the region for a short-term stint. It's costly to have staff leave every couple of years or so. This is usually at the point when they are becoming effective in their jobs and beginning to make real contributions. For companies, it's frustrating each time they face a situation where, instead of having an experienced hand in place, another person who is green to the region must be trained up again.

The Ideal Candidate

Education:	*U.S. degree from a leading university. An MBA from the U.S. a plus, but not a must.*
Work Experience:	*At least 2+ years previous work experience with a Fortune 1000 or reputable company.*
Professional Skills:	*Service industry oriented skills (i.e. consulting, product management, marketing, communications, strategic planning, business development, finance, project management, etc.).*
Language Skills:	*Excellent fluency in English. Fluency in or a "good command" of spoken Mandarin or Cantonese. Reading and writing a plus.*
Asia Experience:	*Significant time (six months or more) spent or previous work experience in Greater China.*
Intangibles:	*Ability to think outside the box. Open-minded. Good problem solver. Fast learner. Able to work well independently. Strong communicator. Equally comfortable and effective operating in both Asian and western business situations. Hard worker. Committed to developing a career in the region.*

Today, firms want employees intent on developing their careers in the region, who will put the time and effort into improving local skills and understanding the business environment. They aren't interested in "bandwagon jumpers," or candidates suddenly motivated by a few *Asian Wall Street Journal* articles and looking for an alternative to the U.S. job market. Hiring managers can spot this type and try to avoid them. I've seen many candidates crash out in an interview because a client just didn't sense their commitment to a career in Greater China. This was usually reflected in the candidates' lack of basic knowledge about the region, which raised questions as to how much thought went into the decision to work in Asia.

Managers also try to sense how comfortable you feel about being in Greater China overall. Having career goals related to Asia is one thing. Living here is another. Companies have gone through it all in terms of hand holding and letting staff go because they were a poor fit for the local environment. Whether or not you are openly asked, family or close ties in the region can be a significant factor in putting the commitment issue to rest with employers.

One Foot In Asia, One Foot In The West

After successfully placing one Chinese American candidate into a marketing manager position with a consumer products company in China, the general manager told me: "That's exactly the type we're looking for — people with one foot in Asia and one foot in the West!" Today, the ideal candidate is more versatile than what multinationals were willing to hire just a few years ago. Their skills are more diverse. They have western-oriented thinking, U.S. educational backgrounds, work experience with reputable companies, and professional expertise in service-oriented and management functions. At the same time, they possess bi- or even multilingual language skills, understand local business practices and attitudes, can participate in local situations, and are able to bridge two cultures. It's a combination of talent difficult to find enough of in Asia.

What The Region Is Offering

Local Education System

Test For Success

Despite a deep pool of intellectual talent to draw from, oddly, Greater China's education systems do not provide enough candidates with the well-rounded professional skills sought by multinationals. Fundamentally, the education system in each Asian country is extremely competitive. It's a situation created out of sheer logistics. There are simply too many students and too few educational facilities. For instance, in Hong Kong, 85 percent of primary school students attend part-time because there aren't enough classrooms to accommodate the number of full-time students. Whether students move on to the next school level depends on how well they do on a single, rigorous measurement criteria: their national exam scores.

Staying Within The Lines

The competitive nature of the education systems significantly affects the type of learning experience students receive. Open, unbounded learning approaches are less emphasized. Instead, with intense pressure to score well on exams, learning is highly focused on the rote memorization of information. Successful students complete assignments according to instructions. As a result, the qualities of creativity and alternative thinking that are stressed in the West and valued by multinationals are not nurtured nearly to the same degree in Asia.

Regional MBA Programs

Not There Yet

You may be wondering to what extent local graduate schools are supplying candidates with the management skills and industry expertise that multinationals seek. Unfortunately, a look at the region's top graduate business programs indicate that it may be a while before Greater China produces enough talent with such training.

In September 1996, *Asia Inc.*, a leading regional English-language business magazine published its annual edition of "The Best MBA Schools." It ranked Asia's top 25 business programs, much like the list of Top 20 U.S. MBA programs published annually by *Business Week*. The title of the cover article was, "Who Needs Stanford?" When I read that, I immediately thought: "Unbelievable, Asian MBA programs are already on par with schools like Stanford?!?" I eagerly surveyed the list.

What I discovered was interesting. Nine of the top MBA programs mentioned were in Australia and New Zealand. Five were in India and Pakistan. Another seven were in South East Asia. One was in Japan and one was in Korea. Entirely absent from the list were any programs from Taiwan or China. Of the schools in Greater China, there were only two: Hong Kong University and Chinese University of Hong Kong. The enrollments of these programs amounted to 79 and 62 students respectively. Essentially, this was the local MBA factory producing investment bankers, consultants, marketing managers, business strategists, and other functional specialists for the region. The Wharton School of Business alone graduates about 800 MBA students each year.

In addition to the small numbers, the training possessed by graduates from local MBA programs falls below the standards sought by multinationals. One human resources manager at a major international bank, upon arriving in Taipei, immediately targeted the city's top MBA programs for recruiting. She believed that attracting local MBA students was a key to her company's regional growth. She expected to meet candidates of a similar caliber to the ones she met at leading U.S. business schools. Most of the students she interviewed, however, had not worked prior to entering their program. As a result, they were younger, less experienced, and less polished than their U.S. counterparts who had previous work experience. After meeting several candidates, she discontinued her local recruiting efforts. Their professional and international scope simply did not fulfill her bank's requirements.

This is not to say that most of Greater China's future professionals won't come from regional programs. These programs are committed to improving and are doing so rapidly. They are quickly learning from established U.S. business schools, through student and faculty exchanges. It will take some time, however, before the region produces both the numbers and caliber of graduates sought by multinational employers.

Chapter 5: The Solution: Bilingual/ Bicultural Chinese Americans

Although the candidate profile that multinationals seek is not found in sufficient numbers locally, the supply of talent does exist. It is seen in the population of young bilingual and bicultural professionals from the West. In response to the pressing hiring demands of companies, they are rapidly establishing themselves as the *new foreign presence* in the region. This *new foreign presence* represents a group that possesses a different profile and motivation from their expat predecessors of five to ten years ago. Beyond just having the professional skills and industry expertise sought, they also offer more local language skills and cultural knowledge, greater likelihood for remaining in the region, and more affordability.

Don't Need To Be Expatted Out

The *new foreign presence* of professionals you see in Greater China today are mobile and have a high degree of flexibility in their lives. Many are in their 20s and 30s. They are typically single or married and without children, and are less tied down with family obligations and financial responsibilities. These professionals do not necessarily seek or expect expatriate terms. Although compensation is important, they are less concerned about a high salary package as a requirement for relocating to and working in Greater China.

Instead, their desire to be in Asia is self-initiated. The candidates my firm deals with from the U.S. all fly out at their own expense to interview with companies. They have a strong understanding of the region and take a longer term view of the career and financial benefits that working in Greater China can bring them. They place stock in their dual cultural and language abilities. Fundamentally, they believe this is where they can best apply their Asian and western abilities and where their greatest opportunities lie. Their top priority is simply to be here.

Highly Sought Profiles

For most Greater China managers, nationality makes little difference when it comes to hiring. What counts is your ability to get results. The bicultural and bilingual professionals that companies are looking for are coming from all over the world. Among those best suited for doing business in Greater China are regional Chinese nationals from Singapore, Malaysia, or the Philippines. Also included are ethnic Chinese from Australia, Britain, or other parts of Europe. From North America, many Chinese Canadians and Chinese Americans fall into the target profile multinationals seek. Among Chinese Americans, they can be divided into two groups: Asian-born returnees and American-born Chinese.

Asian-Born Returnees (ABRs)

From nearly every perspective, western-educated and trained Asian-born returnees are the leading candidates currently desired by multinationals. These are Chinese nationals from Taiwan, Hong Kong, and Mainland China who have lived, studied, and worked in the U.S. "The value of returnees is clear. They have the best combination of Asian cultural and language skills, western corporate training and education, and understanding for doing business in the region. For them, Asia is their backyard, " points out one human resources director who oversees regional recruiting for a major U.S. consumer products company in Hong Kong. "We're always interested in meeting returning Chinese professionals from the States."

The category of Asian-born returnees is quite broad in itself. The best returnee candidates are those who went to the U.S. at perhaps 10 years old or older. Chinese is their first culture and first language. Because of their later move, they possess a much greater, if not complete degree of Chinese language skills, including reading and writing abilities. Having grown up in the region, they are familiar with local culture and practices. Many return to visit regularly and still have family ties in Greater China. This makes them a more stable group with regard to their longevity in Asia. The prime returnee candidates are practically "transparent" from both an Asian and western standpoint. To local Chinese, they are viewed as Chinese. To westerners, they are considered westerners.

Another distinct category of ABRs are those who moved to the U.S. at around nine years of age or younger. Although they are also classified as Asian-born returnees, in most ways they are more similar to American-born Chinese given their number of years in the U.S. Fundamentally, they have a distinctly western upbringing and orientation. Their spoken Chinese language skills are typically better than American-born Chinese. Having left at such an early age, however, they possess poor Chinese reading and writing skills. Their exposure to Asia comes from occasional return visits. Local Chinese in particular are likely to identify them more closely with American-born Chinese.

Finally, there are the Asian-born returnees who have gone overseas to attend college or graduate school. They've had relatively short stays abroad of a few years. The single quality that makes these ABRs attractive to multinational firms is whether they've had U.S.-based work experience with a reputable company.

My firm regularly receives resumes from this last group of ABRs, who possess outstanding academic qualifications obtained in the U.S. Unfortunately, most have little or no business experience within a western professional environment. For many of these candidates, the extent of their U.S. work experience is in computer centers, research labs, or retail stores. In the past, their connections in Greater China were an attention-getting selling point. However, times have changed. Without the work experience in a recognized company, they lack the caliber of professional training required by most multinationals. The exception is if they have obtained an MBA from a top U.S. business school program.

For ABRs in particular, local family ties are a significant factor that determines whether or not they want to return to Greater China. When I say local family ties, however, I don't necessarily mean that Mom and Dad are living in the region. Many ABRs are from the upper class levels of society in Asia. Family connections may refer to "Uncle Ming", a distant relative's close friend who happens to be an influential property developer in Taipei. As a result, family businesses, links to political figures, and connections across industries and borders give ABRs favorable access to resources and opportunities unmatched for them anywhere else. If there's a single group in a position to impact the region's future, it is the ABRs who are diligently expanding their presence and involvement in Greater China.

Jensen Chow: Feels Like Home

Personal History: *Born in Hong Kong. Moved to Taiwan at age two. Moved to Los Angeles at age 16. Living in Greater China (Hong Kong and Shanghai) since 1995.*

Parents: *Mom and Dad from Shanghai.*

Education: *B.A. in Economics from the University of California, Los Angeles.*

Languages: *Native English, Mandarin, and Shanghainese speaker. Good spoken Cantonese.*

Jenson enjoying a moment with a client in a Shanghai restaurant during "hairy crab" season (October 1997)

Jensen Chow's upbringing was always a mish-mash of cultural influences. She was born in Hong Kong, but moved to Taiwan with her family at age two. While growing up in Taipei, she spoke Shanghainese with her parents, Mandarin with her sister, and English at the international school she attended.

When she moved to Los Angeles, at age 16, she she was ready to adapt to her new home. Her "Americanization" went smoothly as she performed well in high school and later attended UCLA where she earned her undergraduate degree. Events continued to go well for Jensen after she began working. As a tax accountant with Peat Marwick in Los Angeles, she quickly attained the goals and lifestyle she set out to achieve.

After four years, however, she began wondering if there was something more meaningful for her. Although she was seeing regular promotions that kept her on a partner track, she felt the limited scope of dealing only with domestic tax issues. She also felt her Chinese language skills were being wasted. Her attention turned back to Asia. In following the region's developments, she sought to work on China-related projects and shift her career into the finance industry. After a brief job search where she flew out to interview with several securities firms, Jensen landed a position as a China analyst with Morgan Grenfell. She moved to Hong Kong in the spring of 1995. Today, she is a China analyst for ING Baring Securities.

"It feels good to be out here," reveals Jensen. "I have the best time talking to the drivers whenever I'm traveling in China. I've also seen many things that make me feel lucky for what my life in the U.S. has given me. And in my job, I feel like I'm really doing something. In whatever small way, I'm helping China enter the international financial markets and develop its economy.

Jensen knows she will likely go back to the U.S. someday. However, her return to the region has already provided her with gratifying experiences. "Before moving out, I had met my grandparents only once. I grew up in Taipei and the U.S., while they lived in China. One of the most rewarding things for me has been the time I've spent with them out here," Jensen says. "During the year I lived in Shanghai, they stayed with me in my apartment for a month that winter. I had a chance to get to know them, and they got to know me better. I'm really glad I've had that opportunity with them."

American-Born Chinese (ABCs)

ABCs, as defined by the term, refer to Chinese Americans born and raised in the States. Their personalities and backgrounds are almost completely westernized. To varying degrees, they may have spoken Chinese language abilities, depending on the extent it was used with them by their parents. If they possess spoken abilities, they typically have only marginal Chinese reading and writing skills.

Many ABCS have the strong educational background and type of professional and industry training sought by multinationals. They have no problem fitting into a western corporate culture. Their attractiveness, however, depends on whether they also possess the bilingual and bicultural abilities to function effectively in local business settings.

I come across many ABCs who possess little or none of the Chinese language and cultural skills that are meaningful for employment in Greater China. With overwhelmingly westernized upbringings, they have little to leverage to make them competitive in the region's job market. It's not that it's impossible for them to pursue opportunities, but like others, they must develop the language skills and an understanding of the business environment if they're serious about a career here. Otherwise, unless they can offer an area of professional expertise that's in demand, they're better off not pursuing the idea of working in the region. Having an Asian face alone is not enough.

Personal Travelogue

I was one of those American-born Chinese who grew up not speaking Chinese, only to regret it later in life. I was raised in Raleigh, North Carolina in the 1960s, when it was quite a rarity to see Asians in the South. I do recall learning some Mandarin from my mom until I was four years old. It's a bit unusual though seeing a little Asian kid speaking English, let alone Chinese in a thick, unabashed southern accent. It was actually my grandmother who eventually told my mom: "It's great that you're teaching the kiddies to speak Chinese. But this is America. Teach them proper English first!" My mom had no objection. In her own mind, I think she was more than a little unsure if her kids were smart enough to speak two languages well.

I'm certain I did cartwheels across the front yard when I found out my mom was going to follow grandma's advice. This meant more play time and one less reason to feel different from the other kids in the neighborhood. Of course, that change of events has equated to thousands of hours trying to learn Mandarin ever since.

When I was 15, my parents began regretting the absence of Chinese language and culture in our lives and sent my brother, sister, and me to Mei-hua Saturday morning Chinese school. I resisted. They suspended my allowance. I decided to go.

After a year and a half, I made little progress on my Mandarin. In a major loss of face for my family, I became a Chinese school drop-out. Oddly, the one Mandarin conversation I mastered was about pets. For some reason, I could rattle off that one in my sleep. "*Ta you yi zhi mao, wo you liang zhi gou* (he has a cat, I have two dogs). *Yi zhi gou shi hei de, yi zhi gou shi bai de* (one dog is black, one dog is white)." Once I got on a roll, you couldn't shut me up. Unfortunately, that dog and cat conversation only came up every so often. Otherwise, I was a virtual mute when it came to conversing in Chinese.

In college, I took a first-year Mandarin course to fulfill the school's mandatory language requirement. My first serious attempt to learn Chinese occurred 10 years later, the summer before I entered business school. I attended Middlebury College summer school for an intensive study program where I learned the equivalent of one year of Mandarin in nine weeks. Unfortunately, without much opportunity to continue practicing after the program, I forgot just about a year's worth of Mandarin in five weeks. That's when I knew the only way I would ever learn to speak Mandarin was by submerging myself in an environment where I could use it everyday (i.e. Greater China).

An Underlying Desire

Through the introduction of numerous Chinese Americans from the U.S. to multinational companies in Greater China, I'm regularly asked by hiring managers why a particular candidate wants to live and work in the region. I believe that local and non-Asian recruiting personnel and business executives significantly underestimate the desire many Chinese Americans have to come out here. For many candidates that we work with, it goes beyond just career opportunity and money. There is also a sense within them that they can find greater personal fulfillment in Greater China. They are genuinely excited about what they have to offer in this environment, as someone who is part Asian and part western. They are eager to apply and challenge themselves to a degree and in ways that they have not experienced in the U.S. "Although my upbringing is very Americanized, I've also grown up with strong Chinese influences," says Natalie Tso, who has lived and worked in Taipei for the past seven years. "In the States, I'm always portraying myself only as an American. But out here, I find that I can also be as Chinese as I want. That gives me a lot more freedom and the feeling that I can better reach my full potential as a person."

Chapter 6 The Paradox: Why Two Ready And Willing Markets Can't Find Each Other

The scenario sounds straightforward enough. On one side, you have expanding multinationals in Greater China hungry to hire professional managers and staff. On the other side you have a large pool of qualified Chinese American talent in the U.S. anxious to find job opportunities in the region. Yet, despite such a seemingly ideal matchmaking situation, an interesting phenomenon is taking place. These two ready and willing markets are unable to find each other.

Greater China Hiring Is Done Out Of Greater China

Although postings for Greater China jobs are occasionally advertised in U.S. newspapers, or multinationals may make periodic recruiting efforts in the States, these hiring activities reflect just a small fraction of the overall job opportunities actually available. For instance, every Saturday edition of the *South China Morning Post* alone (Hong Kong's largest English-language daily newspaper) provides readers with over one hundred pages of job advertisements. You would never come across these and many other such listings in any U.S. newspaper. This highlights the most essential fact about the job market here. That is, the hiring for Greater China is done out of Greater China.

With this understanding, the difficulties met by both multinational companies and job-seeking candidates become clear. How can a match occur when the two sides are on faraway continents? Who has the time to identify and contact someone a half-a-day time zone away? And how effective can you be if you try? Both sides face basic realities which make coming together extremely difficult.

Challenges Facing Greater China-Based Multinationals

Immediate Hiring Needs

To begin with, the job markets in Greater China and the U.S. are fundamentally different. The Greater China job market is considerably more dynamic. Most industries and companies are in high growth stages of development and expansion. As a result, hiring needs have a "here and now" urgency to them. The availability of many candidates interviewing from the U.S. (when factoring in how much time is needed for their relocation) does not respond well to the immediate time frame of companies who must have someone up and running in a position as soon as possible.

Busy Managers

The aggressive, fast-paced nature of the region's business environment also creates a Catch 22 for hiring managers. Although these managers have the most urgent need and greatest decision-making authority to hire, they also have the least time to spend on recruiting. Besides traveling as often as once a week, they are constantly under pressure to meet deadlines and make revenue targets. Added headcount would alleviate their workload, but they are simply unable to make the necessary effort to find candidates.

We see many cases where a manager will express strong interest in a candidate, but a meeting cannot be arranged because of travel or urgent business that suddenly arises. As a result, an initial interview never takes place and the opportunity passes for good.

Infant Recruiting/Human Resources Infrastructures

Overseas subsidiaries are also not as coordinated with their home office as you might think. In fact, most run fairly independent of their U.S. headquarters. This is especially true for operations functioning in an opposite time zone and thousands of miles away. If you've worked in the region before, you know how impractical and ineffective it is to have the U.S. side involved in daily decisions and business activities. The time frame in which events and market developments occur in Asia is much shorter than in the States. U.S. corporate resources are not nearly as responsive as they often need to be. Greater China subsidiaries are, therefore, self-reliant with regard to situations requiring immediate attention.

U.S. operations also tend to be out of touch with the daily realities faced by their regional operations. Doing business in Greater China requires different approaches and ways of thinking that do not necessarily mirror home office management and corporate practices.

Activities related to recruiting, in particular, are not well coordinated between the two sides. In a classic example, one candidate told me about an unlikely, but opportune circumstance that allowed him to relocate to Taipei. He was working for a major U.S. computer products company at the time. To identify a person to start up operations in Taiwan, his company's home office human resources group searched their corporate-wide employee database for a suitable candidate.

"My name was the only one that came up based on their criteria of finding someone who had more than just a technical background and who could speak Taiwanese," the candidate describes. "My selection was entirely ludicrous because our corporate human resources thought that most people in Taiwan spoke Taiwanese, or at least did business in Taiwanese. If they had known that Mandarin was the common language and had searched their database on that criteria, many more names would have come up. Probably several were more qualified than me. But I wasn't telling anyone."

With a shortage of qualified candidates to be found locally, it would seem that multinationals would expand their recruiting efforts to places like the U.S. that offer a supply of such professionals. Regional human resources personnel have few capabilities, however, to search for candidates abroad. As part of relatively young operations, the human resources functions in Asia are not yet sophisticated and mature enough to tap into U.S.-based recruiting resources. Their primary hiring efforts are done locally. In addition, most Greater China human resources personnel are locally educated and trained professionals. They do not have the contacts and access to U.S. schools, organizations, and recruiting channels, which could turn up the type of candidates they'd like to identify. With limited overseas recruiting abilities, conducting a long-distance job search for candidates in the U.S. is a costly, long-odds proposition for Greater China operations.

There are some multinationals that actively recruit in the U.S. These are usually the major U.S. investment banks, consulting firms, and consumer product companies that tap into top U.S. MBA programs. Overall, however, they are relatively few. For the majority of multinationals, it will take time to ramp up their international recruiting efforts.

Challenges Facing U.S.-Based Job Seekers

Time, Distance, and Information Gap

The presence of Chinese Americans in Greater China has increased significantly over the past few years. But with the opportunities to be found, what's stopping many others from coming out? What I've found is that the desire among many is there. The problem is a basic and practical one. They can't connect with the job opportunities from where they are. How does a person overcome the time, distance, and information gap to find the position that will bring them to the region?

Before coming out, I attended every Asia Pacific-related job fair and business forum or seminar I could find in hopes of gaining information on how I might get a job in Greater China. These events usually featured non-Asian, senior-level expat executives and academics who were introduced as "Asia experts." Typically, however, their backgrounds and situations were entirely unlike my own. Their information was macroeconomic, revolving around high-level, corporate approaches for conducting business in Asia. Unfortunately, what I needed was practical job search advice and job market insight that applied to a young professional who wanted to become part of the opportunities and growth being expounded.

Solo Effort

Conducting a job search and landing a Greater China position from the U.S. is mostly a solo effort on behalf of the candidate. It can be a lonely process, where it often feels like you're spinning your wheels without getting anywhere. Just try doing research on the Greater China job market. Although regional employment resources are increasing, they require a commitment of time and effort to utilize.

Many positions available in Greater China aren't even advertised locally. Your ability to know about and pursue them comes from having regional contacts and speaking to the right people, not something that can be done very effectively from the U.S. For someone working full-time, with limited time to search for a job in a market thousands of miles away, this is a fairly disheartening reality.

It's no wonder why multinationals and candidates have such poor success in identifying and meeting each other. To beat the odds, you need to have an understanding of the Greater China job search process, an idea of the resources available to you, and a realistic plan of how to access job openings and decision makers. The best way to obtain these things is by following the examples of those who have successfully made the venture out.

Part III

How To Get Here

Chapter 7 The Things To Consider: Do You Belong In Greater China?

Reality Check

Greater China Is Not For Everybody

A young man from Los Angeles called me after receiving an offer to work in Hong Kong. He wanted to know what type of apartment he could afford at his salary level. I told him that housing in Hong Kong was expensive. At the same time, it was also affordable, depending on the area and type of place he chose. He just had to keep in mind that he wasn't going to get the same size place for what he was use to paying in the States. As an example, a 450 square foot, one-bedroom apartment in the Mid-levels, a residential area that attracts many foreigners, rented for about US$1500 a month. When he heard this, he exclaimed: "My God, how can anyone be expected to live like that?" As soon as he said that, I thought to myself, is this guy in for a surprise. That type of accommodation is actually not at all unusual for young professionals living here. From his comment, he seemed like someone who might have a difficult time adjusting to life in Greater China.

Whenever the topic of Chinese Americans in Greater China arises, I'm the first person to get excited about the challenges and rewards the region can offer. Although

I'm always ready to encourage anyone who wants come out, I can also be the first to let someone know that it might not be the right move for them. The international career opportunities and fast-paced lifestyle make the idea of living and working in the region an alluring proposition. Yet, as gratifying as the personal and professional growth can be, there are also tough realities to face. It's important to know what you're looking for and what Greater China can offer you. The first question to ask yourself is simply: "Is Greater China for me?"

Who Does Well In Asia?

For The Career Minded

A Work Hard, Work Hard Place

I still remember what my mentor told me when I first moved to Taipei. He was the one who initially brought me overseas. When I asked him if he had any words of advice, he merely said: "Be ready to work your ass off." I still tell people who want to come to Greater China the exact same thing.

People often describe the lifestyle here as work hard, play hard. Frequently though, it's much closer to a work hard, work hard existence. Greater China is for people who put their career first. For most, that's the predominant reason why they're here. It's a place where there is every chance to go all out in your job. With major industries expanding aggressively, there is intense pressure to produce results. On top of that, many companies are continually short-handed. Staff are given as much work and responsibility as they can handle. An average work day is at least ten hours. People often work late nights and go into the office on weekends. Many travel regularly. For those with regional or China-related responsibilities, it's not uncommon to be on the road 25–50 percent of the time. When you return, you find yourself catching up on unfinished work that has accumulated. Even after office hours, conversations tend to revolve around business. At the end of the day, it's still the topic that's on everybody's mind.

"The hours you put in can be twice as long. In China, I probably average 70 hour work weeks, and I often come in on Saturdays and Sundays."

Paying The Price

In discussing their rapid career advancement out here, many identify timing and the chances to perform among the key factors that have contributed to their success. However, they are also all quick to point out that their success did not come by chance. They earned it.

"The opportunities and fast career tracks are definitely here," acknowledges a Chinese American consultant working in Shanghai, "but you're paying the price for it. The hours you put in can be twice as long. In China, I probably average 70 hour work weeks, and I often come in on Saturdays and Sundays."

Lisa Lai: Fast Tracking It

Personal History: *Born and raised in Heilongjiang, China's northern-most province. Immigrated to Los Angeles at age 12. Living in Hong Kong since September of 1994.*

Parents: *Mom and Dad from Nanjing, China.*

Education: *B.S. in Computer Science and Engineering from the University of California, Los Angeles.*

Languages: *Native Mandarin and English speaker. Has picked up Cantonese since living in Hong Kong.*

Lisa Lai moved to Hong Kong with one goal in mind — to push her career. She left a computer programming job in Phoenix, with no intention of continuing on that track. She wanted to better utilize what she felt were her greatest assets: her Chinese language abilities, a willingness to work hard, and a conviction that her potential would someday peak in Greater China. After mass mailing more than 100 resumes and interviewing with over 30 companies, Lisa joined Procter & Gamble Hong Kong as an assistant brand manager. She set a goal to make brand manager in four years. She was one year out of college.

As a young professional entering an industry and job function that were new to her, Lisa started at the bottom. She knew she needed to gain experience. She applied her ability to learn quickly and take on multiple responsibilities and soon received a number of exceptional opportunities where her accomplishments were

Lisa Lai (bottom row, third from left) with her Hong Kong Division I field hockey team, the Zeniths, at the Hong Kong Club (January 1997)

recognized. The payoffs came with frequent and healthy salary increases.

Opportunities to interact closely with her managers added greatly to Lisa's job satisfaction. "Everyone is so young. In my office, even the most senior person is only in his mid-30s. They're great role models. To think that within 10 years, I can be where they are now. In the U.S., it's more conservative and the seniority gap seems so unbridgeable."

Within three years, Lisa has managed seven product launches and 15 copies for local and regional commercial shoots. "If you're ambitious, this is a fantastic place," she emphasizes. "Because it's such a dynamic market, you gain experience much faster. In my job, I get the chance to do everything related to a brand."

While she loves her job, Lisa admits that the consuming hours, demanding product launches, and daily pressures take a toll on her personal life. "You're earning what you reap with the long hours you put in. For example, if you average four extra hours a day, after two years you'll do as much as you'd do elsewhere in three years. The downside is that sometimes I can't socialize and enjoy my life the way I'd like. I've felt like going back to the States on several occasions," she confides. To avoid burnout, Lisa has become more involved in her other passion — sports. She makes time to get out of the office to hike or play volleyball or tennis. A year ago, she took up field hockey and now plays for one of Hong Kong's junior teams.

Still, Lisa is quick to put her sacrifices in perspective. "You have to think about your future," she says. "The experience you gain here is invaluable. I feel like I now have the skills and experience to do well wherever I go later on. And ultimately, the whole world is looking at Greater China as a new market. I want to be among the first here to make it all happen." On her three-year anniversary, Lisa was promoted to brand manager, one year ahead of schedule.

One evening in Hong Kong seemed to capture the region's work ethic. I was in the office at around eight o'clock and decided to call a couple of friends to go grab some dinner. They were both still working as well. We got together and spent an hour or so catching up. When we finished eating, at around ten o'clock, everyone revealed where they were headed next. As it turned out, all three of us were going back to the office. One guy had to make calls to his U.S. headquarters beginning at midnight. He predicted they would take until three in the morning. The next day I called to ask him how late he ended up in the office. He said that, in fact, he was on the phone until six in the morning!

For Those Seeking Challenges

Always New Situations to Face

Greater China is for those who enjoy challenges and who have a commitment to learning. Everyday you run into situations you've never encountered before. If you're not comfortable with that, then you'll probably have a difficult time here. On the other hand, if you can be receptive to what's happening around you, then you're likely to see a great deal of personal development.

One Chinese American has felt himself mature significantly from his regular encounters with local colleagues and customers. "I use to have a lot of fixed opinions and pre-conceived notions. They were based on my one-dimensional perspective of the world as an American," he points out. "When I first arrived in Hong Kong, I'd always tell everyone how things should be done. I'd make a lot of wrong assumptions and end up making bad decisions. Now, I ask questions first, I'm more patient, and I think things through more carefully. The exposure to diverse cultures and situations has helped me become much more open-minded both as a professional and a person."

Going Beyond Your Limits

Being open to new challenges can also lead to exciting opportunities. Josephina Shen's finance career was moving along quite well on a "conventional" track. After completing her MBA at UCLA, she moved to Hong Kong to participate in its booming finance industry. She was a vice president, comfortable in her position evaluating and executing direct investment deals for a major Asian investment bank. She was content growing into more responsibility over time. That was before a former colleague asked her to join his firm – a new merchant bank backed by some leading Asian families and regional corporate finance groups. The bank was forming a new Asia fund, initially capitalized at US$100 million. Josephina was asked to join the fund, but to perform key marketing, deal sourcing, and fund raising roles that went far beyond her current capacity.

"I was originally apprehensive about failing and letting down the company. I'd never done these things before, which were significant roles for the fund," admits Josephina. "But my former colleague and the other partners expressed so much confidence and support in my ability to succeed, I decided to give it a try."

Josephina joined the bank in 1996. She has not looked back since. "It's a rare, ground floor opportunity to contribute and develop ideas for a new, fast-growing company. I'm 29 years old, but in a position to act as an owner of a business. I know I'm fortunate. I'm getting the chance to do the same job my former boss did at my previous bank, only 11 years earlier. Whatever happens, I know I'll take with me skills and experience that will open doors I would normally not see open if not for this chance. I use to think very mainstream and shy away from risk. I don't anymore. I'm much more pro-active now about keeping my eyes open to new opportunities."

For The Young Or The Young At Heart

From Dusk 'Til Dawn

Because of the relentless demands of job and career, those who come to Greater China tend to be younger, or at least they think and act young. The candidates we see are mostly in their mid-30s or under. It takes a great deal of energy to work or even just to live here. The pulse of the region is quick. Intense, frenetic, fast-paced, dynamic, tiring, and demanding all appropriately describe the lifestyle. There is a tendency towards burnout among those working in the region. If you're seeking stability or are looking for an easygoing environment, then Greater China is probably not the right place for you. It's more for those who enjoy living on the edge, day-by-day.

Most people who come to Greater China also tend to be fairly free of significant personal obligations and responsibilities back in the U.S. Leaving the States to be out here is somewhat self-indulgent. It usually revolves around the chance to pursue high-reaching personal and professional goals. Whether you acknowledge it or not, by moving to Greater China you make a choice to place family and friends in the

States as a lesser priority in your life. You not only become far removed physically from those relationships, but your emphasis in life shifts more heavily towards your career. For those who have substantial family obligations or whose lives revolve around close relationships in the U.S., these are major factors to consider.

For The Adventurous And Open-Minded

Try Some Fried Scorpion?

A friend told me of a trip he took to Beijing with his boss. They were trying to secure a permit with a government official so their company could establish an office in China. On their last night, they invited the official and his colleagues to dinner. At the time, eating scorpions was very chic. To show that he was "hip" to the local cuisine, his boss ordered a plate of deep-fried scorpions for the table. I asked my friend if he tried them. "Of course," he said, "I had to." "Well, how were they?" I wanted to know. "Not so bad," he replied, "after I got past the stingers."

Now, eating scorpions does not exactly top the list of culinary treats I'd like to try in my lifetime, but one of the pleasures that living in Greater China offers is the chance to constantly learn, see, and experience new things. It's an eye-opening, fascinating place if you're willing to explore and experiment a little. You can immerse yourself in 5000 years of history and culture, and visit inspiring and memorable sites. There's also an abundance and variety of delicious food. And there's a mosaic of perspectives that reflects how people see the world outside of America.

Since I've been in Asia, I've gone shrimp fishing at midnight in the hills outside of Taipei (you actually fish for shrimp with pencil thin rods and a hook). I've celebrated a spring harvest festival in southern Taiwan, where I danced (hopped around actually) with local Ami tribe villagers for two straight days. I drank about a gallon of local brew and feasted on an open-pit roasted boar. I've also stayed in a one-room home of a Chinese family in a village outside Shanghai. It was my first time using a squat toilet (I must admit I felt pretty liberated after that experience)! For many, the adventure that Asia offers is the primary attraction for coming out.

Even for the most diehard adventure seekers, however, many aspects of life in Greater China are frustrating and difficult to deal with. For example, there's a severe lack of a service concept. No matter where you go, you're constantly being made to wait or stand in line. Even those who return after being abroad for a while discover the place to be more congested, disorganized, and abrasive than they remembered.

If you're the type who prefers familiarity and convenience, or the routine and orderly, then you're likely to find Asia a tough place to live.

For most, living in Greater China is an ongoing love-hate relationship. It's about keeping the bad points in perspective and appreciating the good ones. Although you may often want to make comparisons with the U.S., the differences are a major part of what makes Greater China such an interesting place. If you can accept those differences, then there's a good chance you'll enjoy living here.

The Most Suitable Type

It's difficult to predict exactly how someone will adapt to the lifestyle of Greater China. Factors such as knowing people in the place where you live, what time of year you arrive, and how smoothly you settle into permanent accommodations can make a big difference in how quickly and easily you adjust. Lori Quon moved to Hong Kong in 1990. After spending two and a half years in advertising, she decided to start her own business, Brio International Limited, to export men's and women's casual fashions to South America and Europe. Lori once described to me the kind of people she felt were most suitable for Greater China. It's worth mentioning.

Lori feels that people coming to Greater China could be placed in three categories. The first type come mostly for career reasons. They usually have limited interest in the culture or local lifestyle. Rather than try to integrate, their efforts are spent trying to minimize the degree of westernization they must forego as a result of their relocation. Without a diverse, more complete lifestyle to enjoy, there is little else outside of work to sustain their interest in being here. Often, they soon get fed up with the relentless pace, demands, and frustrations of both their job and the region. This type usually doesn't end up lasting long.

The second type come for the adventure. They're here to experience the culture, sights, and people of Greater China. For those just looking for adventure, their contentment can last a while. Greater China and the rest of Asia can be endlessly explored. Eventually, however, these people may become restless. Wanderlust does not last forever, nor can it financially sustain itself indefinitely.

The third type possesses both a desire for professional achievement and personal adventure. These are the ones likely to enjoy themselves the most and who are often the most successful. They also tend to stay the longest. They are driven not only by the career challenges and opportunities in Greater China, but they are also interested in integrating into the local culture and with the local people. Their fulfillment is well-balanced. It's this kind of gratification which makes a person want to stay a long time.

Be Prepared For A Lifestyle Change

I Miss My Morning Bagel And Whipped Cappuccino!

If you move to Greater China, count on almost every aspect of your life changing dramatically. You give up all sorts of things you may be very accustomed to in the States. To begin with, most of your family and friends will now be a few extra thousand miles away from you. Imagine seeing these people only once or twice a year. During the time I've lived in Greater China, I've missed anniversaries, weddings, and special occasions of many people I'm close to in the U.S. Unfortunately, it's just too difficult returning so frequently.

You'll also have to cope with much less space. Say good-bye to living in a large home or apartment (unless you're fortunate enough to have your company pay for it). What may be considered a closet in the States often functions as a bedroom in Asia. Outdoors, you'll find few places that aren't crowded. For most of us, even the concept of escaping the city and "getting away" to the great outdoors is not easy. It's not as simple as taking off in a car. Most likely, you won't have one. Owning a car is typically reserved for the well-off. Import taxes easily double the price of what you'd pay for the same model in the States. Parking is also a pain, and it's expensive. Even if you have a car, there are few places to drive it. Many end up mostly going between two places, their home and the office. Whenever I'm back in the U.S., the first thing I do is rent a car and drive down the freeway with the windows down and the radio blasting.

Perhaps people in New York are accustomed to working long hours, but I used to live in Los Angeles. On a typical day, I'd be out of the office and halfway to the beach by 4:45pm. I don't know anyone in Hong Kong who leaves work before 6pm on a regular basis. Just try taking off that early every day. Forget it! The workload, pressure to perform, and corporate culture just won't allow it.

When I lived in L.A., I was also active in sports. I'd go cycling along the beach two or three times a week. I played tennis on weekends and participated in one or two softball leagues throughout the year. Because Asian cities are so populated, however, outdoor sports are much more difficult to arrange. There just aren't the facilities or convenience to do the same activities we're use to doing in the States. overseas. You can't easily jump onto a tennis court or a ball field. Out here, I'm lucky if I play tennis three or four times a year. If you play golf, you better have a liberal company expense account or generous friends who belong to a club. A round can easily cost over US$100. And that's at the public courses! Try jogging or cycling on the streets. It's a life-threatening hazard, more detrimental than helpful to your health because of the cars and polution. To stay in shape, the best I can manage is going to the gym twice a week (on a good week). So much for my Adonis-like physique.

In the States, I often had time to just hang out and relax. I use to watch a good amount of television: Redskins football games, *The David Letterman Show, Saturday Night Live*, you name it. If you want to watch a live U.S. sporting event in Greater China, then you better be a light sleeper. Because of the time difference, U.S. games are televised after midnight. For the past seven years, I've woken up to see the Superbowl at 6am on Monday morning! And sure, *Seinfeld, Baywatch*, and the *X-files* can now be seen on local stations, but they're episodes from last season. As a result, you tend to fall behind on U.S. trends.

Socially, it's easy to meet people, but difficult to make close friends. Everyone is always busy working and traveling. It's not only them, but you too. Even when you have the time, you often don't have the energy. You end up randomly running into people at house parties or happy hours, making promises to get together in the near future. Unless you go out of your way to schedule it though, it rarely happens.

Making the decision to move to Greater China is all about weighing the trade-offs. The lifestyle is exciting, but it can also be a grind. It's eye-opening and enriching, but it can also be limiting. It can allow you to know a wide variety of interesting and successful people, but it can also be lonely and isolated. Enjoying life in Greater China starts with understanding these trade-offs and then knowing whether you can live with them.

Taking Inventory Of Your Skills

Even if your desire to be in Greater China is strong, you also need to assess what you have to offer. I meet many candidates who claim to have high aspirations for developing a career in the region. Yet, when I ask about their background and skills for working here, many are unable to articulate any. Instead, their responses are short and simplistic:

Candidate: I'm looking for a position in Greater China that will offer me career growth opportunities.

Me: That's good. There are plenty of those out here. Mind if I ask you a few questions first?

Candidate: Shoot.

Me: All right, first of all, do you speak an Asian language?

Candidate: No, but I plan on learning. I'm sure I can pick it up pretty quickly.

Me: Right ... well, have you ever lived or stayed in Greater China for an extended period of time?

Candidate: No, but I came here for a week on vacation once. I do like to travel though and I'm very adaptable to new environments and situations.

Me: Okay ... well, have you ever done any business related to the region?

Candidate: No, but I've always had an interest in this part of the world.

Me: Okay ... well, let's see, ... that's good, ... ummmm, ... so, how 'bout them Mets!

For such candidates, I have to tell them that realistically they will have an extremely difficult time finding a suitable position. The pool of bilingual and bicultural professionals the region is attracting and producing continues to grow. Without fundamental language skills, an understanding of local markets, or regional business experience to offer, there are few compelling reasons why such a person would stand out to a multinational employer.

Even if you have developed some local capabilities, it is becoming increasingly competitive to find a niche in Asia if those skills are not genuinely strong. I meet many Asian and non-Asian candidates whose primary Greater China experience is through U.S.-based East Asian Studies undergraduate or graduate programs. Their language is learned in classrooms. Their understanding of Asia business is entirely through articles and books. Their Asia experience comes from a trek or two through the region. Based on such a background, they believe they possess an advantage for conducting regional business.

Unfortunately, such a peripheral Greater China background no longer carries the same weight that it might have several years ago. Asian skills acquired in the U.S. do not attract the same attention as before. Today, the comparison must be made to the increasing number of native Chinese speakers who offer the same U.S. academic degrees and business training, plus stronger regional exposure. To be attractive to employers here, a more direct and aggressive approach is required. For developing local language skills and business understanding, nothing compares to learning it in Greater China itself.

If you don't already possess local abilities and experience, you need to take a closer look at your job marketability. This doesn't mean you have to give up your ambition to work in the region. As long as you have a willingness to acquire the skills needed, you can achieve the goals you seek here. Quite a few have shown it can be done. However, these success stories all indicate that it takes a real commitment and long-term effort to make it happen.

It Takes Time

Success Does Not Come Overnight

Some candidates I meet are entirely unrealistic about the time frame it will take to achieve the goals they've set in the region. They expect to make quantum leaps in their career advancement despite their lack of the language skills, market knowledge, professional training, or relationships necessary to be successful here.

Often, it just takes time for your break to happen. I know many who have switched into jobs and industries they had little previous background in. They didn't make the jump when they first arrived though. Instead, they first leveraged the strength of their work experience to find a good position that would bring them to Greater China. Once here, they were able to develop their network of contacts, understanding of the region, and knowledge of the industry that interested them.

Of the many success stories I hear about, each one involves hard work and some degree of patience by the individual. Luck or timing contribute to some extent, but there are no real short cuts to their success. Their career development is clear to see. When their opportunities eventually came, they were ready.

Martin Leung began his career with IBM in New York. He worked there for seven years in various software development positions. Frustrated over being typecast as a "techie," he began contemplating Greater China as a better place to pursue his interests in marketing and business development. In 1993, he sought a transfer to IBM's Hong Kong operations.

"The most important thing I did was to figure out where I wanted to be in a few years. After that, I just tried to take realistic steps and show people what I could do whenever I had the chance."

Martin's first position with IBM in Hong Kong was in post-sales support. Although it was a technical position similar to what he did in the States, it gave him the opportunity first and foremost to be in Asia. The position also allowed him to begin making contacts within Hong Kong's information technology industry. A year later, he moved to a U.S. software products company into a sales manager role. There, he was able to gain the sales experience he always sought and play an increasing role in new business development opportunities for the firm.

Today, Martin is a principal consultant for Platinum Technology, a U.S. software company operating in Hong Kong. He is responsible for developing its business strategy and sales plan for new products launched in the region. His role is critical for Platinum's expansion in Greater China. Martin is now looking to move into a regional marketing position, which he is confident will occur soon. "The most important thing I did was figure out where I wanted to be in a few years," Martin explains. "After that, I just tried to take realistic steps and show people what I could do whenever I had the chance."

The Longer You Stay, The Better It Gets

People who choose to stay in Greater China for only two years or less really short change themselves. You give up a great deal by leaving so quickly, particularly after working so hard to pay your dues during those initial years here.

For just about everyone who comes to Greater China, there's a steep learning curve to climb. Your first year is your learning year. Even for those who grew up in the region and left, there's a lot to adapt to and relearn upon returning. It takes time

Felix Wong: Staying the Course

Personal History: *Born and raised in Vancouver, Canada. Grew up in Oakland, California. Moved to Shenzhen in February 1994. Living in Hong Kong since 1996.*

Parents: *Mom and Dad from Shanghai, China.*

Education: *B.S. in Economics from the University of California, Davis*

Languages: *Native Cantonese and English speaker. Grew up speaking Mandarin and Shanghainese at home as well.*

Felix Wong and wife Sophie (on her cellular phone) at his company's Christmas party in Hong Kong (December 1997)

Ever since he was a kid, Felix Wong loved movies. While growing up, he became fascinated by Hollywood. In 1994, however, it seemed like an impossible road going from the soy milk to the entertainment industry. That's the dilemma Felix faced. Working as a marketing manager for Vitasoy at the time, his job was to expand the company's soy milk market in North America. Although he was performing well, he knew he'd never reach Hollywood on that track.

The turning point for Felix began with a job ad he saw in *The Wall Street Journal*. The posting was for a sales manager position with Seagrams in Asia. Felix knew that Edgar Bronfman Jr., Seagrams' Chief Executive Officer and President, was enamored with the idea of getting into the entertainment industry. Although it was an incredible long shot, a job at Seagrams could potentially get him one step closer to the entertainment business.

The catch was that the job was based in Shenzhen, China. Actually, living in Shenzhen was not far beyond the realm of Felix's experience. He first went to China in 1987 to spend a year abroad while in college. During his stay, he didn't go to a newly modernizing city. Instead, he chose Manchuria where he worked in a Chinese and Russian jointly owned caviar plant. "I probably know more about making caviar than any Chinese American alive," Felix muses.

With an interest to return to Asia always in the back of his mind, Felix applied for and landed the Seagrams position. When he arrived in Shenzhen, adjustments were in order. The management team was made up entirely of Hong Kong expatriates. The local business nature and style of selling spirits was also dramatically different from selling soy milk. As much as it was a day job, it was also a night job. Felix was expected to go to night clubs and karaoke bars after office hours to nurture relationships with his best customers, the club owners.

"Most days I'd get up at 7am for work. I'd spend all day planning marketing and sales activities and meeting with management. At 8pm I'd leave the office and start making my rounds to our top customers, which always involved some form of drinking and entertaining. This would go until two or three in the morning. Then I'd get up at 7am again and start the process all over. This happened three to five days a week. It was pretty grueling."

After two years, Felix's break finally arrived. Seagrams bought MCA and Universal Pictures. He immediately sent out feelers to the MCA side. Within a year, an opening appeared. Today, Felix is MCA's director of new business development for Asia.

"Without coming out here, I never could have made the move into movies. Hollywood is a tough place to break into. In Asia though, it's an incredibly exciting time for the studios to blaze new trails. I'm like a twister who knows the terrain and can stir things up for my company. In essence, my job is to bring a bit of Hollywood to Asia."

Looking back, Felix is glad he stayed with his spirits job. "It was like boot camp, a total mental and physical challenge. There were times I'd be laying in bed at three in the morning, after a long night with clients. I'd stare at the ceiling and wonder to myself if I could do this much longer or if I was even on the right track. It's hard to stay focused with so many opportunities springing up around you. But you need to be patient. If you keep going after what you want, anything's possible."

to figure out how to get things done effectively. Most importantly, it takes time to prove yourself and establish a track record.

Once over those fundamental hurdles though, as time passes, you'll find that the picture for you changes dramatically. By your second year, you'll not only start to feel like a Greater China veteran, you'll be considered one too. You'll begin to be able to make significant contributions in your job. In addition, the opportunities and your ability to take advantage of them start to get exponentially better.

We try to tell candidates just coming out, that although they may have a specific destination in mind, not to overlook the journey to get there. Just being here is fun and exciting. It takes a little time and hard work to reach where you want to go. It's important to give things a chance to happen though, and to enjoy the ride along the way.

You Never Know What Will Happen Next

Although most people in Greater China are only able to project an initial two or three-year stay when they first arrive, the majority end up staying longer than they planned. Their decision to remain arises from unforeseen, positive factors. I've heard many say they can't afford to go back. Their comment does not reflect a poor situation awaiting them in the States. Rather, they would have to make significant career and financial sacrifices if they left the region.

Evolving Goals

Christine and Michael Chow initially thought of a stint in the region as an adventure. When they arrived in Hong Kong in the fall of 1991, Christine was a brand manager for Procter & Gamble's China marketing team and Michael was an economic planner for Dow Chemicals. How long they would stay was entirely unknown to both of them.

After seven years, they've seen their life in Greater China develop deeper and deeper roots. During that time, they spent five years living and working in Guangzhou. Today, they're residing in Hong Kong once again. Christine is the Asia marketing director for a major consumer apparel multinational. Michael is still at Dow, but as the director of sales for Asia Pacific. They've also started a family since coming out here.

"Life here isn't about taking the middle road, but going to extremes and enjoying it," describes Michael. "The more clear the picture becomes, the more unclear it is as well. As your career and personal life develop, there's a greater sense of purpose in what you want to achieve. At the same time, you don't know where it will lead. The excitement comes from both ends of the spectrum."

"Your outlook and decision to remain changes significantly after being here a few years," Christine explains. "Once you gain the knowledge and experience, it becomes more personal. Beyond just the adventure, you try to build something that will have a meaningful impact. You start to lay down roots and extend your time frame. So much is happening here now. We want to continue to be a part of it."

Developing Ties That Bind

C.K. Tsang relocated to the region with the Boston Consulting Group, recruited from his MBA program at Northwestern University. His initial plan was to spend a couple of years in Hong Kong. C.K. is now in his seventh year here. "In the U.S., things are more predictable. But in Asia, anything can happen," he describes. "With the demand for bilingual and bicultural backgrounds, your stay is based on opportunity rather than a defined period of time."

"With the demand for bicultural and bilingual backgrounds, your stay is based on opportunity rather than a defined period of time."

In C.K.'s experience, personal factors also play a significant role in the decision to remain. "My wife is from Malaysia," C.K. says. "She's very close to her family. As a result, there's a strong likelihood we'll remain here indefinitely. Several of my friends have also married spouses from this part of the world. They tend to share the same outlook of staying longer."

The "I Belong/Do Not Belong In Greater China" Self-Assessment Quiz

Now that you have a better idea of the type of people who are most suitable for a career in Greater China, let's make your decision process even simpler. The following is a quick self-assessment quiz that may help you determine whether living and working in the region is the right move for you.

1) ***You want to live and work in Greater China, as long as:***
   a) the company that hires you pays for your housing, will fly you back to the U.S. once a year, and there are few infringements on your current quality of life.
   b) the company offers you a good opportunity in which the position and responsibilities give you the chance to perform and show your capabilities.

2) ***When it comes to Chinese language skills, you can:***
   a) carry on a 30-minute conversation fairly comfortably … as long as people stick to topics about your family, the weather, and what you like to do on weekends.
   b) handle a business situation without much difficulty.

3) ***You like a working environment where:***
   a) there are structured, mature operation in place and lots of resources to support you. Otherwise, how else are you going to learn?
   b) you're encouraged to get your hands dirty, explore different areas, and where your only limitation is how aggressive you are at learning and doing things.

4) ***You're at a business dinner in Taipei being entertained by a client. For the third course, they bring out snake's blood soup accompanied by a dish of sliced, boiled pig ears. Your clients are delighted and start digging in. You:***
   a) make up an excuse (i.e. "I had that for lunch," or "I'm sorry, I'm allergic to boiled reptile hemoglobins") and ask the waiter for another bowl of white rice.

b) tell yourself that you'll try anything once, start munching along with the others, and use the soup to wash down that chewy pig's ear.

5) ***You find out you're being considered for a position in Greater China in which you're very interested. The opportunity may come up soon. If the offer is made, you:***

a) need to deliberate on the decision with significant others, get the best price on your house in the market, and prepare yourself mentally and emotionally for the move. If everything goes well, you might possibly be available in three months.

b) are ready to resign from your job, sell your car, close your lease, and say your good-byes within the next few weeks.

6) ***You're standing in line again in the Mid-levels of Hong Kong, waiting for the mini-bus to take you to work. As you wait in line, you:***

a) continuously look at your watch, think incessantly about the time you're wasting, and start thinking about how you wish you were driving to work in your car like you used to back in the U.S.

b) open up your newspaper, accept the wait, and hope it doesn't rain.

7) ***When someone asks you what you're planning to do five years from now, you:***

a) give them a yearly breakdown of what you'll be doing and where you'll be at various stages during that period.

b) admit that things could change as you speak, but you'll likely pursue whatever continues to be challenging and rewarding.

8) ***Your boss gives you a choice of job assignments for the next two years. You would choose the one that:***

a) will involve a single project scope and clearly defined schedule that will last the entire two years. You won't have to be concerned about any major deviations from the plan.

b) may include a variety of different projects that you could be either juggling or moving on from fairly quickly. You won't know when these projects will come up or how long they will last, but they promise to add to your career development.

9) *It's your first week in Hong Kong and one of the first things you find out is that they don't have Wheaties, your favorite breakfast food. Your reaction is:*

a) Damn it, no Wheaties?!? I bet I won't even be able to get a decent bagel out here either!
b) Well, I wonder what people in Hong Kong do for breakfast? I hear there's great dim sum out here. I'll have to check that out.

10) *When looking for a career opportunity, you're the type likely to choose:*

a) an established company that has a proven track record, systems in place, and near-guaranteed, steady single-digit growth prospects per year.
b) a company fairly new in the region, but with an innovative service or product for the market, a young energetic management team, and substantial, annual double-digit growth potential over the next few years.

11) *You've been planning it for weeks, a weekend of great food and some gambling in Macau. Nobody from work to bother you and suddenly ... you receive a call from the office. They need you to come in on Saturday to help get the group's project report out on time. You:*

a) enjoy your weekends too much to give them up! Besides, you need the time off to recuperate, otherwise you won't be fresh for the following Monday. Sorry guys, I'm out of here!
b) take a deep breath, start unpacking your suitcase, and hope that next month you'll have the chance to take a well deserved break.

12) *Greater China attracts all types of interesting people. Socially, you're the type who:*

a) prefers hanging around a small group of the same people. In fact, if they're not available, you'll most likely end up just staying home and watching TV.
b) enjoys meeting a variety of new people, learning about their backgrounds, and getting to know what they're doing in Asia.

Self Assessment Ratings

If you selected 10–12 b) responses, you should pack your bags and get ready for your 12–24 hour flight! Your career goals and personality appear to be well-suited for Greater China. You're likely to enjoy the challenges and excitement of living and working in the region.

If you selected 7–9 b) responses, postpone your travel plans and take a good look in the mirror. Perhaps you should put some additional thought into a thorough, honest assessment to determine whether relocating to Greater China is the right move for you.

If you selected 6 or less b) responses, don't sell the house yet. You should appreciate where you are now and put your efforts into improving your present situation. Mostly likely, you're much better off and are going to be happier with life in the United States.

Chapter 8 The Things To Know: What Does It Take To Get Out Here?

The young man who approached me in Los Angeles after my presentation on *The Greater China Job Market* was perplexed. He had heard me give several examples of Chinese Americans who were doing extremely well in the region. He was also a fluent Mandarin speaker with several years of work experience with a reputable U.S. company. He kept up-to-date with Asia events and business developments. Yet, he was puzzled over why others with backgrounds no more qualified than his were making it to Greater China, while he remained in the U.S. wondering why he was not there too. He wanted to know what they did to get to the region that he wasn't doing?

There wasn't a single answer I could give him. There are several reasons why some are able to land job opportunities, while others are not. Among the many who have successfully placed themselves in Greater China, they tend to share a few common characteristics.

Initiative

Be Pro-Active

Many people start their Greater China job search by contacting the U.S. headquarters of multinational firms regarding employment opportunities abroad. Their inquiries are often never heard about again. Candidates may then fax or mass mail resumes directly to offices in Greater China. Usually, little is known about these operations. They may not even identify a specific person in their correspondence. Afterwards, candidates may make follow-up phone calls to solicit interest in their background. Some may just wait for a response. Their hope is that firms will either meet them in the States or evaluate them through an initial phone interview.

The entire approach is a passive one, unlikely to result in landing a job in the region. Unfortunately, it's also a common one. It's easy to say that you want to work in Greater China if the companies and opportunities sought you out and conveniently showed up at your door. However, that's not the way it happens.

A Greater China job search requires a pro-active approach on your part. Successful candidates leave no stone unturned. They have a drive to be in the region and are committed to seeking out openings. They also utilize whatever resources or networks available to them. The good news is that the information and contacts to connect you with the job market are available and constantly improving. These include newspaper classifieds, business and alumni associations, recruitment firms, and the Internet. To access and make use of them though takes a focused effort.

It's Your Job Search

In giving U.S.-based candidates job search help for Greater China positions, we give them an idea of what the current employment market is like. We tell them how we're able to pursue opportunities on their behalf. We also let them know that, although we are an excellent job search resource, we cannot guarantee interviews with companies. Nobody can. Ultimately, your own self-effort has the greatest impact on your employment success. When it comes down to it, it's your job search, your money and time investment, and your career and future in the balance.

Many candidates who contact us greatly underestimate what is involved in a successful Greater China job search. One candidate repeatedly stressed his desire to work in Asia. His questions about the job market were endless. In each instance, I told him that I felt his background was well-suited for opportunities in the region. When his friend landed a position in Hong Kong after visiting for just a week, it reinforced his feeling that he should be working here too.

Finally, he planned a trip to Hong Kong. For several weeks, he called to ask about how many interviews we had set up for his visit. We were, in fact, able to arrange a good one for him. He was disappointed, however, that there weren't additional meetings arranged. As a result, he decided to cut his trip short, from two weeks to just a few days. Without more interviews, he didn't feel it was worth his while to stay longer.

Before his trip, I asked him if he had contacted any firms on his own or if he met with his friend, who had just returned, to pick his brain for leads. He said he didn't have the time. Essentially, he was counting on us alone to search for him.

The candidate flew to Hong Kong. Unfortunately, the position we arranged for him to interview for was filled by someone else. Sure enough, he came and went without generating any other job prospects or market information beyond what we provided. I felt he missed a great chance to make significant progress on his job search. He had the opportunity to collect names beforehand. Contacting those people would have benefited him substantially. In the end, the result reflected the effort.

Persistence

It Pays Off

When I began my own five-year odyssey to come to Greater China, I started at ground zero. Beyond an appreciation of Chinese values, I had none of the fundamental language, cultural, or business skills to obtain a suitable position in the region. I had to build up those abilities from scratch. Just to learn Mandarin, I took an intensive study language program, hired private tutors, and listened religiously to homemade lesson tapes.

I was also reluctant to come out by taking a job that would be a major step backwards. I wanted an opportunity at a level that would maintain the momentum in my career. I knew I had solid experience and professional skills to offer. But I also knew they would not come into play in a significant way until I could function within

Personal Travelogue

As a first-year MBA student, I had my heart set on working over the summer in Greater China. Unfortunately, only a handful of firms came to campus to recruit for overseas internship positions. I received an invitation to meet with one major consumer products company. At the bottom of my resume I wrote the ambiguous words, "proficient in Mandarin."

Anticipating a test of my language skills during the interview, I practiced my Mandarin responses, drawing from my vast first-year level of language training. As I recall, my conversation with the Mandarin speaking company representative went something like this:

Me: Ni hao. Wo de mingzi shi Larry Wang. (Hi, my name is Larry Wang)
P&G Interviewer: *Ni hao. Ni jintian hao bu hao?* *(Hello. How are you today?)*
Me: Wo hen hao. Nin ne? (I'm fine. And you?)
P&G Interviewer *Wo ye bu cuo.* *(I'm also fine)*
Me: Hen hao, ... (That's nice) ... silence

With only one year of Mandarin under my belt, it was not easy being a captivating conversationalist. Yet, on we chatted.

P&G Interviewer: *Ni de fumu* * *cong nali lai de* ** *?* *(Where are your parents from)*
Me: Uhhhhh, ... dui bu qi, ni keyi bu keyi zai shuo yi ci? (huh?!?)
P&G Interviewer: *Okay, ... well, let's see, ... that's good, ... ummmm, ... so, how 'bout them Mets!*

* I later learned that "fu mu" was a more colloquial term for mother and father. In Chinese class, we had always used "*baba*" and "*mama*." No wonder I was thrown off.

** I had also never heard the expression "*cong na li lai de*" before. I had learned the textbook way, "*ni cong nar lai de*." Clearly, an honest mistake.

The interview brought to light a particularly harsh reality. I was nearly hopeless at speaking Mandarin with a native speaker or with anyone not reciting lines from a first-year Chinese textbook. Add to that my heavy western accent and I don't think I was fooling anyone into thinking I could conduct business in Chinese. I guess that's why my campus interviews for Greater China internship positions only lasted the few minutes they usually did.

the local business environment. Eventually, I found the right opportunity. Yet, it would not have happened if I hadn't plugged away as long as I did.

Persistence does pay off. After graduating from Georgetown University, Evan Ho moved to Hong Kong to work for a property research firm. After a year, he decided to go to Taipei to learn Mandarin and use it in a business setting. He brought with him a basic foundation from two years of previous classroom study.

A couple of months after arriving in Taipei, Evan set his sights on gaining an analyst position within an international bank. He knew it would not be achievable without the ability to read newspaper business pages and company financial statements written in Chinese. To reach his goal, he began a rigorous self-study program to recognize Chinese characters related to banking terms. He did this by obtaining Chinese financial statements from a friend already working at a bank and by copying articles from the business section of local newspapers, which he would bring to class to review with his teacher. In total, Evan estimates that he devoted hundreds of hours practicing to recognize business and finance characters.

After six months, he felt confident enough to apply for banking jobs. He submitted his application for a credit analyst position at a European bank. The bank called Evan in and asked him to write a brief analysis based on a set of financial statements in Chinese. He passed the reading and writing requirement and was offered the position.

Factors Beyond Your Control

Attaining your ideal job may not happen immediately. Timing alone can dictate when the right job opportunity may present itself. The finance industry in Hong Kong is a prime example. In late 1992, China began allowing mainland companies and enterprises to be listed on international stock markets. From 1992 until early 1995, investment banks hired almost indiscriminately in anticipation of the swell of underwriting activity to take place. If you had any type of quantitative skills as an engineer, accountant, or graduating MBA and the ability to speak even a little Mandarin, you were likely to have your pick of several offers.

Unfortunately, China's financial markets underperformed relative to expectations. Banks began to down-size from the over-hiring that took place just months earlier. By the end of 1995, even candidates with finance industry experience had difficulty finding a job.

Greater China markets, industries, and companies are subject to rollercoaster cycles that change quickly and unpredictably. Such factors are beyond your control. Overall, however, the job opportunities do eventually appear, usually sooner than later, for those who keep looking.

Taking The Risk

The entire process of going after a job located on the other side of the world involves weighing risks. The time and distance gap alone means you'll have to invest a good deal of money and effort to get closer to the job market. It could likely require much more of each than you originally anticipate. The interviewing process can last for months. If you're working, then you'll have to use precious vacation days to travel to the region. For those without strong language skills, the personal and financial investment in Chinese classes or private lessons can be considerable. To keep abreast of Asia business news, you may also have to subscribe to regional periodicals.

What's The Risk?

Some feel the decision to move out is not nearly as monumental as people make it to be. There are those who have even made the jump with little previous exposure to the region. For them, there was never a question of risk.

Wilkin Tai graduated with a computer science degree from the University of British Columbia in Canada. He took a job with a financial consulting firm in San Francisco to write programs that analyzed financial statements. His work day lasted from 9am to 4:45pm. His office environment was relaxed, and his life was on cruise control. It was so routine, in fact, that Wilkin soon felt he could end up doing the same thing for the next 20 years. He didn't like that feeling.

Without coming to Asia, I never would have had the skills, desire, or ability to take on the entrepreneurial challenges I have."

While studying for his MBA at the University of San Francisco, Wilkin met several classmates from Asia who opened his eyes to international business. In 1990, based on conversations with several of his South East Asian friends, he decided to move to Singapore to see how real the opportunities were that they often spoke of. Two months after arriving, he landed a position as a financial analyst for a US$300 million emerging markets fund. The fund is well known today as Franklin Templeton, run by Dr. Mark Mobius. Wilkin was one of the first five staff to join the team.

His initial intent was merely to learn how to become a financial analyst and then leverage the experience to find a similar position back in the U.S. At Templeton, however, he was able to ride Asia's booming financial markets of the early 1990s. He kept riding it. Within just three years, he was promoted to a director position. In 1994, an opportunity came up for Wilkin to move to Hong Kong and join a US$400 million start-up fund at Hansberger Global Investors. He joined them as a partner and set up the infrastructure resources needed to do trading for their new asset management team in Asia.

"What I'm doing out here goes far beyond what I could have ever imagined," states Wilkin. "There's no way I'd have done the same things had I stayed in the States. I didn't go to a top 20-ranked business school. When I graduated, my only real goal was to get a job to pay off my student loans. Without coming to Asia, I never would have had the skills, desire, or ability to take on the entrepreneurial challenges I have."

Wilkin's approach to his move out was a bottom-line one. He felt he wasn't giving up anything in the States that was irreplaceable by moving to the region. "Coming out here is all about risk, but what's the risk?" Wilkin asks. "In my case, I was at a point in my life where I had achieved at least a certain level of success. If things didn't work out, I felt I could always go back and find another job like the one I had. In the end, you have to take a good, hard look at your situation. If you have family obligations, then that's something substantial to consider. But if you're young and mobile, you should just do it. Moving to Asia was the best 'risk' I've ever taken."

For most, the decision to move to Greater China comes down to weighing critical personal issues. Will I like living in Greater China? Am I suited for its frenetic pace? Will I miss my life in the States too much? There are also the considerations of how the move will impact your career. Regarding career, however, I can only say that I have not heard anyone say that they regretted the choice to come out, regardless of the length of their stay in the region. As one person put it: "With the globalization of world economies and the increasing competitiveness in the job market, would you rather be someone with international experience under your belt, or without?"

Chapter 9 The Greater China Job Search Trip: Nothing Beats Being Here

Nothing Beats Being Here

When people ask for advice on getting a job in Greater China, I simply tell them: "Come out here." You need to place yourself in the hornets' nest, where the overwhelming majority of hiring activity is taking place. If you're unwilling to make at least one trip out, then realistically your chances of landing a position are slim.

Getting Face To Face With Hiring Managers

Your availability to interview in Greater China is one of the greatest factors that determines whether a company will pursue you. When my firm introduces profiles to clients, managers pay much closer attention to resumes of candidates who will be in the region and can interview at their office within a reasonable time frame. Fundamentally, they don't want to jump through hoops and go through hassles just to meet you.

Hiring managers generally have little interest in prescreening candidates in the U.S. through a long distance phone interview process. It's neither a practical nor an effective approach. It's time consuming, costly, and rarely results in a successful hire. Even if the initial conversation is a positive one, the next step still requires a face-to-face meeting. Ultimately, however, a phone call or two does not provide enough of an assessment to justify the cost of flying a candidate halfway around the world for a follow-up interview.

Peggy Shiu: Getting On The Plane

Personal History: *Born and raised in Hawaii. Moved to Hong Kong in February of 1993. Living in Beijing since February of 1995.*
Parents: *Mom and Dad from Hong Kong*
Education: *B.S. in Real Estate Development and Management, University of Southern California.*
Languages: *Native English speaker. Fluent in Mandarin, learned through a three-month course at the Beijing Language Institute and continuous self-study and daily usage in Beijing.*

Peggy Shiu outside of her office in Beijing (October 1997)

Peggy Shiu knows all about how difficult it is to look for a job in Greater China from the U.S. She grew up speaking no Cantonese or Mandarin. "In my family, we had rice at every meal, but as far as 'Chinese' skills I acquired while growing up, there weren't many," says Peggy. "The idea to go to Asia and my interest to learn Mandarin came about after I graduated from college."

She began her Greater China job search while working for a real estate consulting firm in Los Angeles. She tried leveraging her two and a half years of experience to push for a transfer to her company's Hong Kong office, but was unsuccessful. To generate job leads, she joined several Asian professional organizations and attended numerous events. She even went to L.A.'s Hong Kong Development Council to look up company addresses and contact numbers.

Over a one-year period, she sent out over 100 cover letters and resumes to companies in Hong Kong. "I literally wound up with a book full of rejections. I bounded them together and showed them to a friend one day, who couldn't believe how many there were. He just looked at me and said: 'If you're that determined, then why don't you just go there and look.' Suddenly, that made a whole lot of sense."

Still, Peggy was hesitant to pack up and make the move. Oddly enough, what made up her mind was a seemingly small event. Her mom happened to have a free airline ticket to Hong Kong earned through frequent flyer travel points. With no more excuses to hold her back, Peggy gave her one-month notice and was on her way.

Peggy's first few days in Hong Kong were memorable. Her mom had booked her a US$30 per night hotel in Causeway Bay that was recommended by a friend. When she arrived, she discovered the hotel was one frequented by Mainland Chinese tourists on tour packages. "I wasn't expecting a lot, but it was the worst accommodation I'd ever seen. The room was a closet and the bathroom was a communal squat toilet. I pretty much slept with one eye open that first night."

The one job lead she had did not work out. Fortunately, however, the manager she interviewed with happened to have a room to rent in his apartment. Peggy took up the offer and gladly moved out of her hotel after one day. With more comfortable accommodations, she got busy. She bought a fax and phone machine and started her job search. After two months, she received an offer from Jones Lang Wootten in their Asian Hotel Division. In her new position, Peggy performed property development feasibility studies in the region and gained her first exposure to China. A year later, she moved to Beijing for a new job and to pursue her original intent to learn Mandarin. Today, she's able to conduct business in Chinese. She also started her own company that leases and sells office and residential properties in Beijing.

"The hardest part was getting on the plane to come over. I'm glad I did. You have to be on the ground out here, networking and generating your own leads," advises Peggy. "You're not going to get many solid referrals from the States. It's just too far removed."

That doesn't mean that accessing jobs in Greater China from the U.S. is impossible. It can be done. However, it's considerably more work and far less effective than spending time out here looking. Without U.S. recruitment processes and resources in place among multinationals at present, it's the job seeker who must take the initiative to research the market, find the openings, and become available to interview with employers. It takes a good deal of planning, but the benefits are overwhelming. The bottom line is that traveling to Greater China greatly improves your chances for finding employment. Many managers I know even feel that anything short of coming out on your own to interview reflects a lack of commitment by the candidate.

It's Your Dime

If it's not apparent yet, then I should make it clear that your job search trip to Greater China is a self-financed one. Companies will not fly you out from the States for an initial interview. Should they choose to pursue you beyond the first round, however, they will then pick up travel expenses.

Some candidates are convinced that a company will pay for their trip once the company has spoken with them. This was the case with one candidate I met at an Asian American job fair in San Francisco who wanted to work in Hong Kong. Her background was impressive. She spoke Cantonese and Mandarin and had six years of work experience as a product manager in a major U.S. bank. She had even worked in Hong Kong earlier in her career. Although she had no future travel plans, she insisted she would fly to Hong Kong if a serious opportunity arose.

As timing would have it, one did. I was able to arrange for her a rare phone interview with a multinational commercial bank based in Hong Kong. I made it clear to the candidate that the bank was willing to speak with her with the understanding that she would fly out should the job match appear to be a good one. The candidate readily agreed.

The candidate and client spoke for an hour. There was strong interest from both sides. The candidate told the client that she would indeed arrange to fly out as promised. The client looked forward to meeting her. The next day, however, the candidate called to say she had changed her mind. In principle, she agreed with the idea of candidates making themselves available for the initial face-to-face interview. Having thought it over though, she felt the company should view her differently and pay for the trip, given her experience as a seasoned professional.

That wasn't going to happen. The client was not about to pay the candidate's travel expenses based on a phone conversation. The candidate never came to Hong Kong and no further pursuit by the client occurred.

When To Go?

Candidates always want to know the best time of year to make a job search trip to Greater China. The truth is, there is no ideal time. My firm successfully places candidates all year around. When it comes to hiring, companies take an extremely practical approach. When the market is hot and companies are growing, then there are openings. Over the past several years, that has almost continually been the case for most industries.

If you had to pick a time though, then you may want to target the month of January. Companies and managers tend to be more optimistic at the start of a new year. New business plans are ready to be implemented, and budgets are intact and ready to be spent (having been forecasted from the previous fall).

Managers are also traveling less at this time. It's the period right after American New Year and before Chinese New Year (which typically falls around late January to mid-February), when many people are just returning from one holiday and preparing for another. Business is relatively slow, as people unofficially wait until after the Chinese New Year to begin aggressively pursuing yearly objectives. The result is you're more likely to catch hiring managers, and they're more likely to have the time to speak with you.

The period immediately after Chinese New Year is also recognized as a good time to job hunt in Greater China. This is a time of heavy turnover, as many employees look to change jobs after receiving their year-end bonuses. Keep in mind, however, that while there may be more openings, there is also more competition.

Before any trip, you should check out the holiday schedule in the region *(see Appendix I for Greater China Holiday Schedules)*. Avoid short work weeks like Chinese New Year, American Christmas and New Year, Dragon Boat Festival in June and Autumn Moon Festival in October. One of the greatest disappointments is to fly all the way to Asia and discover that the people you're trying to contact aren't in town.

Paying attention to regional news events also helps you avoid poor timing. The job market can be highly sensitive to economic and political events. As an example, most recently the currency crisis in Southeast Asia and the drop in regional stock markets has resulted in hiring freezes within many finance industry firms, making it almost impossible for new arrivals to find a position in this field.

How Long To Go?

If you're working, then your stay in Greater China will likely be limited to one to two weeks, perhaps three at the most. Although this seems like a short amount of time, it's enough for you to take significant steps in your job search.

A trip of at least two weeks provides some flexibility to catch managers you're trying to meet. For example, if you're interviewing for an investment banking or consulting position, then you'll likely have to see a half dozen or more people. The interview process can easily require three or four rounds. Whether you're able to arrange all the crucial meetings depends on travel schedules and work load.

We've handled several cases where a candidate was in Greater China for less than a week and received a job offer before returning to the States. Typically, they were passing through the region on vacation or business and wanted to use the chance to interview with companies. In these successful cases, the candidate passed us their resume before arriving. The timing was optimal where the candidate's background happened to match an urgent job opening. The company was also responsive in pushing the interview process along.

One candidate called us from the Taipei airport just before his flight to Hong Kong. His Hong Kong stop was only one day. That same week, a multinational client gave us a job listing for a regional business development manager. The candidate's background was an excellent fit. I immediately contacted the client and relayed the candidate's time constraint. A breakfast meeting was arranged for the next morning. The meeting went well and the candidate was asked to see three other colleagues in the afternoon. Those meetings also went smoothly. At the end of the day, just before he left for the airport, the candidate received a verbal offer. Getting a job here isn't usually that easy, but it's possible if things fall into place.

On the other end of the spectrum, we've also seen cases drag out for months. In these instances, the interview process could not be concluded while the candidate was here. Usually, a key decision-maker was unavailable. Once the candidate returned to the States, the situation would quickly turn into an "out of sight, out of mind" scenario. The company would decide to wait until the next time the candidate was in the region or when a manager was traveling to the States to arrange another meeting.

In general, if a company knows when and how long you're available, they'll respond accordingly. If your time is short, they'll do their best to conduct the interview process with a sense of urgency and line up the necessary interviews while you're here.

Preparation

Let Them Know You're Coming

My firm typically pre-circulates resumes and contacts companies one to two weeks before a candidate's expected arrival date. In this time frame, managers can match your background to positions they may be trying to fill. Much earlier and the sense of urgency to meet you may not be there. Any later and they may not have enough time to arrange their busy schedules.

Equally as important is letting as many friends, acquaintances, and contacts in the region know that you're coming as soon as possible. The Chinese have a saying, *zai jia kao fumu, zai wai kao peng you.* It means, at home rely on family, outside rely on friends. In Greater China, you'll find this to be very true. Employment leads, company contacts, and job market information can come from anyone.

Do Your Homework

Before arriving, you should know as much as you can about the job market and the job search process itself. Do your homework and research. That way, you'll maximize your time here from the moment you arrive.

The preparation will also help you in impressing employers. Taking the initiative and generating the interviews is one thing, performing well in those interviews is another. To present and position yourself well, you need to be able to speak intelligently and insightfully about the region and the industry(ies) you're targeting. "I interview candidates all the time who want to get into corporate finance," says Barbara Spurling, vice president of training, development, and staffing of Asia Pacific Region for Merrill Lynch. "I take notice of candidates I meet who can speak with some level of depth about what's going on in the region and about our line of business."

Barbara also feels that candidates should have a basic understanding of her company's business activity in Asia. "With the accessibility of information over the Internet these days, there's really no excuse not to be knowledgeable and prepared," she says.

It's also valuable to understand the mentality of hiring managers. Managers are attentive to the risk that a new employee moving to the region will pose in adjusting to a new job and lifestyle. Professionally, they want people who can fit in and perform with minimal start-up time. By displaying an understanding of the business environment, you can indicate to employers that you'll be able to get up to speed quickly.

You also want to project that you know what moving out here will entail. You should have a good sense of the living situation, work habits, lifestyle, and cost of living in the location you're targeting. Questions concerning these areas are better left unasked when speaking with an employer. Raising them only highlights how difficult the relocation adjustment may be for you.

Greater China Trip Checklist: Before You Go, You Should ...

✔ *Obtain names of and contact as many people as possible in your destination city(s).*

✔ *Contact employers by fax and phone to confirm your travel schedule and availability.*

✔ *Arrange a local phone number where you can be reached.**

✔ *Access Asian publications to update yourself on what's going on in the region.*

✔ *Check for holidays during the period you plan to be in Asia.*

* *See Appendix II for Pager And Mobile Phone Services*

Have Realistic Expectations

No Guarantees

Candidates always want to know our job placement success rate. It's a difficult question to answer. It varies greatly depending on a candidate's work experience, regional exposure, language skills, availability to meet employers, and the job market situation. Commitment and job search persistence also factor in. Most critical, of course, is the fit between a candidate's qualifications and the type of job they're seeking.

When we work with candidates on a job search, many will only travel out if we can line up several interviews for them beforehand. Although our objective is to arrange as many as possible, there is no way for us to assure even one interview as a contingency for their trip. Fundamentally, you can't approach a Greater China job search with such guarantees in mind.

While planning your job search trip, set realistic goals for yourself. For example, if you haven't been to Greater China in a while or have never been here before, then landing a job during your initial visit will be tough. Still, the trip can be very worthwhile if you focus your efforts on researching companies, understanding the job market, and developing a job search strategy. You can also get to know people who can help you gain job lead information and contacts for the future. Beyond the basic objective of receiving a job offer, you want to make sure the trip at least clarifies your marketability for the type of position and industry you're seeking.

At Least Now You'll Know

For nearly every traveling candidate we work with, their trip to Greater China greatly benefits their job search process, regardless of whether they land a position or not. Ultimately, the trip clears up questions about life in the region and the competitiveness of their background for working in Greater China. Spending some time here gives you a real sense of what it will take for you to make it out. For instance, it helps you to determine whether you need more language lessons, more U.S.-based work experience, or perhaps more time to research the opportunities you seek.

We've seen many cases where candidates were unable to secure a job offer during their trip, but increased their efforts based on the first-hand perspective they gathered about the market and their marketability. Plus, they were able to develop a network of resources that was valuable for their continuing job search. As one person said after her trip: "If you come here to pound the pavement, you may kick up a lot of dust, but you'll definitely clarify the fit and opportunity for yourself."

You may even realize you're not as marketable as you thought or discover the lifestyle in Greater China is not as suited for you as envisioned. These are disappointing things to realize, but at least you'll put to rest uncertainties about your situation. In the worst case, you'll save yourself a further investment of time and money in a mismatched pursuit.

Go With Your Strengths

Many candidates come to Greater China seeking job functions and industries completely unrelated to their work experience in the U.S. These may be accountants who want to be investment bankers, industry professionals who want to be consultants, or technology professionals who want to be in front-end, business development positions. In fact, making the move into another job function or industry is more common in Greater China than in the U.S., given the favorable market for job seekers. If you're just moving out, however, it's a lot to expect to jump into a new region and a significantly different position (and perhaps industry) at the same time.

We tell candidates to focus their initial job search on opportunities that best leverage their existing strengths and experience. Your first and foremost objective is to get yourself out here. If you end up with a less-than-ideal job, it's okay. Once you start working, you can become familiar with the local business environment and establish a track record of success. As importantly, you can develop the contacts to help you obtain the position you're looking for. It then becomes much easier to switch into that job function or industry. With enough patience and persistent, it will happen.

Harry Hui's early success in Asia gave him the chance to later move onto a completely different career track. Harry came to Hong Kong in 1992, sent out by his firm as the director of business development for the Asia Pacific region. His company produced labels, plain white labels. His task was to develop a business plan to advise management on how to expand their industrial label business in Asia. He began by spending several months evaluating various market entry strategies. Based on his recommendations, senior management then gave him the mandate to implement his plan. Harry began marketing his company's white labels to plant purchasing managers, who were responsible for buying materials for their package production facilities. It was a challenging position and one he performed well.

It was after his third year in this position that Harry's career path changed dramatically. Through a recruiter, he was introduced to a major multinational music company looking to hire a managing director to define and execute a business strategy for Hong Kong. Although Harry had a love for music, he had no experience in the music industry. The company, however, was particularly impressed with his Asia business experience and understanding of the region. After a six-month interview process where he competed with several other candidates who had considerable music industry backgrounds, Harry was offered the managing director position.

Today, he is the vice president of the Asia Pacific region overseeing eight countries spanning from Japan to India. In addition to determining regional expansion strategies for the company, his key responsibilities are to look for new music trends and to identify performing and writing talent. This may happen at clubs or live performances, which he frequents. Much of his time is also spent working with creative and artistic people. Recently, he collaborated with Wayne Wang, director of *The China Box,* starring Jeremy Irons and Gong Li, to develop the music for the film.

"Without the regional experience I gained from my previous position, my current company would never have considered me," says Harry. "The reason I stayed in the running was because of what I had accomplished in Asia. Ultimately, that was my competitive advantage for getting the job."

Job Now, Money Later

When considering a job that will bring you to Greater China, it's best not to get too wrapped up in the money aspect. We worked with one candidate who interviewed for a sales manager position. Although the candidate had no previous sales experience (she had a strong technical background), the client liked her credentials and intelligence. The position would give the candidate a great chance to learn a new job function, prove herself in a revenue-generating role, and add a valuable element to her career development. It was just the type of position she was seeking.

Before the interview, I told the candidate that it was not the client's practice to offer expat terms to middle managers. I also let her know that she was not likely to receive that type of compensation package from a company anyway given her lack of business development, profit and loss, and management experience. Although she had a solid professional background, she was entirely untested in running a key part of the client's business. The candidate acknowledged the compensation expectations and her own priority to find a position that offered a promising career track.

The initial conversation went well and it became obvious that the client was interested. At the end of the meeting, however, the candidate couldn't resist resorting back to her original view of her value and situation. Thinking that she was gaining the upper hand, she told the client she was only interested in the position if it offered an expat package. In her mind, she felt that a company should pay her a premium if she was going to give up her stable situation in the U.S. for something that would result in a major change in her life. It was a "what can you do for me" attitude that reflected both a lack of commitment towards her move and an unrealistic understanding of the opportunity. Not surprisingly, the client's interest in the candidate ended right there.

When considering a position in Greater China, most important is the job itself and the scope of responsibilities it offers. The questions you want answered are: Who will I be learning from? What other internal and external business areas does the position expose me to? What is the likelihood I will be successful in the job?

You should also look at the company and its regional commitment. Is the operation an established or a start-up one? What is the company's position within its industry? What type of management structure and resources are in place to support you?

Finally, look at the industry and its potential for the near future. Is the industry experiencing growth or at a mature stage? What is the competitive situation in the market(s) you're being asked to develop? If these areas look promising, then the advancement opportunities will present themselves before long. Most important to remember about Greater China is, if you can prove yourself as a performer, then the money will come. This is seen time and time again in the countless numbers of professionals developing careers in the region.

Evaluate Greater China Job Opportunities On ...

✔ **Position** — *Will you gain skills, exposure, and experience that will add to your future marketability?*

✔ **Management** — *Who will be supervising you? Who will you be learning from?*

✔ **Company** — *What is the company's commitment and competitive positioning in the region?*

✔ **Industry** — *What is the state of the industry you are entering (i.e. maturing or expanding)?*

✔ **Self** — *What is your overall confidence level that you can do the job well/successfully?*

Grace Wong: From The Bottom Up

Personal History: *Born and raised in Chicago. Living in Hong Kong since March of 1993.*

Parents: *Mom and Dad from Hong Kong*

Education: *B.A. in Communications from DePaul University, Chicago, Illinois.*

Languages: *Native English speaker. Grew up speaking Cantonese at home. Studying Mandarin in Hong Kong.*

Grace Wong along with Hong Kong Chief Executive Tung Chee-hwa and CNN Asia Bureau Chief Mike Chinoy after a CNN interview in 1997

Imagine surviving in high-priced Hong Kong on HK$10,000 a month. That's the amount Grace Wong earned in her advertising job when she first came out to the region. "It was barely enough to live on, and I was even staying with relatives at the time," recalls Grace. Five years later, at 27, Grace is the executive director of public relations for CNN International for the Asia Pacific region. When asked, she estimates that now she likely nets more than twice what she might be earning in the States at this point in her career.

Grace's current situation was years in the making. She made her first few trips to Asia with her family while growing up. Her first visit to Mainland China took place when she was 18. She came to Hong Kong to find work six months after graduating from college.

"A lot of why I decided to move to Asia stems from my upbringing. My family ran a Chinese restaurant. Although the Midwest wasn't exactly a hotbed of Asian culture while I was growing up, my dad was very involved in the Chinese community," describes Grace. "Those personal influences were subtle, but they really made an impact on me later on."

Grace's big career break came when her boss asked her to start up a public relations department for the ad agency she worked at. It was an area the firm's

Hong Kong office had never been involved in before. At the time, she was 22 years old, with little experience in client public relations. As daunting as the task was, she was excited to take on the challenge. With a colleague, she began writing proposals and pitching business to new clients. Within six months, they billed HK$2 million in retainer business.

"I was very lucky. My immediate supervisor was a great mentor," Grace states. "I was also fortunate to be given an exceptional opportunity to prove myself, one hard to imagine coming by in the States for someone my age at the time. But that's Asia for you. In my situation, not many people have extensive PR experience. It's a young industry in this region."

These days, Grace is approached several times a year with job offers from a variety of multinational companies. She's come a long way in her marketability. "The smartest thing I did was not worry about money right off the bat. I took a job I really liked and felt I could do well. Once you begin to establish yourself, the opportunities just seem to appear."

Grace enjoys the tremendous travel and networking opportunities through her job. She has had the chance to meet people like Mainland China president Jiang Zemin, former Hong Kong governor Chris Patten, and Hong Kong's Chief Executive Tung Chee-hwa, as well as numerous political leaders and senior business executives across Asia. "Sometimes it's tempting to make a move, but I won't do it unless it's for the right reason," she concludes. "You can always earn more money somewhere else, but you have to know yourself well and what makes you happy."

Networking

When we ask candidates after their trip what they would have done differently to improve their job search chances, the most frequent response is that they would have contacted more people beforehand. They would have identified and written to more companies and come up with more names to develop job leads.

Fortunately, looking for a job in Greater China these days is much less of a mystery than it was just a few years ago. For example, there is now an extensive network of Chinese Americans that can serve as an excellent resource to help you find out what's going on in various industries and the overall job market. Most were in your exact same shoes at one time. They understand the search process and what you need to know about living and working in the region.

Guanxi Works

The concept of *guanxi*, or connections, is well known among Chinese people. *Guanxi* can come from family, relatives, classmates, co-workers, and friends, any of whom can open doors and expose you to opportunities. In Greater China, having the right *guanxi* can make all the difference in one's success.

Those of us not raised in the region may feel like outsiders, without the local *guanxi* to attain our career and business objectives. Even for us, however, *guanxi* applies. Connections don't have to be local ones. Most managers within multinational firms are westerners or people who are western educated and trained. Although Greater China is a large, well-populated place, the foreign professional community is fairly centralized in each major city. On top of that, being a Chinese American in an Asian city is like being in a small town socially. Everyone in the Chinese American community seems to know each other. As a result, developing contacts is surprisingly easy for newcomers.

One person described the ability to meet all sorts of people as almost comical. "The community is smaller and the social barriers are lower than in the U.S." she says. "I mean, I know the local nightly anchor for ATV News. She's my sister's roommate!" Networking in Greater China is like that. Each person tends to know a lot of other people. The social scene is active and less stratified than in the States. In Hong Kong, the professional workforce is particularly young, with many middle to senior managers only in their late 20s to late 30s. You can run into them at house parties, happy hours, or boat trips. These are people working for major multinational firms, who have a say in hiring decisions.

You need to be aggressive, and it may take a break or two to know the right people, but establishing a network of contacts can happen quickly. Exchanging and collecting business cards is a way of life in Asia. A friend of mine can work a room at any mixer and produce a stack of 30 cards within a half hour. People hand them out willingly. Within a three-week period, one of our new consultants went through a box of 100 just by attending flat parties and weekend outings she was invited to.

Small World Encounters

Greater China has to be the center of the universe for "small world encounters." Just within the Chinese American community, there's a better than average chance that two people can name-drop at least one person they have in common. Just letting someone know which city or region of North America you're from can produce an obscure connection. I've even seen people meet who discovered they went to the same elementary school back in the States.

Because a good number of professionals here were educated in North America, many large universities and MBA programs have extensive alumni networks in the region. Jackie Dong came to Hong Kong after finishing her MBA program at UCLA to find a position in the finance industry. Before leaving L.A., she visited her career center and obtained the names of several alumni working in Hong Kong. "All I did was go straight down the list," she says. "The first person I contacted spoke with me for an hour and told me everything I wanted to know about the finance industry in Hong Kong. The second person invited me to lunch and passed me the names of a few people to call who might be looking to hire. The third person I contacted offered me a job. I'm now working for him."

That's the way it works in Asia. Never underestimate the potential of someone in helping you in your job search. Ask those you speak with for the names of others you might be able to contact. You never know where a lead may take you. In my business, I use names all the time to get in the doors of people I'd like to see. If I want to call on a new client, I know my chances are significantly greater if I mention someone we both know. The same applies for job seekers trying to meet hiring managers.

The Average Person Knows A Lot

Candidates just beginning their job search process often ask if we can help them set up informational interviews with our client contacts. In truth, senior managers aren't that interested in seeing someone just to provide them with information. They're too busy. If they interview a person, then they want it to be for the purpose of filling a job opening. If it's merely information that you're looking for, then you're better off talking to someone at a more junior level.

There's a tremendous community of foreign professionals working at every level, for nearly every multinational firm in Greater China. And because conversations usually revolve around business, the average person is informed and aware of what's going on in their company and industry. Whenever I need company information or want to know of industry trends, I don't call my executive management contacts. I contact my junior and middle manager ones. Being out in the field on a daily basis, they know as well as anyone the latest developments and news in their industry.

The Kindness Of Strangers

You'll be surprised at how open people are to speak and even meet with you, particularly in the foreign community. I've always found people in Greater China willing to share information and references. It stems from nearly everyone's universal experience of feeling lost, isolated, and friendless when they initially moved here. People can understand and appreciate the plight of newcomers. Many also found jobs through friends and contacts who provided employment leads. They've all phoned a stranger at one time, upon the recommendation of someone else, to ask for help or advice. As one Greater China veteran states: "I hardly know of anyone who didn't sleep in someone's guest room or on someone's sofa when they first got here."

Personal Travelogue

Perhaps the biggest break that helped bring me to Asia was a random meeting with someone I had never met before. I was trying to get a summer internship during the first year of my MBA program and decided to fly to Taipei during my spring break. I had never been to Taipei and didn't know a single person there. I also had no interviews lined up. Undeterred, my well-laid plan was to arrive and then cold-call like a maniac. As soon as I landed, I bought a directory of U.S. companies in Taiwan and began phoning people. After five days, I had managed to arrange a couple of interviews, but nothing close to resulting in a summer job. I had no solid leads. I was due to fly back in four days and was beginning to foresee the impending disaster. "Damn it, I've come all this way to Asia, and now I'm going to go home empty handed," was the anxious thought pulsing through my stressed out head.

By chance, I happened to look in my wallet and noticed a phone number written on a scrap of paper. The number was given to me by a classmate, who suggested that I call her sister's husband when I arrived in Taipei. At the time I was given the number, I thought nothing of it. I just stuffed it in my pocket. In an act of desperation, I called him.

The person invited me to his office. We talked a little about ourselves first. It was very casual. I remembered that he was from San Francisco, so I brought up the 49ers. He perked up. When I saw that, I began pouring on the sports talk. He had been living in Taipei for over three years and was out of touch with the latest news on his favorite team. It worked. We began to really hit it off. Although I was sincerely enjoying talking to him, my main thought throughout our conversation was: "Pleeeease, like me, like me, help me, help me!"

After about thirty minutes, he looked at me and asked, "so what can I do for you?" I told him about my interest in finding a marketing job in a multinational consumer products company. "And by the way," I added sheepishly, "I should probably let you know that I don't speak much Mandarin, have never worked in the region, and have never worked in a marketing position before. Do you think you can help me?"

He paused for several moments to assess my striking credentials and to ponder my situation. He then reached for his Rolodex and began pulling out name cards. While I sat there, he proceeded to call up his marketing friends at Pepsi, Johnson & Johnson, Quaker, Nestle, Procter & Gamble, and Coca-Cola. Within thirty minutes I had seven meetings set up over the next two days. I ended up interviewing with and accepting a summer internship with Johnson & Johnson the day before I left.

Certainly, I was extremely fortunate this guy was willing to help me. Yet, I've heard many similar stories where a new acquaintance was able to provide a key introduction that eventually led to something. I call this benefiting through "the kindness of strangers." Situations like mine happen all the time out here.

Resources/Getting Information

Information And Contacts Are Accessible With A Little Effort

In researching Greater China job opportunities from the States, there are several resources that can give you a good feel for the market. In Hong Kong, the best listing of weekly positions is the Saturday edition of the South *China Morning Post*. The career section averages over one hundred pages of job postings, many within the multinational companies you may have an interest in. Although the positions are for immediate hiring, you can at least get a sense of which companies are looking and the types of positions they need to fill.

If you were to invest in a single resource for your Greater China job search, then you should purchase the American Chamber of Commerce Membership Directory in the city you're targeting. These directories contain the names of executives working in just about every major multinational firm operating in the region. The book's price varies widely for each Chamber. For instance, the Shanghai version costs about US$35, while the Hong Kong version costs about US$250. For that price, the Hong Kong directory includes each member's title, phone number, fax number, company address, and even a photograph *(see Appendix III for Helpful Greater China Associations And Resources)*.

Help Through The Internet

As recently as two years ago, the cost and lack of timely, relevant job market information made researching international jobs from North America nearly impossible. With the explosive growth of the Internet, however, conducting research for a Greater China job has become as easy as turning on your computer.

Getting A Sense For The Employment Market

These days, the easiest way to get an idea of what is happening in the Greater China hiring markets is through the Internet. Many of the region's top daily newspapers, both English and Chinese, have on-line or "interactive" editions. Like their printed counterparts, these on-line editions have classified sections or sections of job postings and employment information. For instance, you can visit the *Scouth China Morning Post*'s Classified Post Interactive site for one of the largest classified job ad databases in Asia. You can search for "marketing manager" positions and obtain ads for openings ranging from "regional sales manager" to "business development manager." A browse through these on-line classified sections provides valuable information on companies that are hiring and the kinds of positions that are available. An intrepid Internet surfer can also find on-line editions to the *Hong Kong Standard*, Hong Kong's *Ming Pao Daily*, China's *People's Daily*, and Taiwan's *China Times (see Appendix IV for Helpful Greater China Job Search Websites)*.

There are also many excellent job listings sites now on the Internet, including ones focusing exclusively on Greater China. Some of these sites have successful North American counterparts, like Career Mosaic Hong Kong. Some are indigenous to the region, like Asia-Net, SinaNet Job Bank, and Job Asia. They provide not only job listings, but information on how to submit resumes for consideration. Sites like Career Mosaic and Sinanet maintain on-line job databases that list positions by either country location or company. In many cases, a resume can be posted directly to a hiring employer by being pasted into an on-line form.

Executive search firms specializing in Greater China recruiting are increasingly developing their own on-line websites as well. Wang & Li Asia Resources, China Executive Search, Pacific Bridge, and Recruit are several recruiting firms that utilize the Internet to list job opportunities, allow candidates to input their data into a job bank, and let employers list company information and recruiting needs for potential employees to view. Various websites also include helpful tax, salary, cost of living, job search planning, and relocation information.

Research Prospective Employers

A wealth of information on prospective employers is also available on the Internet. For example, if you're interested in working for Hewlett-Packard in China, you can visit their corporate website, which links to their China website containing information on their mainland operations. Many companies post their worldwide job listings on their websites. You can even look up a company's products and services, corporate mission/vision statement, and recent press releases.

You can find more company information from sites like Hoover's On-line or Companies On-line. Their on-line databases allow you to research thousands of public and private U.S. and foreign companies. Information provided includes a description of the company's major businesses, key people, historical stock prices, figures on yearly net sales, and net income. Hoover's even lists a company's major competitors along with links to their websites.

If you want to go the extra mile to prepare for an interview or evaluate a job offer with a prospective employer, you can even access a U.S. publicly listed company's 10K report. This mandatory annual report is filed with the U.S. Securities & Exchange Commission (SEC) by listed companies. The report differs from the Hoover's and Companies On-line reports in that they offer in-depth and generally un-pampered reporting of company strategies, revenues, profitability, and operations. EDGAR On-line is the foremost resource of information on U.S. publicly listed companies on the Internet. Their on-line database allows a job seeker access to a firm's 10K report, 10Q report (a quarterly report filed with the SEC), and proxy statements provided to company shareholders. EDGAR's only limitation is that it does not provide this information for private or foreign companies.

Tips For Various Job Seekers

MBAs

Landing a job in Greater China for a graduating MBA from the U.S. is like playing a game of chicken. Can you hold out long enough for an offer in the region, or will you cave in and take a more immediate job offer in the States?

For U.S. firms, the hiring of MBAs is projected well in advance. Companies begin appearing at schools for first-round interviews as early as October. Second-year MBAs who graduate the following May or June are typically available to begin work in August or September. It's a recruiting cycle well-known and understood by both MBA candidates and U.S. firms.

In Greater China, however, the MBA recruiting cycle is entirely out of sync with the immediate hiring needs of multinational operations. This makes it difficult for U.S. MBAs to attract job offers in the region during the early to middle part of their school year, as companies are unable to project staffing needs six to nine months down the road when candidates become available.

When we began our U.S. recruiting efforts, second-year MBAs from top U.S. business schools were a primary target group, representing highly qualified candidates in an active job search mode. During our first year, we worked with numerous students traveling to Greater China over their winter break. Our objective was to set up interviews with regional operations not recruiting directly from U.S. campuses. We were extremely excited about our large pool of top-notch MBA candidates and expected an overwhelming response from our multinational clients.

The result, however, was disappointing. Managers had favorable impressions of our candidates, but their interest to actually meet with them was only mild. In some cases, clients even told us they did not want to see MBA resumes at that time.

Consistently, they emphasized that their overwhelming hiring priority was to fill immediate openings in the face of pressing business objectives. Interviewing so far in advance had little value and was not a good use of their busy schedules. A typical client response to candidate profiles we showed them in January was: "Let me know if they're still interested and available in May."

As far as I'm concerned, next summer may as well be next century, ... I need people who can start working right away."

When I asked the managing director of a U.S. computer software company in January if he wanted to meet some outstanding MBA candidates that I could introduce to him, he said that he did. When I added that these candidates would not be available to start work until late summer, he changed his mind. He just looked at me and said: "Honestly Larry, as far as I'm concerned, next summer may as well be next century. I have no idea what our business or hiring needs will look like at that time. I need people who can start working right away."

When they learn of the immediate hiring time frame of multinationals in Greater China, many MBA candidates then wonder if it's worthwhile traveling to the region to try to interview over their winter or spring break. The answer is that taking a trip out during your holidays does have tremendous value. The more companies and managers you can meet early in your job search, the better off you'll be later on when the timing is more appropriate for firms to hire. As importantly, generating leads and gaining interest early on reduces the anxiety you may inevitably feel as you wait out your job search while classmates who secure U.S.-based positions by March or earlier enter a "just need to graduate" phase.

The last thing a second-year MBA wants is to carry the uncertainty of their future all the way until graduation. But that's what you may have to do. The best advice is to try to ignore what your classmates are doing. You can't compare your situation to theirs. They will receive their U.S.-based job offers earlier than you. The bottom-line reality is that the job search process for Greater China requires significantly more initiative and patience.

The second-year MBAs we work with around the time of, or even after, graduation do not remain unemployed for long in most cases. This is particularly true if they've attended a well-recognized program. Multinationals in Greater China become much more responsive as the time between when a candidate is interviewed and when they can begin working gets closer, and when the fit between a candidate and an opening becomes easier to identify.

Undergrads

For undergraduates intent on working in Greater China straight out of school, getting a job is almost entirely based on your own effort. Unfortunately for you, directing resources towards U.S. undergraduate recruiting and entry-level positions is one of the lower priorities for multinational firms. As a result, you're likely to find few on-campus placement or recruitment channels that will get you to Greater China.

This doesn't mean there aren't jobs available for fresh graduates from the U.S. In fact, you'll find many entry and junior level positions within leading multinational firms. In addition, there are significant advantages for job seekers with U.S. university degrees. Multinationals prefer the educational and personality backgrounds of U.S. graduates, relative to local graduates. U.S. graduates tend to have sharper communications skills and a more pro-active approach to taking on responsibility and completing tasks. They also tend to have more and better summer internship work experience within international firms, compared to the internship experience of local graduates.

On the minus side, multinationals do not have to be concerned over the work visa issue for local graduates. This can be a major stumbling block for young job seekers who do not have residency status in the country they wish to work in. Companies apply for a work visa on your behalf. To sponsor you, however, they must justify to visa authorities why you are more qualified for a particular position over a local hire. Without previous full-time work experience, highlighting your special expertise and skills becomes difficult.

The bigger question for fresh college graduates is whether you should begin your career in Asia or in the U.S. I've heard some people say that you should just make the move out, the sooner the better. Their perspective revolves around the view that the only way to really learn how to do business in Greater China is to come here and do it. Most employers, and those who have moved here immediately after college, however, feel it's not wise to come here too early in your career. They recommend obtaining a couple of years of work experience and developing solid fundamentals as a professional in the U.S. first. As you build experience there, you can keep an eye on regional developments and travel here whenever you're able to assess the job market.

You should also weigh your long-term goals in your decision. If you're fairly certain about building a career in Asia, immediately putting yourself in the thick of things may be the right move. Projecting where you want to be in five or more years is difficult, however, particularly for someone just out of school. Even diehard Asia veterans have to take a good look at what they're doing every two or three years and reassess their situation.

Many new college graduates I meet are anxious to come out while the window of opportunity exists. You shouldn't be concerned about timing or arriving here "too late" though. Greater China will still offer plenty of chances two or three years down the road when you have some experience under your belt. The opportunities are here, and will continue to be. It doesn't help, however, to see all kinds of interesting and desirable positions only to find yourself unable to compete for them.

Without a doubt, Greater China multinationals offer exciting, hands-on opportunities for young professionals to learn and develop quickly. However, the region's dynamic and entrepreneurial orientation can overwhelm those not yet ready for such an unstructured environment. When considering whether you should come to the region straight out of school, think about the kind of person you are. If you're the type who needs a great deal of instruction and guidance, then it's probably not the right decision to move here immediately. If you're proactive, aggressive, and independent, however, then you're more likely to do well.

Interns

Summer internships in Greater China present a good news, bad news scenario. The bad news is that summer internships are not much of a concept in the region. Multinational operations are not yet developed enough to provide structured internship programs. The hiring emphasis is heavily placed on full-time positions that are difficult and time-consuming enough. In addition, most managers barely have time to supervise their own full-time staff, let alone a temporary intern.

The good news is that there is a tremendous need for interns within many companies. Shorthanded managers can use well-trained, motivated interns who can handle special projects, provide business analysis, or conduct research. The concept of employing summer interns does make sense. The need is there. The problem is that managers simply don't have the time to look for such hires.

Therefore, if you want a summer internship in Asia, it's up to you to create the opportunity. I've seen a number of students come out over their spring break and secure positions with companies who weren't even looking to hire an intern. They obtained their internship by meeting needy managers and selling themselves. Their emphasis was on the tangible skills they could offer. They made a case for what they could do to make the manager's job easier. Salary was usually not a key issue. In many cases, students were merely looking to cover their costs (i.e. housing and perhaps a bit more), in return for a chance to gain as much exposure and experience as possible.

Within my own MBA internship search experience, I first tried to secure a summer job in Taipei through on-campus interviews. The number of companies hiring for Asia-based internships, however, was sparse. Those firms I spoke with were not looking for someone like myself, with poor language skills and no regional work experience. They sought foreign national students who had local backgrounds and were more likely to return to their home country after graduation.

Beyond these few campus interviews, I then began writing directly to branch offices in Taipei. I mailed over 30 letters only to receive a handful of lukewarm responses. Those that wrote back either expressed a lack of interest or politely informed me that my resume would be kept on file. Without another option, I flew to Taipei over my spring break. I arranged several interviews through a connection who knew marketing managers at several consumer product companies.

During the interviewing process, not one manager I spoke with had an idea to hire me for an internship before I walked into their office. Nearly every conversation began with a remark like: "Rick said I should talk to you, what's on your mind?" In these meetings, I spoke of my intent to work in Taipei for the summer and pitched my analytical skills, marketing sense, and unbridled eagerness. Most managers were only able to offer me advice, or another contact or potential job lead to follow up on. All were receptive.

At Johnson & Johnson, the marketing director happened to have recently launched a new shampoo product that was showing disappointing sales results. There was some market research data that she wanted to reevaluate. She felt there might be some important, overlooked information that could help improve the positioning of the product. Noting my quantitative background (I began my career as a mechanical engineer), she thought I might be a good person to re-analyze the data. After our second meeting, she made me an offer. I accepted. I was paid modestly, but was provided free housing (actually, I stayed at my boss's father's summer apartment).

Over the summer, I re-examined the market research data and did, in fact, uncover some additional findings. I used the information to develop a tighter positioning strategy and a new ad campaign for the product. My boss even asked me to consider staying in Taipei and forego the second year of my MBA program to oversee the product's re-launch.

Based on my own experience and those of others, I'm a firm believer in the willingness of managers to employ summer interns. The problem is in their time limitations to hire for such positions. That's why it's critical to take the initiative to travel out and meet with these managers. I remember how anxious I was throughout my trip. As risky and stressful as it was though, it was the best move I ever made in my efforts to gain work experience in the region. My internship would not have happened if I didn't fly to Taipei. The Asia and marketing experience I acquired that summer were key supplements to my resume and eventually helped me attain a full-time position in the region after graduation.

Part IV

What Else You Should Know

Chapter 10 The Outlook For Key Industries

I'm sure you've gotten the message by now. Fantastic opportunities are attainable for bilingual and bicultural professionals in Greater China. But what and where exactly are these opportunities? Writing about the developments of key industries and markets is another book in itself. In identifying positions, however, I will provide some overall background and point out significant trends of several major industries. I focus specifically on commercial service-oriented ones. As business sectors relatively new to the region, they are experiencing high growth and a shortage of locally sourced talent. It is within these industries where professionals with Asian and western backgrounds and capabilities are in greatest demand.

Finance

Big And Getting Bigger

Hong Kong is the Asia Pacific region's undisputed financial center (excluding Japan). It's the fifth largest banking center and the seventh largest stock market in the world (second largest in Asia in both cases after Japan). The island's financial regulatory environment makes it an attractive place for institutions and individuals in the business of investing money. Hong Kong's Central district is the Wall Street of Asia where within a few hundred meters radius you'll find 85 of the world's top 100 financial institutions.

For several years now, Taipei has relaxed strict laws and regulations that have adversely affected foreigners operating in its financial market. Opening accounts, repatriating money, and obtaining approval for power of attorney are just a few obstacles considerably more difficult for foreigners to deal with. Although substantial progress has been made in easing capital flow and operating restrictions for foreign banks and individuals, Taiwan's finance industry is still without a complete set of laws and the know-how to match Hong Kong's user-friendly investment environment. Although Shanghai is seen as an up-and-coming financial center, its financial environment is even more immature and bureaucratic than Taipei's for foreign participants. Regulatory changes will not occur in either place overnight. Therefore, as long as it maintains its current environment, Hong Kong is well-positioned to continue as the region's financial center.

Investment Banking

The practice of investment banking is relatively new to Greater China. The sudden, aggressive expansion of U.S. investment banks was triggered by China's decision to open its financial markets for foreign institutional investment. In October 1992, the mainland government issued a list of the first 22 Chinese companies and enterprises, or "red hongs," to be allowed to launch initial public offerings (IPO). The period that has followed can best be characterized as a rollercoaster ride for these investment banks who quickly ramped up and then down their regional operations.

One Chinese American corporate finance director recalls the rush by U.S. banks to jump-start business in 1993. "I call it 'The China Year'. I was working in Hong Kong back then for a computer company. Although I had no finance background, I was pursued by nearly every expanding bank, simply because I could speak Mandarin. They'd show me a menu of jobs to pick from in corporate finance, trading, sales, capital markets, direct investment, you name it. I was like a kid in a candy store. They'd even ask me if I had Mandarin-speaking relatives or friends who might want to do investment banking in Asia!"

For anyone seeking a finance industry job, it was an ideal time. Any level of Mandarin skills, combined with a quantitative or finance-related background, was almost a sure ticket for multiple interviews and job offers. "The rush during that period was the closest thing to indiscriminate hiring as you can get," recalls the director.

Within a year, however, boom turned to bust. The difficulties of developing China's financial markets began to show. Over-zealous optimism was replaced by financial and operating realities. Initial issues of mainland-listed companies underperformed or took much longer than anticipated to structure. An about-face took place, as an equally rapid downsizing by many banks began occurring as fast as the earlier build-up. When the corporate finance director began his banking career in mid-1993, his company had about 100 staff in Hong Kong. By late 1994, that number escalated to over 500. After another year, head-count was reduced to under 350.

The retrenchment phase of U.S. financial institutions in Hong Kong appears to have passed. Investment banks are more experienced and focused now in their regional efforts. In late 1996, a second list of government-approved Mainland China companies for public offering was released. Once again, there is renewed corporate finance activity related to mainland IPOs.

U.S., European, and Regional Banks

The reputations among the U.S., European, and regional banks vary quite a bit. From an employment perspective, each has their pluses and minuses. The European banks such as Wardleys and Barclays de Zoete Wedd (BZW) have a longer regional presence compared to the American banks. Their operations are considered more conservative and are thought to be more patient, with a longer term strategic outlook. Their less impulsive and reactionary practices have been reflected in their steadier response to the market's ups and downs over the past several years. As a result, they are traditionally viewed as more stable places to work over their U.S. counterparts. On the downside, their compensation packages tend to be lower.

Regional banks such as Hong Kong and Shanghai Banking Corporation (HSBC) and Jardine Fleming are known for having a strong Asia presence through their local relationships and long-standing activity in the region. Their management style also tends to be more localized and conservative.

The U.S. banks are the relatively new kids on the block. They entered the region brash and eager, expecting to dominate the market. From early-1995 through late-1996, they were among the hardest hit by the performance downturn of the mainland's financial markets. Although their growth plans are still aggressive, business activities are being executed more strategically as their regional understanding and presence has matured.

Equity Versus Fixed Income Markets

At present, equity markets dominate the region. Traditionally, Greater China has seen tremendous amounts of cash floating around and seeking investments. As the number and quality of equity investments have fallen recently, debt markets have begun to grow. Although considerably smaller, the growth rate of fixed income markets is more substantial and will continue to be rapid.

Leland Sun relocated to Hong Kong as the Greater China head of fixed income sales for Goldman Sachs in early 1993. "At that time, people predicted that the fixed income market was just about to take off," recalls Leland. "It has grown quite a bit since then, but not as much as expected. The region's understanding and comfort in fixed income markets has taken time to develop. Today, however, I believe the signs indicating the need for fixed income financing are stronger and clearer than ever."

Equity Research

Security industry insiders will tell you that the overall quality of the region's equity research is poor. There is much less information to work with and less technical training provided to analysts. In addition, most companies maintain low and inconsistent standards for recording financial information. The financials of many businesses are suspect at best, with creative accounting approaches commonly used.

There is also great difficulty in gaining company information. The same information that can be easily found through secondary research sources (i.e. libraries and agencies) in the U.S. does not exist to the same degree in Asia. As a result, equity research in the region is far from an exact science. Instead, analyst must exercise a much higher degree of interpretation.

Direct Investment

When the initial round of publicly offered China companies performed below expectations, many attributed the poor showings to the mainland government's substantial influence in the selection of enterprises that were listed on the market. From an investment perspective, these were not the soundest companies. Many of the issues were of low quality. In addition, China's young securities exchange environment, intended to enforce regulatory standards, was still weak. This meant that investors were basing decisions on questionable, if not totally inaccurate, information.

The result has been the emergence of direct investment and private equity funds. If the market was not going to offer the best investment choices, many investors reasoned that they may as well take their money and make their own selections. This would give them much greater control in choosing investment targets.

The recent South East Asia currency crisis has created an abundance of exceptional bargains for direct investment firms, as local companies are in dire need of cash. "We recently purchased an Indonesian securities firm," says a manager at one direct investment group. "We essentially paid half the price of what they were asking for one year ago."

Fund Management

For years, local investors and financial institutions relied on inside information and connections to make buying and selling decisions. Stocks and other financial products were often traded on the basis of non-financial analysis factors. In addition, tight regulations prevented foreigners from actively participating in local financial markets.

More recently, however, Greater China financial markets have opened up, becoming more accessible to foreign investors in particular. The crackdown on the long-time practice of identifying investment opportunities through speculative, insider information is also lessening the advantage for local investors. Investment decisions are increasingly being made based on financial analysis fundamentals. The result is a fairer playing field for international players.

Although still relatively young in Asia, the fund management industry is growing steadily. Traditionally, Asians have preferred to make investments through personal means. They are less trusting of and less comfortable with institutional investment structures and their views. The growing sophistication of markets and products in the region, however, has increased the popularity of fund managers. Investors need a higher degree of professionalism and expertise to stay abreast of fast-moving financial markets.

Private Banking

Asia is first and foremost a haven for individual money. As such, it is seen as the world's most promising private banking market. Wealth held by individuals with more than US$1 million to invest is projected to grow at least 11.5 percent annually over the next few years (the U.S. is expected to grow by 5 percent or less). With the embrace of capitalism by over one billion people, one can only guess how many individuals in China will become millionaires in the coming years. As Robert Chiu, senior vice-president and general manager for Republic National Bank of New York puts it, "China will be the mother of all private banking markets."

As individual wealth is being created in Asia by the minute, the private banking industry is showing excellent growth. It responds to the closer, more personal approach in which Asians like to do business. Breaking into and succeeding in private banking in Asia does not necessarily require connections. "Personal contacts may help you in your first year or two, but what happens when your connections dry out?" asks Ivy Tai, an executive director of private banking in Hong Kong. "What counts most is the personal drive and commitment to provide impeccable service and consistently sound investment advice to clients."

Finance Industry Opportunities

Asia's expanding finance industry is a volatile one. Its dynamic nature results in down cycles, where finding a position can be extremely difficult if the circumstances are not right. Simple timing can be the key. The past year's occurrence of events out here serve as a prime example. For the first three quarters of 1997, hiring within the finance industry was as strong as it had been at any time over the past three years. The recent currency crisis in South East Asia, however, has resulted in a shake-out in the region. Obtaining a finance industry position is not impossible at this time, but it is as tough to accomplish as during any other period.

Generally, however, the industry's growth in the region offers opportunities for professionals who want to break into a career in finance. For example, securities firms have tremendous difficulty finding experienced equity analysts with strong financial statements, company analysis, and report writing backgrounds, on top of regional knowledge and local language skills. I've met numerous professionals who were able to leverage accounting, consulting, market research, and various other industry backgrounds to obtain positions with leading international banks.

As many have confided, these opportunities would not likely have happened elsewhere.

During strong economic times, you can look at almost any area of finance and see the hiring needs. These include corporate finance, project finance, capital markets, mergers and acquisitions, syndicated banking, asset management, credit lending, financial advisory, as well as middle and back office support roles. Given the front-end, client or market interface nature of many of these positions, the candidates most successful at attracting opportunities have fluent Mandarin or other local language skills, a fundamental understanding of Asia Pacific financial markets, and experience working in the region.

Consulting

Boom Time

"The consulting industry is seeing a boom time," according to Alex Liu, former vice president and partner at The Boston Consulting Group in Hong Kong. "When I came to Hong Kong in 1990, the practice of consulting was still relatively unknown. The industry was in its pre-infancy stage in Asia. Today, I would describe it at a young, adolescent stage. There's still so much room for growth"

Over the past several years, major changes have occurred within both the types of consulting services delivered and the types of clients paying for such services. According to Alex, when he arrived, about 90 percent of the engagements he dealt with involved basic market research, market entry strategy, corporate strategy, or business development work. These engagements were primarily for international firms fairly new to the region.

As the businesses of multinationals have matured, the emphasis has shifted towards improving operations. Today, business development and market entry-related engagements might make up only about 50 percent of work demanded by clients. The other 50 percent revolves around process improvement, re-engineering, and management-related issues. Companies are more at a stage where they know what they want to do in the region, they just need to do it better.

Similarly, a few years ago, about 90 percent of consulting industry revenues came from multinational firms attuned to paying expensive professional service fees.

More recently, however, there has been a shift towards increasing numbers of Asian and regional clients. This shift has coincided with the deregulation of previously protected public sector industries that have been restructured to create a competitive market of services to customers. Local companies in telecommunications, power, and infrastructure industries are now using consultants to modernize their business approach and adjust to the new competitive environment. For these same reasons, large Asian family conglomerates have also begun to tap into the international business expertise that consulting firms provide. Alex estimates that about 50 percent of consulting industry revenues are now earned from these public sector companies and regional conglomerates.

Most countries do not have the business base for consulting firms to justify a fully staffed practice in those locations. Instead, firms operate out of one or two places, where consultants are assigned throughout the region according to project needs. The two leading locations are Hong Kong and Singapore. From these bases, firms are able to cover engagements that extend from China and Korea to Indonesia and India.

In 1995 and 1996, several international consulting firms established offices in either Beijing or Shanghai. Although there was a great deal of optimism over revenue potential in China, the development of business from local clients willing to pay for consulting services has yet to materialize.

Consulting Industry Opportunities

Nevertheless, there is clearly more demand for consulting talent in Greater China than supply. With regional operations intent on maintaining their high international practice standards, finding qualified consultants locally is not easy. The regional hiring approach is no different than from in the U.S. The best and brightest backgrounds from top undergraduate schools, MBA programs, and reputable companies are also sought. Added to the challenge is finding professionals with local business understanding and language skills.

"The quality, level, and excitement of the consulting work is magnitudes better in Asia," says Alex, in comparing his consulting career in the U.S. and Asia. "The chance to be on engagements in such a diverse and dynamic international market always makes the work extremely challenging and interesting."

Consumer Products

The China Market

When talking about Greater China's consumer market, you're essentially talking about Mainland China. With 1.2 billion people, manufacturers and consumer goods companies from around the world are taking a shot at becoming leading players in the mainland.

For consumer goods companies, it's a market share game being played right now. The general strategy is to enter early and create brand awareness. To do this, many companies are practically giving away product in order to win consumers and gain name recognition. The fierce competition has caused prices to go down, not up, for many items. It's a long-term strategy. As consumer spending levels continue to rise, these multinationals hope to reap the benefits of their efforts in the near future.

The Greater China director of strategic planning for a major consumer products multinational breaks the mainland into three distinct markets; developed, developing, and underdeveloped. The developed market — primarily major cities such as Beijing, Shanghai, Chengdu, and Tianjin — are areas where consumers are at income levels where they can afford to purchase products. This segment represents about the top one and a half percent of the population. For this market, companies are trying to stake out a leadership position and develop it into a cash cow.

The developing market, represents the next five percent of China's consumers who are interested in trying new products, but do not quite have the financial means to purchase yet. For this market, the objective for companies is to get consumers to use their product (i.e. through promotions, specials, etc.). When their disposable income increases, there will already be some brand loyalty among these customers. The underdeveloped market represents the rest of China's consumers. This segment of the population will not emerge as a consumer base in the foreseeable future and should be ignored at this time.

For consumer product companies in China, distribution is the key. However, it's not as easy as stocking products on supermarket shelves and in department stores where they are readily available to consumers. Most mainlanders buy their food and household items in small, neighborhood mom-and-pop shops. In addition, retail and wholesale channels are weak and inconsistent in their presentation and positioning of products. Customer service and general product knowledge is also poor. Companies able to develop better delivery channels are the ones who will do well in China.

Compounding the challenge for companies is the size of the mainland. "China is so huge. It's nearly impossible to know it all at once," according to John Chan, chief representative for Fosters Beer in China. Over the past year, John has been involved in Fosters' expansion planning and market development in the mainland. "There are over 200 Chinese sub-cultures, and they're very different. I know of places where, if you cross the street, you'll find people speaking a completely different Chinese dialect. If you think that using the same marketing approach throughout the country is going to work, then you're going to be surprised and disappointed. Eventually, you have to regionalize your marketing strategy within China."

Consumer Products Industry Opportunities

The consumer products industry in Greater China is less sophisticated than in the U.S. The emphasis for many firms is on training and managing sales teams, developing retail and distribution channel relationships, and product promotions. Markets are also smaller and more dynamic relative to the U.S. Because of this, marketing professionals often have the opportunity to be involved in all aspects of a brand (i.e. market planning, product launch, advertising, public relations, etc.).

There is an overall lack of quality brand management and marketing professionals in the region. Local marketing talent tends to be good at execution, but weaker in the critical areas of strategic thinking, planning, management, and creativity that multinational consumer product firms require. For China, the need is for staff with a strong understanding and experience in distribution channel development. With 87 percent of the population living in the countryside, firms are going everywhere in pursuit of consumers. The challenge is to identify people who can understand and deal in a variety of diverse cultures, attitudes, and markets.

Information Technology (IT)

An Awakening

Over the past five years or so, Greater China has gone through an information technology awakening. The region has embraced technology as a competitive weapon to bring itself up to speed in today's global economy. As a result, it is one of Greater China's fastest growing industries. Witness the entry and rapid emergence of major players such as Dell, Microsoft, Compaq, and Cisco over the past few years.

Asia's fast adoption of new technologies reflects an interesting phenomenon. Where just a few years ago it was several product generations behind the West, the region is leapfrogging older technologies in acquiring newer ones. "Asia is not burdened by the legacies and years of investment that the U.S. has to deal with," says James Yao, Asia Pacific vice president of marketing for Anixter Inc, a world leader in network systems integration. "That makes it easier to skip weaker technologies and implement new ones much quicker. For instance, in software only the latest releases are used. In hardware, the newest computer models are purchased. And in networking, the most modern equipment is installed."

Computers

Although the personal computer market around the region shows strong, steady growth, China is the market generating the real excitement for computer product companies. The mainland's PC sales are rising exponentially. In 1995, annual sales totaled about 500,000 units. In 1997, an estimated 2.5 million units were sold. By 2002, sales are predicted to hit 10 million. To make a comparison, annual PC sales in Japan today total about 7 million units.

Much of the optimism stems from the fact that mainland PC sales are almost entirely driven by corporate and government business purchases. The consumer market has not even begun to be tapped. The understanding of computers is still new to local consumers, similar to the level U.S. consumers were at ten years ago. The explosion of China's PC market over the next few years will coincide with increased consumer purchasing power and awareness.

For multinational software firms, piracy and copyright infringements are a glaring problem. At present, it is estimated that a staggering 98 percent of all software distributed in China is pirated. The market is still highly attractive to multinationals, however, since even a two percent improvement on piracy violations means a doubling of revenues for the industry. Despite the high copyright infringement rate, software firms are still able to be profitable through services and support paid by users. Many newer entrants take a guerrilla sales and marketing approach, essentially grass-roots business development that builds a presence and name recognition without the support of a large infrastructure and spending budget. When the market does explode, these firms will already be established and well-positioned.

Ker Gibbs spends a good deal of his time lobbying governing bodies and speaking to the media to create awareness over copyright infringement. Ker is the managing director of Asia Pacific for Claris, a Silicon Valley-based software firm with annual worldwide sales of US$250 million. He foresees the mainland's environment changing once more local companies begin developing their own software products. "To protect its domestic companies, the government will toughen laws to crack down on violators," states Ker. "Although these new domestic players and products will increase competition for foreign firms, this is exactly what we'd like to see. The legitimate market and revenues for software companies will grow. The firms who will profit are the ones with the best products, and sales and marketing abilities. Companies like mine are more than happy to compete on those criteria."

Telecom

The sophistication of telecommunications in Greater China is impressive. Hong Kong is the region's telecommunications center and the first major city in the world to have an all-digital exchange network. Its fiber optics network gives it tremendous external phone line capacity and it has among the world's highest penetration rates for pagers and cellular phones. Taiwan itself has 1.2 million mobile phone users, expected to increase to 5.8 million within one year.

Although glaringly under capacity at this time, the mainland will invest a tremendous amount in its telecommunications infrastructure over the next few years. This will include the installation of about 10 million new telephone lines a year. And in perhaps the region's ultimate example of bypassing older technologies, its Post and Telecommunications Ministry is already raising the question: "Why install telephone lines when we can go wireless?" Such directions have to be considered and pursued if the mainland expects to meet the overwhelming challenge of its telecommunications needs.

Fueling the industry's growth is the deregulation occurring throughout the region. Long-time, local public service providers are no longer being protected or bolstered through government subsidies. Hong Kong deregulated the domestic phone services monopoly of Hongkong Telecom in the summer of 1995 by granting licenses to three new operators. Taiwan will completely open its telecommunications markets by the year 2001 as part of its effort to join the World Trade Organization (WTO).

Service areas being liberalized include the public switching telephone networks (PSTN), mobile phone services, and satellite network services.

Internet

So far, the Internet market in Asia is more hype than reality, according to Darwin Singson, former Asia Pacific IT industry consultant for Dataquest, the world's leading information technology market advisory group. "Currently, Internet usage is almost entirely driven by multinationals and businesses. Home usage is still extremely low compared to what it is in the U.S. A key to greater usage in Asia is the development of localized content. To date, most is in English." Darwin points to Hong Kong and Singapore as the largest Internet markets in Asia, based on their higher level of IT sophistication and greater PC usage levels in both businesses and homes.

Systems Integration

For multinationals establishing operations throughout the region, there is a need to network and access information between office locations. With firms in the early stages of expansion often directing resources to business development areas initially, IT work is often subcontracted to outside vendors. This has created a great demand for systems integration and IT consulting services.

Information Technology Opportunities

Many IT companies enter Asia after first launching their hot products and leading technologies in the U.S. and Europe. For most computer products and telecommunications companies, their strategy in the region is to develop business through key distributor networks and government relationships. Such firms need business development managers able to establish sales and distribution channels that provide access to local markets. Candidates who have industry contacts and familiarity with the competitive environment of individual countries are actively sought.

Finding experienced IT service professionals is a real challenge in the region. Excellent opportunities are available for IT consultants, systems integrators, and project managers who can design, oversee, and implement large information systems and applications development projects. "Local IT professionals tend to be strong technically, but lack a well-rounded business background and strong management skills,' says Janet Tan, director for Andersen Consulting's technology group in Hong

Kong. "Or they might have the business and management abilities, but can't deliver specific IT expertise. In our industry, the overwhelming need is for people with both solid technical training and good business sense. IT professionals from the U.S. tend to have a stronger combination of these skills."

Although nobody can predict the future of the mainland's IT industry, information technology firms know they must be active in the market now. Ker Gibbs sees great opportunities in China for business development professionals who understand Silicon Valley and know U.S. technology companies. "I was at a computer trade show in Beijing recently and met several people representing major U.S. technology companies in the mainland," he says. "Their IT backgrounds weren't extensive or overwhelmingly impressive. But they had the willingness and determination to contact U.S. firms and say that they could get results in China without having to incur a lot of expense to the company."

Accounting

Chronic Shortage

Foreign-invested enterprises are setting up in China, new joint ventures are constantly being established between Chinese and foreign partners, and mainland companies are seeking to go public through their listing in overseas stock markets. At the heart of all these activities is the essential need for professional accounting services and effective internal financial infrastructures.

The volume of business activity in Hong Kong, China, and Taiwan has created a demand for qualified accounting professionals and finance managers that severely exceeds the available supply. "There is a tremendous shortage, in particular, within the major international public accounting firms for professional staff," says Bill Seto, partner at Ernst & Young in Shanghai. Most of the business for these firms is audit-driven, according to Bill, with about 95 percent of business coming from ventures involving foreign companies. As a result, an understanding of western accounting standards is important.

Similar to other industries, China is where the dynamic growth for the accounting industry is happening. This not only includes the auditing area, but tax services as well (as increasing numbers of foreign professionals relocate to the mainland). Where public accounting firms used to remote control their mainland business from Hong

Kong, over the past couple of years the trend has quickly shifted to developing China operations. "Our Shanghai office grew in staff by 70 percent in 1997," continues Bill. "We're projected to match that growth this year as well." This places an emphasis on Chinese language abilities, including Chinese reading skills.

The practice of accounting in China requires experience and good judgment. Rarely is there a straightforward case. Among the challenges that accounting professionals in China face are the less advanced financial systems of clients, a less disciplined and less mature commercial business culture, and a less open business environment. As a supervisor or assistant manager, you must also be prepared to perform a job with less resources, in terms of research material or technically knowledgeable specialists. In addition, you can't rely on secretaries or junior staff preparers as much because of limited English skills and poor understanding of modern business practices

Accounting Industry Opportunities

Although junior staff levels in public accounting firms are usually filled through local hires (work visa issues arise as a problem for fresh graduates from overseas), senior accountant and manager level positions are generally filled through more experienced, western-trained professionals. Overall, it's difficult for the Big Six firms to find good staff in Hong Kong and China since every employer is seeking the same candidate from a limited supply that is available. In Singapore, one Big Six firm is said to have recruited expat housewives and trained them to prepare U.S. tax returns!

With U.S. work experience and training, you should have the self initiative, professionalism and strong communication skills to give you a fast track edge over local colleagues without the same degree of exposure and training. As a result, the chance to see large engagement and people management responsibilities early in your career can be tremendous. The greatest opportunities are in China for experienced accounting professionals who can develop and train local staff.

"I wouldn't say the partner track is necessarily any faster in Asia compared to the U.S.," says Bill. "But every step along the way out here you'll be better compensated, assume more responsibility, and play a more significant role in the practice. For instance, we're in the high growth stage of building Ernst & Young's practice in China. There aren't many markets where you can play a key role in an operation experiencing that level of development."

Law

Never Enough Lawyers

When he began at Skadden, Arps' Hong Kong practice in 1993, the international legal profession in Hong Kong was at a Phase I stage according to Arthur Wang. "At that time, there were no more than five U.S. law firms with operations beyond a legal professional and a secretary," describes Arthur. "But with the finance industry's growth in the region, the legal industry has grown with it and reached a Phase II stage. Today, there are at least triple the number of practices, with nearly every major U.S. law firm now having a presence in Greater China. Not only that, the size of each firm has increased by ten-fold, growing from up to 10 to 15 professionals per office."

Hong Kong is the focal point for lawyers practicing in the region, even if your interest is China. The mainland has strict regulations allowing foreign law firms to operate offices within the country. Most firms doing work in China have their lawyers travel in-country frequently from Hong Kong.

A U.S. law degree only allows a lawyer to legally act as a foreign legal consultant, but does not allow you to practice law in Hong Kong courts. However, this limitation does not prevent U.S.-trained lawyers from representing and advising companies on essential legal and business issues. The value-added areas provided by foreign-trained lawyers are in their legal counsel and international expertise. Court-related activities such as litigation are typically handled through locally-licensed intermediaries.

The most common types of legal work in the region fall into three areas. They are project finance, related to banking and financing for power plants, roads, aircraft leasing, and infrastructure projects; corporate finance or securities, involving the execution of equity and debt products for corporations and governments; and direct investment or corporate, or joint venture and investment-related work for multinationals expanding in the region.

Corporate and securities law makes up roughly 95 percent of the work practiced by law firms in China. Corporate law is the more stable business area, primarily involving the advising of multinational clients on China law related to direct investment or joint venture formation with a local Chinese partner. Securities law is the more volatile practice, since business is dictated by fluctuating capital markets in the region. More recently, there is a trend for mergers and acquisitions business that's being driven by the mainland government's decision to let failing state-owned enterprises go bankrupt. As a result, there will be a considerable amount of reform work to buy and sell off pieces of these operations.

With relatively few legal professionals in the region, there are exceptional chances for responsibility and a greater variety of tasks early on (i.e. direct client contact exposure, high profile cases, etc.). "There were 550 lawyers in just the one building I worked at in New York. In that type of environment, it takes time and the right exposure to distinguish yourself," says Arthur. But as the only Mandarin speaking lawyer in Skadden Arps' newly set up Hong Kong office, Arthur quickly found himself involved in several high profile China cases. China's investment industry was in its early development stage. He was assigned to be the lead lawyer in the mainland's first global bond offering. He also performed the country's first corporate convertible bond offering. "There were virtually no pre-existing laws related to these issues in China at the time," says Arthur. "In many ways, the cases we worked on defined the laws. We provided the framework and advice, and it was deemed right."

If you're interested in China work, Mandarin is essential, including reading abilities. You'll be constantly dealing with dual language documents, written in English and Chinese. The amount of new laws evolving in China is staggering, with reforms in all industries and areas of business occurring daily. Because the translated English version may not be easy to interpret, you often have to revert to the original Chinese version for clarification and understanding.

Arthur sees another phase of significant growth coming where practices will become more full-fledged. Currently, more U.S. law firms are setting up representative offices in Beijing and Shanghai (at least 10 by Arthur's estimate). As the region's legal industry continues to mature, he also sees local language skills and cultural understanding as increasingly critical, with the likelihood of getting a job on technical legal skills alone progressively more difficult.

Legal Industry Opportunities

"There is a 'big time' need for law professionals in the region, especially ones who can do China work," according to Frank Rocco, former general counsel at Pepsi Restaurants International. "For multinationals doing business in the mainland, there are so many traps and bureaucracies you can fall into. There are also issues, such as protecting the environment and the remittance of local currency, that you'd never even know to ask about, let alone address. A strong legal counsel with the experience and capabilities to maneuver in China can help a company avoid significant problems."

When looking for an associate position out here, it's better to get interviewed and hired from the U.S. It's not unusual for second year law school students to arrange summer associate internships where time is split between the U.S. and Hong Kong. Law firms often hire these interns upon graduation for full-time assignment in Asia, after an initial stint in the U.S. practice.

The downside to a law career in Greater China relates to the topical nature of practicing law in general. In other professions, you can work hard out here for several years and leverage much of the experience you gain back in the U.S. when you return. In law, it's different. Once you step outside the U.S. legal environment, it becomes increasingly difficult to jump back in as time passes. In the end, the legal experience you gain in Asia does not have the same value in the U.S. compared to if you had practiced in the U.S. all along. "I've been in Asia five years. If I returned to the States today, I'd need to study for six months to familiarize myself with changes in the U.S. legal environment before I could practice there again," admits Frank.

The upsides, however, are apparent. "The fun meter for practicing law out here is 10 times greater than in the States. The sheer newness of so many business developments in the region makes the cases you work on much more challenging and interesting, rather than routine and boring. For instance, you're not just executing a contract, but a contract in China or Jakarta. That adds a lot of spice to what you're doing," concludes Arthur.

Media/Entertainment

Appealing To Local Audiences

News reporting and broadcasting in the region by international players has been occurring for several years. Only within the last couple of years, however, have these major media and entertainment companies established production operations in Greater China. U.S. broadcasting powerhouses like CNN, CNBC, ESPN, and MTV began producing programs in Asia only as recently as 1995. Most undertook an Asia Pacific strategy, where one station would broadcast programs across the region. It didn't work. How can you compare viewing markets in Korea or Taiwan with those in Indonesia or the Philippines? Now cable operators are taking a more localized approach that caters content towards specific audiences. For instance, STAR Chinese channel's targeting of Mandarin-speaking audiences in Taiwan and China has proven to be very successful.

The challenge for all operators is in increasing viewership. A major difficulty is the inverse relationship between those who can afford cable services and those who watch television. More affluent professionals work long hours and tend not to have time for TV, while high viewing, lower income households aren't as willing to pay for cable services.

Another obstacle is that the establishment of a credible advertising model, based on viewership ratings and media buying standards (like those that exist in the U.S.), is only in its early stage of development in Asia. As a result, many stations are not yet able to earn significant revenues through traditional advertising dollars. As a necessity, they look at alternative strategies to generate cash flow, such as through licensed product sales, events sponsorships, and TV commerce.

The region's television industry will take time to develop. Media firms are still pursuing a viable business model that will create long-term success, yet will allow them to sustain and develop local operations in the short term. Where the initial thrust was in setting up production facilities, the main challenge now is in developing stronger programming, sales, and marketing. With the viewing market not yet mature, it's the TV companies operating the most cost effectively who are doing the best in the region.

Asians have always had a great appetite for western films. The popularity of western movies has reached the point where it is difficult for local film makers to get their movies distributed in local theaters. Still, for entertainment giants like Warner Brothers and Universal Pictures, developing business in Asia is slow progress. Much effort and investment are being directed at basic issues, such as building more and better theater complexes.

Media Industry Opportunities

If you want to break into TV media, Greater China is an opportunistic place to do it. The industry is relatively young. The breadth and depth of production and reporting talent is in short supply. I've met many who entered the industry and advanced rapidly despite lacking a media background. In Hong Kong, you can even find positions in English-speaking stations that do not require Chinese language skills. Increasingly, however, media firms are valuing those who offer local language ability and, therefore, more versatility in reporting and covering stories.

Mark Tung was working as a lawyer in Hawaii when he decided to pursue a news reporting career. His friend knew the executive producer for a weekly Hong Kong program called *Eye On Hong Kong*. "The show was looking for a guy who looked Chinese and spoke Cantonese and English," recalls Mark. "I happened to qualify on all counts." After a series of interviews and screen tests, he got the job. Since his TV career began in 1993, Mark has written and produced documentaries and served as a field reporter. He currently anchors the nightly news on ATV, one of Hong Kong's two local stations.

Print media also offers great chances to develop reporting and writing careers. Freelance writing work is fairly accessible throughout the region. Although salaries may not be high initially, excellent experience and exposure to regional contacts and events can be gained quickly.

Public Relations (PR)

Young and Growing

Public relations is a young industry in the region that's seeing rapid growth. In Asia, "public relations" is often perceived as coordinating and managing events, such as hiring celebrities to promote products or attend openings. The types of high-level PR strategic planning and communications skills many multinational firms require are not as common.

PR firms are constantly short of staff at all levels, particularly experienced professionals. The problem is the industry's high employee burnout and turnover rate. In addition, with the difficulty of finding expertise locally, many U.S. or European firms bring out managers from other international operations to Asia. As these expats return home, gaps are created at middle and senior manager levels.

In the mainland, the PR industry is underdeveloped. Almost 100 percent of PR services are paid for by multinationals, or joint ventures in which the non-Chinese side foots the bill. However, the industry is seeing tremendous growth. One major international agency grew revenues by 54 percent in 1996 from the previous year.

"The restraint is in people to service the business, not in the client demand," says the managing director of the firm's Beijing office. His advice to those interested in a PR career in the mainland: "Become a master of the PR business first, rather than a master of China. Once you have the solid skills, you'll find a tremendous need among pubic relations firms in China to train and manage local staff. Ultimately, it's your ability to develop the local team that will lead to career promotion opportunities."

Recently, the industry is seeing the new entry of local PR agencies. It is also undergoing greater segmentation and seeing the need for both low-end (i.e. news releases, organizing banquets and functions, etc.) and high-end services (i.e. public affairs consultancy, crisis management, government relations, assisting foreign firms to obtain licenses and deal with distribution issues, etc.).

Public Relations Industry Opportunities

Greater China's PR industry offers outstanding chances for those with strong creative, writing, and account management skills. It's a young field where most people are in their twenties and thirties. "Multinational PR firms look for bright, young people who are willing to work long and hard," says Grace Wong, CNN International's Asia Pacific executive director of public relations. "It's an easy industry to break into out here and one where tremendous responsibility and exposure can come quickly. In addition, significant career advancement opportunities and rewards can happen within only three to five years. PR also opens a lot of doors for you. As a discipline that emphasizes strong communications skills, it's highly transferable to fields like marketing and consulting."

Advertising

China On My Mind

International advertising agencies have had a presence in Greater China for many years, with operations firmly rooted in Taiwan and Hong Kong. Recently, agencies have ramped up operations in China as well, in response to the flood of consumer products companies, electronics manufacturers, and restaurants building a presence there. Since 1995, leading agencies like DDB Needham, Saatchi & Saatchi, and Lintas have all established mainland operations. The potential for these agencies is huge, but currently slow going. "There are many sensitivities that make advertising in China frustrating," says a client services director working in Shanghai. "For instance, they won't allow any advertising that claims you're the best. We had one client whose product's success was built entirely on the claim that it was 'the best of Scotland.' We couldn't use it."

Candidates with an international background and broad mindset offer a competitive advantage in an industry that values creativity and an understanding of consumers. Bicultural and bilingual backgrounds are also key. Where just a few years ago, many Hong Kong agencies did regional work, much of that business has moved to Singapore. Today, China is increasingly the focus for Hong Kong offices. One account manager estimates that 90 percent of her agency's people are western-educated, and just about everyone is fluent in Chinese.

Advertising Industry Opportunities

As with the public relations industry, the advertising industry in Greater China has a high turnover rate. It's not unusual for an agency to lose 30–40 percent of its staff each year. Hiring needs are constant and at every level. "Getting into advertising is not difficult, but the early going is," says Wendy Yang, associate account director for DDB Needham in Hong Kong. "You work incredibly long hours and starting salaries are low. But if you like a fast-paced, exciting, fun environment, where you're constantly learning new things, then it's a great choice. And if you can stick with it, you'll find yourself moving up fast. A friend was recently named the client services director for an agency in China, in charge of the entire client services department for his office. He's about 30 years old. That level of responsibility might take 15 years or more to attain back in the States."

Regional Outlook

What About The Downturn(s)?

While I was on a Greater China job market information tour of U.S. MBA programs in November 1997, the Hong Kong stock market began bouncing up and down. During each presentation, the first question people would ask was how job prospects in the region were being affected. The market's instability was an indication that the region's economies were operating on extremely tenuous grounds. Vulnerabilities and weaknesses in Asia's growth engine began exposing themselves, particularly throughout South East Asia. At the beginning of each day, I would call back to Hong Kong to find out what the outlook was among multinational firms. More recently, the region's currency crisis has made headline news and raised additional questions about the prospects for businesses operating out here.

In speaking with many multinational managers, their view of this downturn is similar. They know regional business results in 1998 will not match those of recent years. They are communicating this scenario to their home offices in order to set appropriate expectations. However, this is not to say that companies are panicking. There is not a mass retreat from the region or rampant downsizing going on across industries.

Long-Term Commitment

Companies are indeed absorbing and factoring in the fluctuations in the region's economic picture. Many have paused to assess the overall situation and outlook for 1998. However, most firms are adhering to their long-term view of their presence and business opportunities in Asia.

"We've made a clear decision to continue to grow in 1998 at the same rate we projected one year ago, before the recent slowdown," says Graham Brandt, managing director of consulting services at Microsoft in Hong Kong. "As with most companies in Asia, revenues will be tighter this year. But that doesn't change our long-term strategy which we're committed to. As a result, now is the time to invest in infrastructure and people. We remain optimistic in our regional business outlook. Otherwise, we wouldn't be here."

For similar companies committed to the region, Asia still remains the world's largest emerging economy. The fundamentals are there. They include the world's largest population, an affordable and highly educated workforce, strong cross-border networks among the Chinese, and a history and culture rooted in trade, society, and making money.

Slower, But Healthier Growth

Asia's economic upsurge has happened over a relatively short time period. Success has almost come too easy for many countries who have become overconfident as a result. Economies have overheated to the point where prices and spending have hit unjustifiable heights. The "correction" going on now is bringing these areas in line to more reasonable levels.

In parallel, many companies have either overestimated regional markets, expanded too fast, or both. Their early success came quickly as well. "When we began out here, markets were completely untapped. Market share and new business came relatively easily. Revenue growth averaged nearly 100 percent annually over the past four years," says a regional marketing director for a large U.S. consumer products company. "Suddenly, that growth has slowed to low double-digits. Although that's a significant downshift from the past, it's still an attractive rate of expansion. Over the long-term, it's healthier. It allows us to build better infrastructures, make sounder expansion decisions, and select stronger business relationships,"

Silver Lining

With a long-term view and belief in the region's fundamentals, there is a silver lining to the currency crisis. The economic downturn is forcing local countries, markets, and governments to get their act together in order to correct the harsh economic situation they've helped create. Inside favoritism, protectionism, under-the-table business practices, and inappropriate directing of funds and resources have long occurred throughout the region. There are too many close relationships between government and banks. In places like Indonesia and Korea, in particular, a few families and organizations (i.e. chaebols) dominate and write rules to the exclusion of others. Rapid growth gave these countries the feeling that they had a better system for economic development than the rest of the world.

Such activities favored local companies and industries, making it tougher for foreign players to penetrate markets and operate profitably. The hardening economic realities are eliminating many of these inequities. To reach the next stage of growth, local systems and practices must change. Countries will fail if governments don't reform industries and practices. More openness and competition are needed. When the dust settles, multinationals will be able to compete on a fairer playing field. This, they welcome wholeheartedly.

Operations Renewal

In the meantime, the focus for many companies is to solidify and improve their infrastructure. Many are undergoing an "operations renewal" process. Despite the current economic downturn, setting up strong distribution channels and partnerships, establishing efficient operations, and developing a capable management team remain as necessary objectives for success and profitability in the region. Multinationals that have expanded quickly are using this period to strengthen and better position themselves for the future, when markets and economies shape up.

Regarding staffing issues, companies can be more deliberate and selective in bringing aboard excellent personnel. Although companies might officially have a hiring freeze in place, unofficially this is not necessarily the case. "We continue to look for good people. The approval process to bring someone on board may require more steps and sign-offs, but we're not going to pass up on attractive talent," says a human resources manager for a U.S. investment bank in Hong Kong.

Costs Too High

The downturn is also causing multinationals to take a renewed, critical look at their cost structure and spending. For many companies, general and administration costs (G&A) are way out of line with sales growth. That has become even more apparent during the currency crisis. One of the greatest areas of susceptibility is the exorbitant cost of maintaining expatriate employees.

"One of our first moves has been to lay off several expats," says a regional human resources manager for a consumer products company. "We have some who receive as much as HK$200,000 (over US$25,000) in housing allowance per month. On top of salary and a host of other benefits, some even get up to HK$50,000 (about US$6,500) in hardship allowance. This is for living in Hong Kong! Multiply that kind of total cost by ten, the number of expats we have, and you begin to wonder if that amount of spending on expat packages is necessary, or even smart. Just think of how many locally hired professionals can be employed for the same amount of money."

They're Still Looking

The current slowdown is trying for businesses, particularly smaller companies and firms whose business cycles go from quarter to quarter. But the overall picture is far from desperate. News that highlights the region's finance industry, receives the biggest and most alarming headlines. From the plight of several banks, it appears as if the sky is falling across the region. It is, in fact, a grim period for many financial institutions in Asia that are poorly positioned with their product mix and investment choices.

Word on the street, however, is that some of the larger U.S. investment houses are actually planning to expand. They see this as a great time to pick up excellent talent.

For other industries, the situation is much stronger. Charmaine Chan, a *South China Morning Post* reporter, was surprised at what she found while researching a story on Hong Kong executive recruitment firms in mid-February 1998. "I expected to hear that times were bad and that multinationals weren't hiring. I was surprised to find that a lot of recruiting firms were still very active, with some even predicting substantial growth this year." Although the finance industry had definitely slowed, Charmaine discovered that hiring in information technology, telecommunications, and consulting industries were still strong.

During the weeks up to and immediately following Chinese New Year in 1998, the heaviest period of news surrounding the currency crisis, the South China Morning Post still averaged more than 100 pages of job advertisements. Beyond the finance industry, job search requests from Wang & Li's multinational clients continue to be strong. "The situation is not as bad as the U.S. media paints it," says William Han, who came to Hong Kong in February to find a job in the executive search industry. "You may have to be more focused and aggressive, but there are still a lot of jobs that need to be filled here."

Do You Bet On Or Against Asia?

The Asia Pacific region and Greater China will continue to experience downturns, some more serious than others, that will impact confidence in the region. These downturns are a part of the regional picture as economies and markets develop. Despite the uncertain times that occur, however, the outlook remains an optimistic and long-term one for most companies and individuals here. Of all the areas in the region, Mainland China, Hong Kong, and Taiwan have maintained attractive economic growth throughout. They continue to be the strongest holdouts among Asia pacific countries. As someone in Hong Kong said to me recently: "Look at all the crises that have been made light of in Hong Kong, such as the period following Tiananmen Square, the time surrounding the 1997 handover, and the passing away of Deng Xiaoping. Yet, Hong Kong and China continue to beat the doomsayers. For the overwhelming majority of individuals who have bet on Asia by being in Greater China over the past 10 years, their careers have taken off."

Throughout the region, a shake out is going on, where business practices and corporate strategies are being more closely scrutinized. Firms that have been merely opportunistic in the past are having a harder time competing now. The more favored companies are ones with sound business approaches that deliver superior products, services, and value. For such companies, outstanding business opportunities in the region continue to present themselves.

For job seekers, the same holds true. Excellent career opportunities continue to exist in Greater China for those who can deliver the right skills. The shift in the region towards a more competitive environment ultimately creates greater openings for affordable, localized professionals. More so than ever, the compensation packages of home office-sent expats are standing out as excessive, non-essential costs. Companies will continue to pursue the type of personnel who can build their operations and business successfully. Throughout the changes and developments taking place, bilingual and bicultural Chinese American professionals respond to the critical hiring needs of multinational firms in the region.

Chapter 11 The Four City Comparison: Hong Kong/Taipei/Shanghai/Beijing

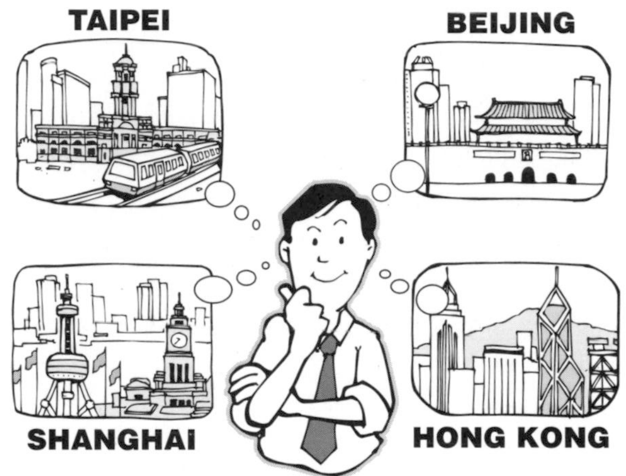

Many U.S. candidates I speak with want to know which is the best location to live and work in Greater China. I can only tell them what each major city offers. The lifestyle, as well as personal and career development implications in Hong Kong, Taipei, Shanghai, and Beijing are dramatically different. It depends on what you're looking to accomplish. Is your objective to develop Chinese language skills? Take on a fast track career? Immerse yourself in a local Chinese environment? Be part of a rapidly changing place? Or to what extent are you considering each of these areas? This chapter describes the four destinations that most Chinese Americans choose when moving to Greater China.

Hong Kong

The Place

Hong Kong can be described as New York City and Mainland China rolled into one. It's a bustling, western and cosmopolitan metropolis and a local Chinese enclave packed together. It's also the most densely populated city in the world. Just walk around any of its urban areas and you'll have no difficulty confirming that fact.

Look across the harbor towards the Hong Kong side from Kowloon and you'll see an impressive skyline of shiny, new office buildings and high rises. The city is modern and international. At the same time, it has its distinct local flavor. Scenes of sturdy old men on the streets pushing heavy carts, people in the park doing morning *tai chi* exercises, and vendors selling goods from stalls in narrow alleyways are common.

Hong Kong has an energy you can feel. Hong Kong people always appear to be in a hurry, rushing about and talking on their mobile phones. The city is also more convenient and well-run than Taipei or Shanghai, while at the same time less structured and more free-wheeling than Singapore.

The Business Environment

Built For Business

After spending some time working in Hong Kong, it may seem to you as if it was developed for the sole purpose of doing business. An entrepreneurial spirit and energy dominates the scene. The British government may no longer have a legal presence in Hong Kong, but they built and left behind a system that strikes an optimal balance between the government and business community. Equitable rules leave firms relatively free to conduct business. The result is an environment geared to helping both institutions and individuals do business effectively and expediently. As a minor example, when I registered my company in Taipei, it took me six months and several thousand dollars to obtain a business license. In Hong Kong, I wrote a check for a couple of hundred dollars. Within a few days, I received a pre-registered license which I merely signed and wrote down the name of my company.

Hong Kong's legal system, based on the rule of law and an independent judiciary, provides a solid framework of fair play and enforcement that allows businesses to run securely. Its low corporate and personal tax rates also make Hong Kong a profitable place to operate. The simplicity of its tax structure adds to an already favorable situation that attracts investments and promotes business initiative. In the end, Hong Kong offers a playing field for firms and individuals, where the key factors for success come down to ability and determination.

Regional Business Services Center

Hong Kong's business friendly environment has earned it its position as the regional center for commercial activity. It is not only the region's leading hub for finance, but also for telecommunications, media, business services, technology expertise, management, and transport. Just about every major multinational in Asia has its regional headquarters, if not a significant presence, in Hong Kong (some 2300 according to a June 1997 *Business Week* article entitled "Why Multinationals Are So Gung Ho"). In addition, it competes with Singapore as the top location for many multinationals conducting business throughout South East Asia.

Fundamentally, Hong Kong is a commercial and financial center, not a manufacturing one. Given its limited size, it has emerged as a "knowledge economy" that has developed value-added business sectors serving the rest of the region.

Gateway To The Mainland

Hong Kong is also the indisputable gateway to Mainland China. This is not a result of the handover. Hong Kong and the mainland have been intimately involved in each other's success for quite some time. As its third largest trading partner, Hong Kong plays a significant role in facilitating trade between the mainland and the rest of the world. Today, Hong Kong handles about 50 percent of China's exports.

In addition, Hong Kong's provision and facilitation of capital, technology, sourcing services, management know-how, and logistical support continue to be critical to China's modernization and growth. Many multinationals spearhead their mainland operations and business expansion initiatives from the island. Employees are often based in Hong Kong and may travel to the mainland as often as once a week. Collectively, Hong Kong-based companies and individuals possess just about the most extensive expertise and experience of anyone operating in China.

Doing Business

The work ethic in Hong Kong is driven and dedicated. Multinational corporate cultures are westernized, with most managers within these firms having educational backgrounds from abroad. As a result, Hong Kong's business environment is more "professional" than in other Greater China cities. At the same time, business in Hong Kong is also done in a highly entrepreneurial manner. It is known for being competitive and fast-paced.

Just a few years ago, non-Asian language speakers could easily find employment in Hong Kong. Although it's still possible in certain fields (i.e. information technology, media, etc.), it's becoming increasingly difficult to do overall. Mandarin or Cantonese are now a prerequisite for many professional jobs within multinational firms, which require staff to conduct business within local markets and directly with local parties.

Job Market

Hong Kong offers the most dynamic job market in the region, perhaps even in the world today. As a center for business services to the Asia Pacific region, it has exceptional career opportunities for professionals with backgrounds in finance, consulting, marketing, legal, accounting, communications, and information technology. With numerous multinational headquarters in Hong Kong, many positions offer regional responsibilties and exposure. Or if your sights are set on developing a career centered around China, there are also many front-line positions aimed at this market.

The Lifestyle

Within Greater China, Hong Kong is the easiest city to adjust to coming from the U.S. Although Cantonese is the common spoken language, English is the primary language used in business. Even outside of work, it's fairly convenient to get around in English. If you don't speak Mandarin, that's okay. But if you do, it's a useful back-up when interacting with locals. Many now speak Mandarin, having anticipated the 1997 handover back to China.

The lifestyle in Hong Kong is the consummate definition of work hard, play hard. People who come to Hong Kong in particular place their career as number one. The average person works at least a 10-hour day, and twelve is not uncommon. Many are involved in business with the mainland or throughout the Asia Pacific and travel frequently.

Socially, Hong Kong is the city that never sleeps. It's a place to party hard. For night life, Lan Kwai Fong is the dusk till dawn dining, drinking, and dancing hang-out for foreigners. Drop by The Milk Bar, Post 1997, or California's at 1am on any weekend and you're sure to find each place packed with late-night revelers.

Hong Kong's foreign community is large, with its presence both seen and felt. In the districts of Central, Admiralty, Wanchai, or Causeway Bay you won't be able to look in any direction without spotting numerous *gweilos* (a.k.a. foreign devils). One attractive aspect of Hong Kong is that it's a melting pot that attracts a diverse mix of talented and adventurous people from all over the world. Americans, Britains, Australians, Indians, and regional Asians are among those foreigners with the greatest presence. In addition, Hong Kong's Chinese American community is by far the largest of any city in Asia.

U.S. citizens represent the largest foreign business group residing in Hong Kong, estimated at 41,000 permanent or temporary residents as of mid-1997 — U.S. Department of State.

If you like to meet interesting people, Hong Kong is your 24-hour cocktail party. Networking and socializing are a way of life. "During my first six weeks here I met more people than I did in the previous year back in the States," recalls Jenny Lin. Jenny came to Hong Kong from Boston to look for a media industry position. "I was out five nights a week, going to cocktail parties, junk trips, happy hours, store openings, you name it. There was always a function going on or people to get together with."

One drawback, however, is the difficulty many find integrating into the local community. Beyond business hours, there's a definite segregation between foreigners and local Hong Kong residents. While many attribute the lack of interaction to the language barrier, foreigners I know who speak Cantonese also experience the same feeling of separation. In general, Hong Kong people seem to keep their personal lives more to themselves. With its British colonial history, Hong Kongers are not as curious about or enamored by the thought of knowing westerners in the way that Taiwanese or mainlanders can be.

Many find Hong Kong's lifestyle and environment to be a bit harsh. You'll frequently hear complaints about how rude and pushy people are. Rarely will you hear the words "personable" and "warm" used to describe Hong Kong as a place.

If you like to eat, then you'll have no problem satisfying your palate. It feels odd whenever I see people eating at McDonalds or Kentucky Fried Chicken here. It seems a shame to have the same hamburger or piece of chicken that's available anywhere in the world when Hong Kong offers a tantalizing variety of international foods. The one downside is that spending on food and entertainment can get expensive. Eating out can put a dent in your finances if you regularly go to restaurants that cater to foreigners. It's no effort at all to drop US$100 in one night, as dinner, cover charges, and drink prices add up quickly.

Crowded within a half-mile radius of Central district, you'll find the regional offices for hundreds of multinational firms. If you're calling on clients, chances are you can reach them all within fifteen minutes by foot, taxi, or mass transit railway (MTR).

Although the city's compact size makes life easier, Tony Shen, a consultant living in Hong Kong since 1994, cautions against the tendency to live a "Central Centric" life. He refers to the sterile lifestyle, nearly devoid of any Asian flavor or influences, that many foreigners have. "A lot of people in Hong Kong only know life in Central, where it's extremely westernized and convenient," describes Tony. "We live in Central's Mid-levels, work in Central business district, and hang out in Lan Kwai Fong. Our entire existence happens within ten minutes in any direction. I know people who have been in Hong Kong for over a year and have hardly ever been to the Kowloon side. This type of sheltered living kind of defeats the purpose of coming out to experience Asia in the first place."

It's also easy to fall into a limited existence, where your days are spent in the office and your evenings are spent socializing at dining and drinking establishments. However, the territory does offer a variety of outdoor activities. There are great trails for hiking and scenic spots on both the Hong Kong and Kowloon sides. Rock climbing, water skiing, boat rides (referred to as junk trips), or cycling are also accessible with a little effort on your part.

Hong Kong Is For ...

If you're looking to be where the action is, then Hong Kong is your destination. Among the candidates my firm works with, over 80 percent target Hong Kong as their top choice. Their reasons relate to the career opportunities and exposure to China and the rest of Asia that Hong Kong offers. It's the place to be if you want to push your career. I've heard many people say that its work ethic surpasses that of New York City, the place most recognized as the optimal location for go-getters.

Many also prefer Hong Kong because it's more westernized lifestyle makes it easy to adapt to. It's a place, however, where burnout is high. Some find Hong Kong's lifestyle one-dimensional and shallow. It offers a challenging experience, but not necessarily one that will give you a good sense of the culture, language, and people of Greater China.

A Word About the 1997 Handover

Three weeks after the historic handover of June 30, 1997, I was talking with friends about the changes we've felt since the British left the territory and the Mainland Chinese moved in. One person summed it up. It was as if the event never took place. For those of us who live here on a daily basis, there has hardly been a discernible difference between our pre- and post-handover lives. Life has carried on in a business-as-usual manner.

China has given Hong Kong a Special Administrative Region (SAR) status, a "one country, two systems" approach that essentially allows Hong Kong to operate under a separate economic system and to preserve its "way of life" for the next 50 years. As stated in The Joint Declaration (an agreement negotiated between the British and Mainland Chinese governments in 1984), the "one country, two systems" policy also allows Hong Kong people to rule the island. As a result, Hong Kong's pre-1997 business and government structures have remained primarily intact. The open and entrepreneurial business environment the territory enjoyed before the handover continues to exist.

In the U.S., people often talk about the limitations imposed by the mainland on Hong Kong's democracy and freedom. However, the free, upbeat lifestyle we enjoy also continues. There are some media restrictions, and it is prohibited to openly protest against China's government. For the average person in Hong Kong, however, doing business is their primary focus. Few in the foreign community were involved in any type of political protests before the handover. This has remained the case since. Therefore, for most, the impact from those changes in civil liberties has been non-existent.

Post-1997 confidence in Hong Kong by the regional business community has also remained high. Hong Kong is a tremendous economic prize for China — the proverbial goose that lays the golden egg. For Beijing to disrupt and harm it is almost unthinkable. Many also point to the success of Hong Kong as a major source of pride for the mainland. The world is watching. As such, China is intent on proving that Hong Kong can continue to operate beyond British rule as an attractive commercial and investment center. Many believe the handover has even enhanced the island's status as the pre-eminent gateway to the mainland. As an indicator, Hong Kong's property market remained strong during the period leading up to the handover, as major businesses and investors sought an even bigger foothold in the territory.

For most people in the region, there's an acceptance and even pride over Hong Kong's return to the mainland. Activities and news from China do not have the day-to-day impact on people's lives that those in the West might think. Hong Kongers in particular are practical and realistic. They are fully aware of the mainland's enormous, unpredictable presence. Without making China sound like a trivial consideration, however, they are used to it.

Those most concerned about their future have already done something about it. The real confidence crisis over Hong Kong's future happened in the early 90s, just after Tiananmen Square. That's when fear was greatest that China's actions towards Hong Kong might be extreme. In response, many went abroad to claim citizenship in places like the U.S., Canada, and Australia. Recently, many have returned. Should an unacceptable situation arise, they now have their insurance policy of dual citizenship.

For those who never left, Hong Kong is simply their permanent home and will continue to be so, regardless of whatever changes that may take place. For foreigners here, we can return to our home countries should an unforeseen change of events occur.

Perhaps the view towards China and the handover by people in Hong Kong and the Asia Pacific region is best described as "cautiously optimistic." Nobody underestimates or ignores what the mainland does or says. At the same time, if companies and individuals based decisions on what China might do, then they wouldn't be here. China might do anything. On the plus side, events and decisions appear to be based increasingly on economic, rather than political factors. Most believe this trend will continue.

The uncertainty of China might be compared to the threat of a major earthquake that Californians constantly face. Like those in California, people here continue with their lives and plan their future despite the most unwelcome possibility. Perhaps everyone is in denial, but there's too much opportunity and upside potential not to be here. One Chinese American in Hong Kong puts a positive spin on Beijing's unpredictable nature and actions. "There will always be a certain fear factor, but that's good," he says. "It keeps this place from being overrun and the competition down for those of us in the region."

Taipei

People often remark that Taipei is disorganized, or *luan qi ba zao* (chaotic or helter-skelter) as they say. They point out that it's polluted and crowded. They complain about the city's poor infrastructure and traffic that can frustrate even the most level-headed commuter. In fact, it's true. Taipei is all those things. Despite these shortcomings though, I'm a big Taipei fan. It's the place where I picked up my Mandarin, gained an understanding of local business ways, and learned about Chinese society and people. And it's where I've made some of my best friends in Asia. They're the type of friendships I believe will last a lifetime.

The Place

Taipei is a place whose characteristics lie somewhere between those of Hong Kong and Beijing. In contrast to Hong Kong, Taipei is a Chinese city developed by Chinese people. It has a much more distinct and traditional Chinese flavor and personality. Compared to Hong Kong, it's less cosmopolitan and less international. It is also not as socially sophisticated and materialistic. For example, rather than Mercedes Benzes and BMWs, a river of motor scooters flows through Taipei's streets and alleys.

Compared to Beijing though, Taipei is more modern and bustling. It has a much greater degree of westernization, with its share of neon lights, glimmering commercial buildings, and international store fronts. Public transportation is quite convenient. In spite of its evolving, modern landscape, Taipei maintains its personal feel. It's not a difficult place to get to know. You'll find numerous neighborhoods and alleyways that are home to small, privately owned shops and businesses. These quaint, residential pockets give the city a great intimacy.

The Business Environment

Steady As She Goes

Taiwan's economy use to be agriculture and manufacturing driven, but over the past decade emphasis has been placed on developing its technology, electronics, and service capabilities. The government has been successful in targeting and subsidizing several strategic industries. For example, today, Taiwan is a world leader in producing semiconductor, computer, and computer-related products, such as motherboards, keyboards, scanners, and computer mice.

With its 21 million people and steadily developing economy, Taiwan offers a strong, vibrant consumer market for multinational firms. Taiwan people have a penchant for American foods, consumer products, music, and entertainment. The internationalization of Taipei in recent years has been obvious. For instance, when I arrived in 1990, the only restaurant that served a reasonably authentic hamburger or western meal was Swenson's (that's right, as in the U.S.-based ice cream parlor). My big treat to myself each week was to go there on Sunday mornings for an American breakfast. Now, western food is available at one of five TGI Friday's (interestingly, they're the happening place in Taipei), the Hard Rock Cafe, Trader Vic's, Ruth's Chris, Tony Roma's, or dozens of other international restaurants. Walk down a sidestreet and you'll also find all sorts of quaint and cozy pubs, wine bars, and cafes.

Pizza was a rarity back then, beyond one or two Roundtable or Shakey's Pizza locations. Now Domino's and Pizza Hut scooters zip around the city delivering take-out. Just a few years ago, the only premium ice cream available was Dreyer's. Now you can buy Haagan-Dazs at just about any convenience store. Other western businesses that have appeared include Tower Records, Sir Speedy Printing, Subway Sandwiches, and Nine West shoe stores. In 1997 alone, the Warner Brothers Store, Blockbuster Video, and Century 21 Real Estate opened their doors in Taipei. During my last trip, I even passed by a Hooters Restaurant! Personally, I'm waiting for a Dunkin' Donuts to set up business.

Short Of Aspirations

The government has long spoken of establishing Taipei as a major Asia Pacific business center for international investment and regional operations. Despite the city's intent, so far this has not happened. Major hindrances include the limits and restrictions the government puts on foreign businesses operating in Taiwan. It's not easy for multinationals. The business environment is bureaucratic and slow-moving, while tariffs and import taxes are high. Many industries remain highly regulated. With recent liberalization activities in the financial securities and telecommunications industries, this seems to be changing. It's happening, but much slower than most would like. So far, only a handful of multinationals have chosen Taiwan as their regional headquarters.

Undermining the situation is Taiwan's testy relationship with Mainland China and its status as a renegade province rather than as a recognized country within the international community (the official stance by countries who do not want to upset the mainland). Such a status excludes Taiwan from many international trade and business organizations and prevents the government from gaining crucial international exposure. These complications also result in occasional instabilities. For example, the mainland's military reaction to President Lee Tung-hui's 1995 U.S. visit to his alma mater, Cornell University, and Taiwan's first-ever democratic presidential election in 1996, both had a significant negative impact on the country's financial markets and overall business environment.

A third obstacle inhibiting its aspiration to become a regional business center is the lack of an open and efficient process allowing foreigners to work in Taiwan. Review of work permit laws began in 1992, at the urging of the Taipei-based American Chamber of Commerce. Today, however, the government still has a long way to go towards liberalizing its foreign worker rules. As a result, firms often balk at hiring non-Taiwan citizens, regardless of how qualified they are. This has a significant and detrimental effect on the international competitiveness of Taiwan companies and industries.

Doing Business

While you can manage well with only English in Hong Kong, Mandarin is a necessity in Taiwan. Professionally, you'll be extremely limited if you're unable to speak any. Although most locals study English through high school and college, their level of proficiency is not as high as you might expect. In recent years, Taiwanese has also become a growing business language. Though much of the country's development is attributed to the contributions of Mandarin-speaking *wai sheng* Chinese who immigrated from the mainland in the late 1940s and early 50s, recent progress has been fueled by *ben sheng* (native) Taiwanese. As one Taiwan-born, U.S.-trained investment banker notes: "To do business with companies in the south, you have to speak their language. That language is increasingly Taiwanese, not Mandarin."

Business attitudes in Taipei are also distinctly Chinese. Taiwan people are polite and conservative, and tend to avoid situations that can offend or lose face (either theirs or yours). For example, communication is not very direct, with people typically reluctant to speak their minds.

Benjamin Chu has worked in Taipei as a consultant over the past two years for an international management consulting firm. "The biggest difference is adjusting to the *guannian* of the local customers and staff," he points out. "It's the concepts or attitudes that people here are ingrained with. For instance, I've been trained to speak up and express my views if I feel an issue is important to raise. But here, if a person is not happy about something, they won't tell you directly. They'll tell somebody else to tell you. It often takes a day or two for their feedback to get to you, probably communicated in a more casual, less risky situation."

"Locals are also not used to challenging issues," Benjamin adds. "If they don't understand why you're doing something, they won't necessarily let you know. They'll either carry out your orders verbatim, or sort of ignore you and approach it the way they think it should happen. It's not done this way maliciously. They just don't like confrontation."

In Taiwan, having a network of contacts is extremely useful in helping you gain trust, establish yourself with clients, and enhance your ability to do business. I've lost track of how many friends in Taipei have received business, job leads, or hot investment tips through relatives, in-laws, ex-classmates, or acquaintances.

The Job Market

Ask an American what a high unemployment rate is, and they might respond with 5–7 percent. Ask a European and they'll likely say 9–11 percent. In Taiwan, where continuous economic growth resulted in about a one percent unemployment rate for many years, the news that the two percent unemployment mark was passed in early 1997 made headlines and caused some panic. It was a historic "high" for Taiwan unemployment. Media stories contemplated how and why this happened. Worrisome job seekers contacted our Taipei office concerned over whether they would be able to find a job.

Despite the occasional scare stories and recent bumps in the economy, there continues to be excellent job opportunities in Taiwan. We constantly meet candidates who think nothing of resigning from their job to search for a better position, salary, or title elsewhere, even before they've secured tangible options. They are that confident they can find an attractive position. That's the nature of Taiwan's job market. Industries from banking and securities to telecom and information technology continue to develop, a trend that is expected to continue.

In past decades, management jobs in multinationals were usually filled by expat managers sent from U.S. headquarters. As firms in Taiwan increasingly look to localize their operations, senior management opportunities for local-born, U.S.-educated and trained managers are proliferating. Today, the general managers for the Taiwan operations of AT&T, Motorola, J. Walter Thompson, and Nike all fit this profile.

The Lifestyle

Though people in Taipei work hard, the hours you may average each day in your job do not compare with those experienced in Hong Kong or China. As a result, the pace of Taipei life is slower and more relaxed, with fewer career pressures and demands. Where Hong Kong people are constantly busy, Taipei people have more time to pursue other aspects of life. There's a stronger sense of community and greater emphasis on personal relationships.

Taipei's personal touch also stems from the people, who are known to be warm and hospitable. They call it *ren qing wei*. Although locals may not come across as open as westerners, they are not closed. Most Taiwanese have a sincere curiosity and interest in learning about you. They want to know where you're from, why you came to Taipei, and how life in Taiwan compares to life in America.

Although Taipei's foreign community is fairly small relative to other Greater China cities, the foreigners living there are active and visible. They fall primarily into two categories. There are the English-teaching, Mandarin-studying students who tend to live around the areas of Taiwan Normal University and National Taiwan University (a.k.a. *Shi Da* and *Tai Da,* respectively) and the multinational expatriates who live comfortably in the suburbs of Tien Mu, about a 20–30 minutes drive outside of Taipei city.

Increasingly, there is a growing community of younger foreign professionals, which includes many Chinese Americans, who choose to live in the city. These are people who have remained in Taipei to work after their Mandarin studies or have moved to Taipei on their own to seek career opportunities.

One of the most appealing aspects about Taipei's social scene is the intermingling of the different sub-cultures. For instance, your ability to blend within the local community is much easier than in Hong Kong or the mainland. There are chances to meet and know people at all levels of society. As with doing business in Taiwan, the key is your ability to speak Mandarin. Most people I know have a diverse mix of local, non-Chinese, and Chinese American friends. It makes the integration into Taipei society smooth, interesting, and fun for anyone willing to put the effort into developing relationships.

As the economy continues to go strong and the society matures, people are spending more time and money on leisure activities. Taipei consumers have become sophisticated in their demands for entertainment and night life. In response, disco and techno clubs, jazz joints, and cigar bars have sprung up all over the city. If you prefer local entertainment, there are night markets, karaoke places, and *xiao ye's* (late night eating places) that stay open most of the night.

Personal Travelogue

After spending my first year in Taipei, I decided to write one of those Christmas letters to friends and family back in the States. I wanted to describe what my new, transplanted life was like. In digging up this piece, it reminds me of what a great experience I had in Taipei and why I continue to be so fond of the place.

THE THINGS YOU DISCOVER*

(December 1, 1992)

Oh, the things you discover in far away places,
The new flavors, new smells, new customs, and faces!
Things that make your life new every day,
Let me give an example if that's okay?!?

There's a place I know, sitting smack dab in the ocean,
Went there last year on a long thought out notion,
Looks like a sweet potato when viewed from the sky,
Has a tropical climate with temperatures high,

The people there speak in a tongue called *Guoyu*,
Mastering the high and low sounds can really annoy you,
But it is the language over one billion use,
That's over a billion new people to know if you choose!

* A tribute to Dr. Seuss, who passed away earlier in the year.

In fact, in this place everywhere there's a crowd,
And the hustle, bustle noise of activity is loud,
But it doesn't take long to get use to the flow,
And make many friends you'll call your *peng you*,

And all over the place you'll see motorbikes,
The way folks pile on them you've not seen the likes,
Imagine on one scooter a family of four,
Riding as if they were in a Honda four-door!!!

Now when you enter a house, *tuo xie* is the custom,
That's removing your shoes, in case they have dust on 'em,
And when giving your name card use not one hand but two,
It's a sign of respect, the polite thing to do,

You can walk into stores and hear *huanying guanglin*!
It's a greeting that staff are all taught to sing,
The meaning is just a kind of welcoming thing,
When they all say it at once it has quite a nice ring,

And the things you can see in a far away land,
Every trip out the door brings new things at hand,
So many fun things to do, you just have to look,
Just go out and find them, they're not in some book!

Have you been to a *ye shi*? That's a night market you know,
There's one down in *Shi Ling*, with vendors row after row,
Clothes, toys, and knick-knacks are among things to buy,
You might even bargain them down if you give it a try,

And there's a place you can go known as KTV,
Where you can sing your heart out for an hourly fee,

It's best in a group, you don't have to sing well,
Just enthusiastic and loud, and no one can tell,

Or you can go walking with friends through *Ding Hao* at night,
So many people milling around is really a sight,
The sidewalks are covered with goods all laid out,
With merchants to tempt you as you stroll about,

And don't forget! ... the things you can taste in a far away spot,
So many dishes and styles, there are really a lot,
Beijing, Hunan, Szechuan, Cantonese,
Are among just a few types that are certain to please,

Now have you ever tried a fried bread called *shao bing?*
With a bowl of hot *dou jiang* and a long donut-like thing?
It's particularly tasty at night when it's late,
After dancing or singing has made your appetite great,

Or for noisy dining go to a *pi jiu wu*,
A place to eat spicy food and drink local brew,
And play drinking games of a type called *hua quan*,
It just takes a quick mind and two very fast hands,

And down a sidestreet you'll find many *lu bian tan*,
Where people cook and sell treats from their one person stand,
You can buy *hong dou bing*, or a few *zhi ma qiu*,
Try some *ji dan gao*, right there or to go,

Yes, far away places can be quite grand in their ways,
They can touch you, and grow you, and even amaze,
As long as you're willing to take both bad and good,
You'll find their best secrets, the way that you should.

In addition, many U.S. movies now have releases in Taipei that coincide with opening dates in the States. Major entertainers pass through frequently. Sting has given several performances in Taipei. (During one concert, he came on stage and greeted the crowd by yelling out "Taipei, *ni hao*!" The phrase was taught to him by my friend who was assigned to be his translator). In 1997, the Three Tenors (with Diana Ross) played to a sold-out crowd. Over the summer, Jewel sang at Taipei Stadium as a stop on her world tour. During my first year in Taipei, there were only three local TV channels. I remember a highlight of my week was watching *L.A. Law* reruns at midnight on Saturday evenings. Now over 70 percent of all homes in Taipei have cable — one of the highest penetration rates in the world. You can choose from more than 50 international channels, including sports, movie, and cartoon ones.

Taipei Is For ...

Most people I know who move to Taipei come for personal reasons over professional ones. Many were born in Taiwan, where they still have close ties. They return because of family considerations or opportunities to be gained through their familiarity with the city and its business community. I know many Taiwanese who, after spending years abroad, returned to pursue business ventures aided by personal relationships.

For super-charged professionals seeking to either conquer the vast mainland market or gain regional exposure, Taipei is a smaller, more confined destination. It is, however, a great place to prepare yourself for a future in Hong Kong or China. The language, culture, and approach to business between Taiwan and the mainland are similar. As such, Taipei is a key source for multinationals seeking staff who are able to do business in China. There are many who begin their time in Asia in Taipei and then relocate to other regional locations two or three years later.

When I first contemplated moving to the region, I chose Taipei as the place to get my feet wet. I wanted to learn to speak Mandarin. I knew I'd never pick it up in Hong Kong, where it's easy to be around westerners and speak English all the time. In Taipei, the choice before you is a straight-forward one. If you don't adapt locally, you'll get left out.

Taipei offers a number of well-established and credible language training centers. Most importantly, however, you can be assured of a submerged Chinese cultural and language experience. Multinational firms, local companies, and government agencies all offer opportunities to jump straight into a strictly Mandarin-speaking business environment. Learning to deal with local customers and staff is invaluable towards building a career in Greater China.

I also wanted to maintain momentum in my career and professional growth. By going directly to China, I felt I'd spend too much time and energy wallowing in the inefficiencies of the country, rather than conducting business. Taipei offered a relatively mature and active business environment a step or two ahead of what Shanghai or Beijing offered. Ultimately, I felt Taipei was the best place for my overall professional and personal development in the region.

Oh yes, one other factor weighed in my decision to choose Taipei over Hong Kong or China. To date, you can only get Burger King Whoppers in Taiwan.

Mainland China

Ask any foreigner living and working in China what it's like and you open up a can of worms. The responses flow effortlessly. "It's difficult." "It's frustrating." "It's tiring." "You sacrifice your quality of life." Although the lifestyle is rapidly improving, of all Greater China locations, the mainland remains the only one still considered a hardship.

"Many aspects of living in China eventually get to you," admits Lisa Lum. Lisa is a regional sales manager for Johnson & Johnson Medical (China) based in Beijing. Her sales territory is Northern China. "The country is developing quickly, but it's still frustrating and inefficient. Although I've been fortunate to work with many hardworking and conscientious people in my job, the overall orientation you find towards responsiveness and service is terrible. You'll run into many people who are ingrained in a lifetime employment, iron rice-bowl mentality. Their entire effort is geared towards how to beat the system and avoid working."

"Work-wise, your workload never ends. There's always more to do. It's not unusual to work seven days a week to where you hardly have the time or energy for a social life. Often times just going to the gym, hanging out, or getting together with friends are out the window. And although there's a great deal of local culture to appreciate, you begin to miss western movies, magazines, books, or just news from outside the country. If you don't leave every three months or so and get away for a break, you start to feel yourself burnout."

The work pace and lifestyles of foreigners in China are indeed extreme. Lisa counted 110 trips within the country over the past year. She estimates being on the road 60 percent of the time. Christina Fang is the site development manager for Kentucky Fried Chicken (KFC) restaurants for Tricon Restaurants International in the mainland. She's based in Shanghai and is responsible for developing a system that will eventually allow KFC to open 200 new restaurant sites a year. Over the past year, Christina traveled to 35 cities in China and flew an average of once a week. When I asked Christina what she did in her free time, it was not surprising that her deadpan response was: "I sleep."

"I feel like I'm in the middle of history being made ... It's like I'm reading an incredibly gripping novel and have only gotten half-way through. I just can't put it down at this point."

Ask these same people why they're in China, however, and the flip side comes to light just as easily. "It's fascinating." "Culturally rich." "Unlimited potential." "Opportunities wherever you turn." "Fantastic professional development." "Career-wise, China has exceeded my expectations," points out Lisa. "The challenges here are big ones. They're completely different from what you've ever encountered in the States. The situations you face push you like you've never been pushed before. I find it very satisfying."

"For my career and personal development, China is everything and more than what I hoped for," Christine concurs. "My career has taken off here. We're making China policy and setting up the base that will conceivably raise the country to new heights. That feels extremely rewarding."

Some describe their presence in China on a grander scale. "I feel like I'm in the middle of history being made," says a Chinese American working in Beijing for the past four years. She's not yet ready to return to the U.S. "Economic growth on this scale will never happen again. It's like I'm reading an incredibly gripping novel and have only gotten half-way through. I just can't put it down at this point."

Despite the upsides, any move to China comes at a cost. "You make significant sacrifices in your quality of life," admits one Chinese American who has lived in Beijing for the past three years. "You'll face greater pollution, higher stress, less time with your spouse or children, even poorer medical coverage. That's a trade-off not many people are willing to make."

Business Environment

Biggest, Fastest, Greatest

Without a doubt, China is the driving force drawing companies, investment, and resources to the region en masse. Every multinational marketing presentation about the country echoes the same facts; 1.2 billion consumers, growth that averages approximately 10 percent annually, and the world's fastest growing economy over the past 15 years. Within just six years, China's economy has doubled. Its foreign trade increased 18.3 percent in 1995 to US$280 billion.

Other more specific forecasts reflect the size and pace of China's growth. Its cosmetics industry is expected to grow five times by the year 2003, to between US$7 and US$8 billion. Over the next decade, China will install approximately 10 million new telephone lines a year. The number of computers purchased is expected to hit 10 million units by the year 2002, roughly doubling every two years until then. These are the types of numbers being contemplated by multinationals with ambitions of becoming significant regional players.

It's an exceptional and exciting time for China. With multinationals targeting it as their next major market, a high stakes game is being played. Some companies are even banking their future on their success in the mainland, which could catapult them into a world leadership position.

The Long Haul

Doing business in China is not a simple game to play though. Talk to knowledgeable China hands and you'll find that most companies are currently losing money there, with some losing very big. Those who are making any are investing it back into further expansion. Still, multinationals are not holding back. With tremendous amounts of money and resources already sunk into operations and market development, most remain committed and optimistic. Over the past couple of years, a good number of multinational firms began moving their China headquarters from Hong Kong into the mainland itself, with Shanghai and Beijing being the top locations. Companies are even extending key operations and sales offices far beyond the major cities, to locations where operating costs are lower and where they are closer to target markets.

The outlook for China players is a long-term one. It has to be. The mainland's consumer markets continue to blossom. The potential for companies is enormous, but there is a way to go. Multinationals need to be active now, building brand awareness and a consumer base. Nobody wants to play a catch-up game a few years down the road. By then, it will be too late. However, the truth of the matter is that nobody really knows what the country's economic story will be. Inevitably, it's a gamble by all players who are banking on China's continued development and increased prosperity.

Doing Business

A True Test Of ...

More so than Hong Kong or Taiwan, operating and doing business in China involves an adjustment of western thinking, perceptions, and approaches. Applying other standards to the mainland is a big mistake. Rather than try to change the place, you have to be committed to learning. "Chinese people are very *keqi* (polite)," reveals Greg Li, who has spent the past five years doing China business in the areas of manufacturing, property development, and financial services. "You may think you have an idea of what's going on, but you'll never know what people are actually thinking unless you sit back to listen and observe. Otherwise, you'll make a lot of wrong assumptions and poor decisions."

Conducting business successfully in China also requires an open mind. However, it's much easier to say than to do. "There's a big difference between having an open mind and living open-mindedly," adds Greg. "When you're actually dealing with the inefficiencies, being pushed around while waiting in line, or getting disconnected in the middle of an important call, it's not always easy to put your situation into perspective. Even if it's happened to you a hundred times before, it's hard to avoid feeling frustrated or upset."

Rick Wong looks back and laughs about some of his early experiences in China. He was sent to Pudong in 1994 to oversee the construction of a new factory his company was building to produce and distribute ice cream in the mainland. "Working in China is a true test of your adaptability, resourcefulness, and patience. It's riding a bus on a dusty road while a little kid is taking a pee down the center aisle. It's having a key distributor give you the duck's head as the honored guest and everyone waiting for you to eat it. Sometimes it's outright miserable, like staying in a hotel for three months where the tap water comes out brown, the pillows smell like cigarettes, and there's only one state-owned TV channel to watch. But it's from hardships and dubious situations like these that you really see yourself grow."

When In China, Do As The Chinese Do

In China, you may also have to consider some major adjustments to help you fit into the business culture. One Chinese American living in Beijing faces the constant presence of cigarette smoking in his business encounters. It is so prevalent that he's considered taking up smoking himself. "It's a great ice breaker," he says. "They're always offering. It almost feels like you're insulting them if you don't accept." The same goes for drinking alcohol. During dinner engagements and after-work gatherings where relationships are built and deals can be closed, you may have to execute some toasts and *gan bei* (bottoms up) a few rounds with your guests.

Even how you present yourself can make a statement. When going to business meetings attended by local Chinese, one investment banker always tries to dress down in order not to make the other side feel uncomfortable. "I almost never wear a tie, even if it's with high-ranking government officials or top ranking company management," he says. "Usually, it's just a sports jacket and an open-collared shirt," he describes. "The spiffy Armani suit just doesn't send the right message."

Times Are Changing

Many candidates considering a career in China want to know what is the extent of corruption that occurs in business there. When capitalism first began to take hold among the masses, the mainland government's encouragement to drive citizens to be "rich and glorious" was being taken a bit too far. Corruption at all levels was overt. In the summer of 1996, however, the government began a "Strike Hard" campaign to curtail unsavory business practices. Several government and business officials at the highest levels were persecuted during the campaign. Today, as state-owned enterprises continue to become privatized and more accountable for bottom line results to management and investors, managers are less inclined to take kickbacks if they expect to keep their jobs. The result is an improving environment for foreign companies to conduct business.

Mainland China Job Market

The dynamics of the mainland's job market are quickly evolving. Salaries for Mainland Chinese staff are rising quickly, in some cases approaching levels offered for comparable positions in Hong Kong. At the same time, compensation packages for expats are being gradually reduced as the living standard in China continues to improve. For instance, where the hardship allowance component of expat packages may have averaged 25–30 percent of base salary two years ago, it is now closer to 15–20 percent in major cities.

The local professional talent is also maturing rapidly. "The Mainland Chinese graduates I meet are among the best I've seen in the region. They're as good or better than ones from Hong Kong, Taiwan, or Singapore," says Mei Wong, a partner at Tasa International, a top executive search firm in Hong Kong. Mei specializes in recruiting local Chinese managers for multinationals operating in China. "They're extremely smart, hard working, and hungry. They just lack the business exposure."

No Magic Pill

Currently, foreigners occupy most middle to senior management positions within multinationals. There is, however, no "magic pill" or ideal choice to be found yet when it comes to hiring at these levels. Everyone has their opinion about the effectiveness and value of each foreign group working in China. Although the culture, business style, and language of Taiwanese are well-suited for China, some feel they're antagonistic and look down on the locals they manage. Others feel that Singaporeans and Hong Kongers are out of touch with Chinese culture and are also arrogant towards mainland staff. In addition, Chinese Americans can be too westernized, Japanese too rigid, and Caucasians limited in their communications abilities.

Even qualified Mainland Chinese managers have their weaknesses. One has to do with their sense of loyalty. After decades of austere living, false hopes, and ephemeral government stances, many older mainlanders place little faith in the future. In their experience, situations such as the current economic prosperity may not last long. Therefore, if there is an opportunity present, better to seize it now. "It's difficult entrusting your China marketing strategy for a key product or business to someone who may easily jump to your competitor for an additional US$100 a month," points out one multinational executive.

Ultimately, it is the young, up-and-coming mainland managers who are the acknowledged solution for multinationals trying to staff their China operations. However, the number of qualified, capable ones are few. The Mainland Chinese are willing, but do not have the experience levels required by multinationals to run their operations yet. Mei predicts that this will change dramatically within the next five years or so. "The first wave of local Chinese staff joined these multinationals only within the past five to eight years," she notes. "In another five years, they'll have about the number of years with a multinational you'd want your middle and upper-middle managers to have."

"There are a few areas where overseas and returning Chinese will continue to have a significant advantage in China," Mei continues. "One is the ability to manage relationships, particularly communications and expectations with home office executives in both the region and in the U.S. With less international exposure under their belt, this is an area where local Chinese have greater difficulty. Another is the ability to plan and think strategically, also a weak area for many mainlanders."

Shanghai

Most China experts peg Shanghai as the future commercial business and financial center for Asia, even replacing Hong Kong in these roles over the next 10–20 years. In 1996, Shanghai's economy grew 13 percent (3 percent faster than the national GDP) and contributed 10 percent of China's tax revenue. It attracted US$7.5 billion in foreign investment. In addition, the city has the full attention and support of Beijing. "The government is putting everything it has behind the success of Shanghai," points out a Chinese American working in Shanghai. "It's a matter of face and pride. Although Hong Kong is now part of the mainland, it was built by westerners. The Chinese want to see the new pearl of China develop under its own system. They want to show the world how well they can do this."

The Place

"Shanghai's modernization and internationalization reminds me of Taipei's stage of development ten years ago, except happening at twice the speed," according to a Chinese American who moved to Shanghai from Taipei in 1995. "It is perhaps the most focused city in the world today."

Shanghai's infrastructure has undergone tremendous development over the past several years. Physically, the city is changing before your eyes. A building is completed or demolished practically every other day. Numerous road, bridge, building, and construction projects have been recently finished and are preparing Shanghai to serve its role as a vital commercial center.

Across the Yangtze River, the city of Pudong has literally risen out of the swampland over the past five years at an estimated cost of US$10 billion. It is being promoted as the mainland's future financial center. Two bridges and two tunnels have opened over the past year to bring Pudong within twenty minutes of downtown Shanghai. Soon, a subway system will also connect the two sides.

The Business Environment

Shanghai attracts business people. Entrepreneurship and capitalism permeate the city. Many foreigners who begin their China experience in Beijing to improve Mandarin skills and satisfy their curiosity for Chinese culture, eventually end up in Shanghai where the business action flourishes.

As of September 1997, there were 2,133 U.S. companies registered in Shanghai according to the Shanghai Municipal Government.

Shanghai's foreign business community is exploding, as many multinationals select it as their headquarters, joint venture, or representative office location from which to execute their China strategy. Many firms are moving their mainland operations from Hong Kong to Shanghai as markets and operations mature and the cost of doing business there decreases. Its central location in the mainland's most densely populated and rapidly developing region provides access to a major segment of the country's consumer market.

Within China, Shanghai is also the easiest city in which to do business. It's the mainland's most sophisticated city "by leaps." Unlike Beijing, activities are more economically, rather than politically driven. Having said that, compared to Hong Kong or Taipei, Shanghai is still a relatively difficult place to work. Although its infrastructure has improved considerably, even simple communications and services are new, underdeveloped, and unreliable.

The Lifestyle

Like Beijing, the western and cosmopolitan aspects of Shanghai have evolved quickly. The quality of life continues to improve dramatically, with the expanding accessibility of western-style food, entertainment, and conveniences. Today, you can eat at The Hard Rock Cafe, Tony Roma's, or a number of foreign restaurants. This wasn't the case a year ago. Shanghai's first western-style indoor mall, the Westgate, now offers shopping in a variety of popular international retail stores and boutiques such as Burberry's, Valentino, Nautica, and Fendi. For recreation, there's a softball league that plays every weekend. You can even play paint ball within a short drive from the city.

Although not nearly as large as Beijing's, Shanghai's foreign population is growing rapidly. Foreign professionals are flowing into the city as multinational firms set up or expand operations. As one indicator of the increasing numbers, Shanghai's American Chamber of Commerce is the fastest growing AmCham in Asia. During the last eight months of 1997, the Chamber saw its membership jump from 600 to over 1,000 members. One Shanghai expat estimates that he runs into at least one new arrival each week.

The lifestyle in Shanghai, however, is not nearly as diverse as Hong Kong and Taipei. As with other mainland cities, there is the feeling of isolation from the rest of the world. The government still restricts international TV and print media access.

Shanghai Is For ...

Shanghai is for people looking to get in on the ground floor of exciting business developments and opportunities in what is predicted to be the largest consumer market in the world. It's for those who want to be on the leading edge of change in China. "You can feel the energy and potential of Shanghai," says a Chinese American sales manager for an electronics manufacturer who has lived there since 1995. "Amazing things are going on everywhere you turn."

Beijing

The Place

During my first visit to Beijing in 1985, I remember walking down the middle of Dong Chang'An Road, the major boulevard that cuts across Tiananmen Square and The Forbidden City, in the middle of the day. There were few cars that passed by. Instead, casual bicycle traffic moving on adjoining bike lanes set the pace of the city. When I made a trip in the fall of 1996, a stream of cars four lanes wide zoomed by the square. Along with Shanghai, Beijing is transforming almost overnight. Each time you blink, more changes have taken place.

Where Shanghai is often compared to New York, Beijing gets compared to Los Angeles. The city is spread out and offers a slower, more relaxed lifestyle. It's not as congested either. Beijing is also likened to Washington D.C., a city of government and politics. Conversations among locals revolve around the latest news within the government and the country. Only recently has there been a noticeable shift towards business by Beijingers. "Five years ago, you practically degraded yourself if you were a local and talked about money," remarks a Beijing veteran. "Now, everyone is aboard the capitalism train. They're just starting to get oriented towards bettering their lot in life."

The Business Environment

Beijing is the headquarters location for multinationals needing to develop key relationships with government officials and authorities. In particular, Beijing attracts companies whose business focus revolves around infrastructure projects, manufacturing, or heavy industry. For these firms, their success in China is based on their ability to obtain licenses, permits, and contracts with the appropriate ministries.

James Yao: I Left My Heart In Beijing

Personal History: *Born in Taiwan. Moved to San Francisco at age 12. Living in Greater China since November of 1990.*
Parents: *Mom and Dad from Taiwan.*
Education: *B.S. in Electrical Engineering at M.I.T.*
Languages: *Native English and Mandarin speaker.*

When asked about the ability of Chinese Americans to be successful in China, James Yao is clear about what it takes. "Doing well in China requires a compassion for Chinese people. During my first six months in China with Oracle, I spent most of my time on personal development. The China operations was growing fast and I was constantly interviewing and hiring. I still remember when each new hire showed up for their first day of work, one of the first things I'd do is take them to a barber shop for a haircut. Whenever I went to Hong Kong, I'd pick up shirts and ties for them. I'd teach them how to answer phone calls, even how to comb their hair. It was challenging, but it was also fun and rewarding.

James Yao at an Oracle User's Conference he organized in Beijing, up to that time the largest computer trade show in China with over 5,000 attendees (Spring 1993)

I could tell I was having a real impact on their lives."

"I remember one woman came to an interview in overalls and sandals. She lived on a farm and had made a great effort to come to the city from the countryside. It happened to be raining that day. When she arrived, I walked her to the bathroom so she could wash off her feet."

In the interview, she was fantastic. She had gone to Beijing University and studied computer science. Of nearly 200 local candidates I met, she was the only one who could articulate to me what a relational database was. I hired her on the spot. She ended up being the best hire I ever made. Today, three years later, she's holding a key management position in Oracle China. If you met her now, she looks like any of the other directors from Hong Kong, Singapore, or Taiwan."

James credits his being Chinese American as a major factor in his ability to get closer to the local Chinese. The similar language he spoke made him more approachable. His Chinese also made it much easier for him to deal with customers. "In China's information technology industry, most local customers are used to dealing with white faces," says James. "I still remember how totally surprised they were that I could speak with them in Chinese."

James believes that his efforts to get to know his colleagues also helped a great deal. He watched Beijing operas, ate at local restaurants, and went horseback riding with them. He even worked at developing a Beijing accent. "The worst thing you can do is come to China with a superiority complex. Those that do are bound to fail," he says frankly. "Speaking another language doesn't make you a better person. You need to have a caring for Chinese culture, people, and heritage. That will translate into sensitivity, which translates into employee effort and teamwork. In China, there is little loyalty to a company, but there is loyalty to people."

The Lifestyle

More genuine, more easy-going, and less materialistic are how Beijingers are often described in relation to people in Shanghai. Given their more down-to-earth personalities, many foreigners feel they are able to build closer friendships with locals in Beijing than in Shanghai. Although Beijing is more laid back as a place than Shanghai, in some ways it is considered more cosmopolitan because of its large, diverse mix of both local government and foreign embassy people. Beijing is where China's cultural and political elite reside. Living there offers the chance to meet all sorts of accomplished and fascinating people.

Beijing contains the most foreigners of any city in China, with estimates ranging from 100,000 to 250,000 (that includes a large Japanese and Korean population). The size of the foreign community is attributed to the three large, distinct groups it attracts: the expat business people, the diplomatic corps, and students.

"There's so much to do if you're the least bit adventurous or curious," according to Kathy Chen, who moved to Beijing in 1993. "You can go antique shopping at the Ghost Market on weekend mornings where people from the countryside bring their antiques and knick-knacks. Forty-five minutes outside the city you can horseback ride through a sea of rice paddy fields. There's also great hiking and picnicking in the countryside or along the Great Wall. Overall, there are endless cultural gems in Beijing such as more museums, historical sites, parks, and cultural events and activities than you have time to see. I like riding my Flying Phoenix bike around the city to explore sidestreets and neighborhoods. Or you can just hang out with friends to *bao jiaozi* (wrap Chinese meat dumplings) and have lively conversations about Chinese society, people, and culture."

Beijing has quickly become a more comfortable place for foreigners compared to how it use to be. "In 1991, almost everything shut down by 8pm," recalls Charlene Foo, former Associated Press Beijing correspondent and a 10-year Beijing veteran. "Now, there's a night life where places stay open most of the night. It use to be an effort just to make a local phone call. Now you can direct dial nearly anywhere in the country. Back then, there were also many things you would crave, but couldn't get. Today, there are McDonald's, Kentucky Fried Chickens, and Pizza Huts everywhere. Cheese was only available at the Friendship Store. Now you can get it all over the city. You can even buy Oreo cookies and Corn Flakes in the local supermarkets. Within the past year Dunkin' Donuts, Chili's Restaurant, and Subways have come to Beijing. Just recently, I saw a Kinko's Copy Center on Dongsanhuan North Road!"

If you're looking for a hip local crowd, you can try San Li Tun and have an imported beer or cappuccino at a sidewalk table outside one of over 20 western-style places named Jack & Jill, Bella's, Upside Down Café, or Daisy's Pub. "I remember driving down that street one night in March 1996. It was pitch black," recalls Charlene. "Then, three months later it was lined with bars, pubs, and restaurants. It was as if after the spring rains all these places mushroomed out of nowhere. A mini Greenwich Village appeared."

Beijing Is For ...

Beijing attracts a more diverse group of foreigners than Shanghai does. Whereas Shanghai attracts primarily business types, many in Beijing come to learn about and experience Chinese culture and people. Many also go to Beijing to study Mandarin. It's the best place to pick up a standard Chinese accent.

If you're expecting a bustling place with the night life of Hong Kong, Beijing will disappoint you. It's much more residential. Although the night scene is growing, it's more limited and not as centrally located as in Hong Kong or Shanghai.

Gary Mui sees his time in Beijing as a worthwhile investment for his career. Gary moved to Beijing in March 1996 to study Mandarin at Beijing University. Three months later, he began working as an assistant manager at Banque Nationale de Paris (formerly Beijing Peregrine Investment Consultant Company). His office is one of the first foreign banks to market mainland investment and financial advisory services to multinationals seeking local partners. "It's the frontier for investment banking services in China right now. Just a year ago we were a relationship office. Today, we're initiating business and introducing deals. I support and help investigate all aspects of these opportunities and do the marketing directly to clients who want to enter China. I'm also gaining an understanding of how to do business in China through the local managers I work closely with."

All Of The Above

I know many Chinese Americans who are very familiar with all four major cities through their years of Greater China business and personal travel. Increasing numbers have lived in more than one of these destinations. They may learn Mandarin in Taipei and later move to Hong Kong's more dynamic business environment. Or they may first get a feel for the region in Hong Kong, before jumping into China through an assignment in Shanghai or Beijing.

It's hard to predict where you'll end up. During my first four years in Asia, I was perfectly content living in Taipei. I never felt the urge to move elsewhere. Once I started Wang & Li, however, I immediately knew Hong Kong was where I needed to be. It's where I've been the past three years. In another two years or so, I can picture myself moving to Shanghai. The stage of your personal and career development can largely determine the road you will travel in Greater China. Each city presents unique characteristics and opportunities that make living in those places fun and rewarding *(see Appendix V for A Four Cities Comparison)*.

What About Singapore?

You may have wondered at some point why I don't place much of an emphasis on Singapore as a destination. In fact, when speaking with candidates who are contemplating a move to Asia, I frequently recommend Singapore as a place to consider. This advice is usually directed to those intent on being in Asia, but who are without strong bilingual and bicultural Chinese backgrounds to live and work comfortably in Greater China.

As a regional center for companies doing business in South East Asia, the requirements for local language skills are much lower and less critical in Singapore. English is used in many business situations in the Philippines, Malaysia, Indonesia, or Thailand. Because, the languages and cultures of South East Asian countries are so diverse, it's nearly impossible for someone to have an extensive background in more than one location. For multinationals operating in these countries, the professional skills and functional expertise offered by a candidate are most important. Next, is a strong understanding of the cultures, economies, and business environments of as many of these countries as possible.

For those accustomed to a highly westernized lifestyle, Singapore is also an easier place to adjust to. It's an organized, clean, convenient, and efficient metropolitan city. Its infrastructure is considered one of the best in the world. English is the common language spoken both in business and social situations. It's also a very "family-friendly" place for those who heavily weigh an environment for children.

Perhaps the most compelling reason Chinese Americans choose Greater China cities over Singapore, however, has to do with competitive advantage. If you possess strong Chinese language skills and cultural background, they would likely be underutilized in Singapore, where your business focus would probably be directed towards South East Asian countries rather than Greater China. It's a place that offers good business and career opportunities, but where your value-added abilities may not work for you as prominently.

In addition, although Singapore aggressively positions itself as a gateway to China and as a regional headquarters, it falls considerably short in both areas relative to Hong Kong. Geographically, historically, and culturally, Hong Kong is much closer to China than Singapore. Hong Kong has more than twice the number of regional headquarters as Singapore. Hong Kong is also a larger financial center and a larger media and communications hub. Although several companies did move operations, or portions of them, from Hong Kong to Singapore prior to the 1997 handover, these were relatively few. They attracted much more media attention rather than reflected a trend.

Chapter 12 The Ten Most Often Asked Questions

Sorry to disappoint, but this isn't a Letterman Top Ten List. However, if you're contemplating a move to Greater China and have some basic, but important questions on your mind, then this could be the most helpful chapter in the book. Based on countless candidate interviews, seminar Q&A sessions, phone inquiries, and emails, these are the ten most commonly asked questions that people coming to Greater China have on their minds.

1) How Good Does My Chinese Have To Be?

The bottom line on Chinese language skills almost goes without saying — the more the better. If you plan on doing business in China or Taiwan, speaking Mandarin is essential. It's a prerequisite for most junior to middle management positions that require you to deal directly with local clients, vendors, distributors, and colleagues. And although English is the common business language in Hong Kong, there is a strong preference for professionals who speak Cantonese. Mandarin-speaking abilities are again highly preferred given the extensive focus on China business for multinationals operating in Hong Kong.

Increasingly, Chinese reading and writing skills are becoming important. In many finance, marketing, advertising, public relations, legal, and media positions, reading is close to a necessity in order to research and respond to local trends and activities in the market. Writing is a "nice to have" skill, but is not a requirement by most employers.

"If you're serious about getting up to speed and doing business in Chinese, then you should think about spending at least one year in a Chinese-speaking environment."

If you're unsure about whether to learn Mandarin or Cantonese, choose Mandarin (unless you have strong personal reasons for learning Cantonese). Knowing Mandarin will make a difference almost anywhere you go in Greater China, whereas the benefits of Cantonese are primarily limited to Hong Kong and Guangzhou.

Occasionally a candidate will tell me: "I don't speak Mandarin now, but I plan to pick it up." Unfortunately, Mandarin isn't exactly the type of language you "pick up." It's more of a lifelong pursuit. I meet many candidates who have studied Mandarin in the U.S. for several years. They believe their language skills are at a point where they have a competitive advantage for doing business in Asia. On their resumes, they use words like "proficient" or "conversational" to describe their level of ability. When interviewing them, however, more often than not they only speak at a "classroom" level. As a result, these days, when I see "proficient" or "conversational" at the bottom of a resume, I usually interpret that to mean "can't really speak well."

Although studying Mandarin in the U.S. is an excellent start, it shouldn't be overvalued. Eric Chu worked as a consultant in Shanghai where he's lived for three years. He learned his Mandarin over five years of dedicated study and practice in both the U.S. and Asia. This included one year in Taipei, where he took four hours of class a day and focused his efforts solely on language study. He has a strong opinion about learning Chinese strictly in the U.S. "What are people expecting to do with their U.S.-learned, classroom Chinese when they come to Asia? Use it in bars and clubs?" he asks. "If you're serious about getting up to speed and doing business in Chinese, then you should think about spending at least one year in a Chinese-speaking environment."

Personal Travelogue

On my first day at Wang Laboratories' Taipei office, the general manager called a meeting to introduce me to his management team. After he made a few brief comments, I was called upon to tell my new local colleagues something about myself. As I stood up, I sensed their uneasiness at having to deal with a native English speaker. But I had a surprise for them. I was no home office-sent expat, totally unfamiliar with the Chinese language and culture. I was ready. I had been practicing this moment for weeks, you could even say years.

In my well-rehearsed Mandarin, I spoke for several minutes about my upbringing, educational background, family history, and even favorite hobbies. My two years of classroom Mandarin study were seeing their crowning glory. My recitation was like a dramatic reading from Shakespeare. I was pleased and proud of my performance. When I sat down, I felt vindicated for the countless hours of hard work during which I had toiled. I anticipated their response, thunderous applause and awestruck admiration. Perhaps even a standing ovation. I was certain I had impressed everyone.

And there it was, a sigh of relief on the faces around me. A visible feeling of relaxation permeated the room upon the realization that I was one of them. Now it was their turn. One by one, each manager stood and described to me their responsibilities. A flood of high-speed Mandarin, no, make that super high speed Mandarin, came spewing forth.

From outside appearances, I listened intently to each speaker. I nodded occasionally to acknowledge what was being said. I laughed heartily with everyone else when witty remarks were made. I even guffawed and slapped my knee one time, nearly doubled over with laughter when one colleague made a lighthearted joke directed at me and the rest of the room reacted.

Inside my head, however, I was in a panic! What the hell were they saying?!? More to the point, what language were they speaking?!? I wasn't picking up any of it! This was nothing like the Mandarin on my first-year lesson tapes. They were speaking three times as fast!

I felt a warm, prickly sensation on my neck and moving down my back. Perhaps the only sign of my discomfort came from my rapidly tapping index finger that pounded the conference table. It was a reflex movement, my finger trying to hit the pause button on a tape recorder, as it had done hundreds of times before. Only this time there was no response. I couldn't stop it!

What a nightmare. Here I was, in the midst of my professional peers and unable to understand a thing being said. What to do? Speak up and admit stupidity. Lose total face? With each passing second, the option to jump up and say, "I'm sorry, I haven't understood a word any of you have said. I'm just wasting your time," became more difficult to do. I pressed on and listened with greater intent. Perhaps I needed to concentrate harder. Great idea, it only made me feel more like I was in way over my head. It was the first of many instances in Taiwan where I had that feeling.

Without diminishing the critical importance of language fluency, in my experience, near native proficiency is not entirely needed in all cases. It depends on the situation and people you're dealing with. I've never claimed to be completely fluent in Mandarin. I have learned over the years, however, to make the best of my language abilities in most encounters. I've entered many business meetings where, although I don't exactly get raves about my Mandarin, I'm able to establish a rapport and communicate effectively with the local Chinese party.

In such situations, I'll socialize with a client informally in Mandarin before the meeting starts. It helps them feel comfortable and allows me to make a connection. When the meeting begins, I speak English, deliberate and clear English. They feel okay with it because, like me, their listening comprehension is better than their spoken ability. When they respond, I let them know that it's fine for them to speak to me in Mandarin, which I can understand well enough. The result is we end up both speaking comfortably in our native tongue, while listening in our second language. The communications is more natural and effective than both sides speaking in our second language.

This was the approach I often took in Taipei where the English skill level was fairly high and where I was usually dealing with managers who had a good degree of international exposure. This same approach might not be as appropriate in many situations in China.

There are some exceptions with language skills. These may include senior management (i.e. director level or higher) or regional positions where daily dealings are typically with other senior managers, high-level clients, or corporate executives back in the U.S., rather than with handling hands-on business matters with local parties. Within these management roles, industry and regional knowledge are more critical. Management experience and professional expertise outweigh the lack of language abilities.

There are also professions and industries that do not always require local language fluency. For instance, in finance, positions in sales or trading where the clients you deal with are outside of Asia, may not require you to speak Chinese. You could also include internal operations or support positions, where interaction is primarily limited to colleagues within the company.

In the information technology industry, the introduction of new technologies and products from the West create a demand for those able to transfer leading-edge IT expertise to the region. In these cases, specialized, hard-to-find technology or project management capabilities also overshadow the absence of local language skills.

Derek Tom is someone who came to Asia without Chinese language abilities, but found a position by offering a skill that was in short supply. After graduating from the University of Hawaii, Derek worked as an account executive for an advertising agency in Honolulu. His passion, however, was in computers. His particular interests were graphic design and print production.

After a vacation to Hong Kong, he made his move out. One agency was looking to computerize its creative production environment in order to be more cost efficient and competitive. A position had not been defined yet to manage the effort. During his interview, the company was impressed by Derek's MAC computer platform background. With his advertising experience and interest in graphics and print production, they felt that Derek could do the job. He received and accepted an offer from the firm as a computer graphics specialist. Over time, Derek more fully defined his job scope. "As long as I was doing things beneficial to the company, they let me do what I wanted," explains Derek. Today, he is the information technology manager overseeing regional computing needs for BBDO Asia Pacific, another worldwide ad agency.

Although situations like the ones I often faced in Taipei and like Derek's do occur, the importance of language abilities cannot be overemphasized. The most repeated advice from Greater China veterans is that if you don't possess Chinese language skills or if they're weak, work on them. For many, it's the single biggest obstacle to overcome out here. Learning Chinese is not only a tremendous asset for your career, it will allow you integrate locally as well. More than any other factor, it will help you achieve your professional and personal goals in Greater China *(see Appendix VI for Greater China Mandarin Language Programs).*

2) How Expensive Is Living In Greater China?

There's no beating around the bush on this one, it's expensive. This applies to every major city in Greater China. Having said that, a great deal of latitude exists on how much you can spend on things from food to housing. It depends on how you choose to live. For instance, housing in Hong Kong is much more affordable if you're not living in the popular Mid-levels area, perceived to be a shorter, more convenient commute to the Central business district. There are far better rental values to be found further down the Mass Transit Railway (MTR) line, in places such as North Point or Quarry Bay. You can also try places in Aberdeen, Kennedy Town, or Discovery Bay. The distance to the business area is further, but the actual commute time may only be a 10–20 minutes difference.

Whenever I'm back in the U.S. and the check comes at a restaurant, I inevitably stare at it as if I've just robbed somebody. After being in Greater China for so long, eating out in the States seems incredibly reasonable. Out here, you're the one who always feels like you're getting ripped off.

Similar to renting a place, how much you spend on food also depends on preference. Eating regularly at western restaurants is a quick drain on your wallet. For example, whether it's Taipei, Hong Kong, or Shanghai, a sandwich or burger and a soft drink at a sit down western restaurant costs around US$15–20. Whenever I take someone to lunch, it's almost impossible to get away without spending less than US$50 on a basic meal for two. Recently, a friend and I went for dinner at a Thai restaurant in Hong Kong. We ordered an appetizer, a vegetable dish, noodles, and a fish. We had one beer each. When the bill came, the total was over US$100! This was for Thai food!

If you like Chinese food, however, there's plenty that's excellent and only costs one-third to one-half the price of a western meal. If you're like me and enjoy rice dishes, noodles, stir-fried vegetables, and dim sum, then there is a tremendous variety and selection of local restaurants and shops to choose from. I've had many great meals at these places where I've eaten my fill for less than US$10.

Overall, relative to major U.S. cities such as New York, San Francisco, or Los Angeles, the cost of living in Greater China is higher. But in comparison, the difference is not outrageous. Just keep in mind that the manner in which you choose to live ultimately determines how expensive Greater China will be for you *(see Appendix VII for Price Comparison On Common Supermarket Items)*.

3) Will The Company Pay For Housing?

Unless you're being hired at a senior management level by a multinational company or are working for a U.S. consulting firm or investment bank, you can almost always put the idea of receiving expat housing out of your mind. Housing paid by the company is an increasingly uncommon practice.

The last time housing costs were routinely covered by companies in an industry at all levels was about four years ago during the investment banking boom. U.S. banks expanding into Greater China hired quickly and offered housing packages for anyone relocated from the States. One 25 year old Chinese American was transferred out in 1994 by her U.S. bank in New York, where she had worked for two years in a mid-office support position. To accommodate her move, the bank provided her with a HK$60,000 (about US$7,700) per month housing allowance. When China's financial markets underperformed, banks found themselves in a sudden reversal of fortunes that involved downsizing and cost-cutting. Six months after her arrival in Hong Kong, the young woman was released and looking for a new job. The bank could no longer justify her housing expense.

The lesson learned was one that many firms in other industries have already known and practiced for several years. To be profitable, it is not possible to pay expat housing costs for all levels of employees.

On the other hand, multinationals understand that housing costs in the region are high. To compensate, most companies today offer employees a lump sum salary amount that factors in some type of housing allowance or subsidy. From an employer's perspective, it's your choice whether you spend 25 percent or 75 percent of your salary on rent each month. Their objective is to offer compensation that they believe will provide you with a fair standard of living for your level of experience and skills. These salary packages typically allow you to find reasonable living accommodations.

The one exception on housing paid by the company is for postings to China. Whereas life in Hong Kong and Taiwan is no longer perceived as a hardship by employers, living in the mainland still is, given its lower standard of living and quality of life. To entice foreign employees to work there, housing costs are typically covered for most foreign hires.

4) How Will My Greater China Work Experience Apply Back In The U.S.?

When returning to the States from Greater China, you have to be realistic about what you offer when re-entering the U.S. business and corporate world. Going back means you leave a region of higher economic growth. Your highly valued Chinese language and cultural abilities and much of the business relationships and expertise you've developed are removed. Instead, you enter a mature, flatter economy in which you operate without those significant advantages. Realistically, it's a less optimal business environment for you.

That doesn't mean your Greater China experience and accomplishments aren't valued. They can be leveraged and utilized in the U.S. as well, just not nearly to the same degree. Where you were given greater responsibilities while in Asia, you'll likely need to readjust your expectations for the different market and situation you face back in the States.

Many professionals are able to highlight their Greater China experience to get into top-ranked MBA programs in the States. Many also find that the fundamental work experience and exposure they've gained abroad are invaluable, regardless of the international scope that that experience may carry.

Juli Shaw arrived in Taipei in 1991, straight out of UC Santa Barbara. Over the next six years, she developed an advertising career in both Taipei and Hong Kong with Saatchi & Saatchi. She began by covering major Hong Kong accounts, before being given the P&G account for laundry detergents in China. Juli quickly rose to the level of client account director.

When she moved back to L.A., she was immediately introduced to a job at BBDO as an account supervisor handling international business for Mars Candy.

Although she lacked U.S. media experience, she emphasized the similar media programming process in Asia which she did have experience with. In the end, BBDO valued her packaged consumer goods background and hired her.

Similarly, in her next job as a product marketing manager with Live Pix, a Silicon Valley graphics software company, it wasn't the international aspect of Juli's Greater China experience that the firm was attracted to. Live Pix also valued her packaged consumer goods background and well-rounded marketing communications skills. They especially liked her experience working with P&G. From a salary perspective, she feels she remains equal or a little ahead of her counterparts.

"Transitioning back into the U.S. job market is a matter of positioning and marketing yourself," says Juli. "You may have to explain much of what you did in Asia to those who interview you, but your exposure and achievements will eventually come across."

In assessing the value of their professional achievements in Greater China, many believe it improves their future prospects back in the U.S. When work experience is looked at, the pluses gained are clear. Will you be more competitive as a professional in the U.S. as a result of your time in Greater China? Will you have developed greater capabilities having had the exposure and management responsibilities here? Will most companies in the U.S. value your international experience? International experience continues to become increasingly valuable for multinational firms taking a more global approach to their business. With today's more interactive world, most feel that their professional backgrounds are much stronger having worked in Asia.

The longer you stay in the region, however, it does become more difficult to jump back on the corporate track in the U.S. To find a way back, many are taking creative, alternative career approaches. Rather than relying on "Corporate America" to evaluate and place their experience, they are joining smaller, more flexible, internationally-focused companies that allow them to continue leveraging regional skills and expertise. Typically, these companies provide services where they may act as a link between the U.S. and Greater China. Areas like consulting, business development, investment, and trading are ideal for providing such cross-cultural, cross-border business services. Others take an entrepreneurial route and set up their own businesses. They've left the corporate track for good and are writing their own ticket back home.

5) How Important Is An MBA?

Contrary to what many people might think, less emphasis is placed on an MBA in Greater China than in the U.S. Greater China is a very grounded place when it comes to doing business. Practical experience and performance count the most.

The newness of many business activities, industries, and markets in the region means that there is often no one to tell you how to get a job done. Classroom courses and textbooks cannot tell you how to negotiate deals in China, introduce services to clients unfamiliar with the value of what you're offering, or get distributors to represent your products over their friend's products. In Greater China, you'll find scores of people without an MBA who have attained success through their hands-on expertise, understanding of local practices, network of contacts, and hard work. Some managers I speak with are even wary of MBAs. They feel that MBA graduates are too corporate and office-oriented, and less willing to perform unglamorous, yet necessary tasks.

In consulting and investment banking, however, an MBA is needed for career advancement into senior levels, similar to the way it is in the U.S. One Chinese American with four years of manufacturing industry experience joined a major U.S. consulting firm in Hong Kong as an analyst. After three years with the firm, she's considering her next step. She feels the pressure to go back for an MBA. "There is an unwritten rule in consulting that you can't move up without one," she says. "The choice is to either go to business school or change industries."

When considering the benefit of an MBA towards your career in Greater China, first look at your existing skills, both professional and personal, and determine if an MBA will help you add capabilities relevant to the region. In my case, my MBA was a definite plus in helping me get out here. During my two-year program, I was able to arrange a summer internship in Taipei, improve my Mandarin through classroom and self study, expand my understanding of the Greater China business environment, and extend my network of contacts in the region. I came out much more marketable and prepared for a Greater China career as a result.

Perhaps the bottom line is that getting an MBA never hurt anyone. It's clearly a credential better to have than not to have. The training that a top business school program provides in a range of areas is indisputable. However, if you're looking at an MBA as a ticket to get you to Greater China, it's not a must by any means. If you want to build your expertise in Greater China, the best way is to come out and learn by doing. Many have done so successfully. The best teacher is the region itself.

6) How Long Of A Commitment Do Companies Expect?

During the interview process, it's almost guaranteed that someone will ask you about your commitment to working in the region. In pre-qualifying candidates, I've heard some say they intend to be in Greater China for the next five to ten years. Rather than reflect commitment, their statement has the reverse effect. It highlights their naiveté about the region and their plans for living and working here.

The reality is that, for most of us, it's difficult to know if we'll even be here two years or more down the road. There are too many unknowns. Will China markets continue to open up and develop? Will Beijing and Taipei establish direct communications and travel links? Both the macro picture and your own situation change too rapidly and dramatically each year to make such long-term predictions.

Similarly, hiring managers do not expect you to state that you have intentions of staying five years or more. What they want to know is whether you have a strong commitment and orientation towards developing a career in Asia. What they're trying to sense is how well thought out and serious you are to be here.

In truth, what says more about your longevity in Greater China is not what you can say about your future, but what you've done in the past. Experienced managers and human resources personnel can easily spot "bandwagon jumpers," or candidates considering a career in Greater China because of a tight job market in the U.S., or because they suddenly think this is the place to be. Such candidates readily claim to be committed to a career in the region. Yet, when asked if they've spent much time out here, speak a Chinese dialect, or know what's going on beyond what can be read in magazines, they have little to say. Without the indication of previous activities related to the region, future claims carry little weight.

Conversely, candidates with a real desire to be in Greater China are easy to identify. These candidates typically have worked on improving their language skills and travel out on a regular basis. They can discuss regional affairs at a deeper, more knowledgeable level. For candidates with such a track record, their claims of pursuing a long-term career in the region are much more credible. As one candidate said to me during his interview, "I've put five years of my life into studying Mandarin. I didn't do that just to come here for a brief adventure." Hard to argue with that kind of logic.

7) How Long Is The Window Of Opportunity?

Many believe the most exciting time of growth in Greater China will occur over the next ten years. Along with it, they see the value of bilingual and bicultural Chinese Americans in the region increasing. However, they also express a sense of urgency. Companies are becoming more selective in their hiring. At the same time, competition is growing all the time, as more local Chinese are gaining experience in leading multinational firms or are going abroad to attain the same U.S. university degrees and MBAs held by Chinese Americans. Multinationals such as Procter & Gamble and Pepsi have even set up "training universities" in the mainland to develop local staff more quickly.

Joe Wong, the regional director of human resources in Asia for Tricon Restaurants International (TRI) in Hong Kong, cautions Chinese Americans against wasting the opportunities before them. Before moving to Hong Kong two years ago, Joe spent three years as the human resources manager for Northern Telecom in Beijing. "Many Chinese Americans I see in Asia today are under-prepared and overconfident," says Joe. "They're able to find jobs, but unless they develop stronger local skills and regional exposure, they're in for a difficult time. In four or five years, companies will be able to find more and better local hires. Look at the ones returning from overseas even today. They're hungry, smart, and have the home-court advantage in their relationships, language skills, and understanding of the place. Plus, they're considerably less expensive."

Joe has a particular warning for Chinese Americans who develop their career solely in Hong Kong. "Those content with remaining in Hong Kong need to be careful," he says. "The biggest market and focus for multinationals is China. If you're not involved there, the job market for you becomes considerably tighter. Regional jobs are relatively few to begin with. In addition, companies are beginning to establish regional centers elsewhere (i.e. Beijing, Shanghai, or Singapore). To sustain your marketability, you have to get out in the field. Without knowing about and being close to what's going on at the country level where company revenues and operations grow, your value becomes short-lived. The key to staying competitive is to continually build on new skill sets. It's all about being able to do things that others can't do." As an example, Joe identifies the need for good implementers and trainers in China who can pass on functional skills to local staff.

Although James Yao feels the future outlook in Greater China for Chinese Americans is very positive, he also warns those about being complacent. "You have to know your value-added out here, then constantly improve on it. When I got to Taipei in 1990, I was a breath of fresh air to customers. Besides just technical skills, I also brought sales and marketing skills that the local computer industry did not have back then. I even remember organizing Taiwan's very first multimedia presentation, using a barcode projector to show MAC images onto a screen. Today, many others have similar strong technical and sales and marketing backgrounds. But since then, I've acquired general management and China experience. My ability to stay ahead of the pack is a result of the new expertise and skills I continually work on gaining."

The New China

Local professionals are rapidly maturing into the caliber of managers that multinationals are seeking. Steven Song is a prime example. If you meet Steven in person, or even speak with him by phone, you'd swear he spent many years of his life outside Mainland China. By any measure of western standards, he is confident, articulate, and well-presented. At 26 years old, he's the regional director of sales for Lucent Technologies (China), responsible for the sales and distribution of PABX and related network infrastructure products to nine provinces in northern China. Steven also happens to be 100 percent, true blue (or true red), born and raised Mainland Chinese.

Steven's father studied in England as a visiting scholar early in his career. His international demeanor rubbed off on his son as well. When you ask Steven how he acquired such a western style of communication and thinking, however, he credits a different source. "While working in Shanghai, I spent a lot of time in pubs," he describes. "I learned a lot just by hanging out with my western colleagues and talking about the economy, European soccer, or cars. They were interesting and I gained an understanding about business and the world from them."

Beyond just his sales record, Stephen stood out in other ways to his management. "Steven has a fantastic ability to break down barriers between Chinese and foreigners. He's an excellent communicator," says James Burton, the general manager who hired Steven for his first job as a sales assistant with GPT, Britain's largest telecommunications manufacturer. "He's also the pro-active type. He'll always find a way through a problem to get the job done. That's not a common characteristic found in most local staff."

For multinational employers like James Burton, the future is clear. "When multinationals here talk about the top candidates to hire for their China operations, they're really talking about people like Steven," says James. "Steven is *The New China.*"

It Won't Happen Overnight

The quality and quantity of Mainland China managers will not appear overnight though. The reality of their widespread presence within multinational management ranks is still a long way off. A recent report by management consulting firm AT Kearney which studied 24 major multinational firms found that, despite years of effort, none had fully localized their management teams. Within 14 of these firms, foreigners still held all key positions. According to a McKinsey & Company study, some of the most successful companies operating in China have even increased the total number of expats they employed over the past six years because of the continually growing size of their operations. Although localization is a goal, foreign professionals are needed to provide the leadership and experience required to properly build operations and run businesses in the mainland at this time.

8) Should I Work In The U.S. Before Going To Asia?

With most multinational infrastructures still at an early growth stage in the region, Greater China is not so much a training ground, but a "doing" ground. Career development out here is like a crash course. Training for young professionals does not come from a classroom or structured program. Whatever training that is available usually happens on-the-job. Essentially, you are expected to get up to speed and add value right away.

Therefore, obtaining work experience in the U.S., where business fundamentals tend to be sounder, is a good idea before coming out. That experience will carry you a long way out here by giving you credibility and something to offer. Lynda Lee is the regional marketing director for Clorox in Hong Kong. For Lynda, her U.S. work experience has been the cornerstone to her career in Asia. "My greatest asset is the four years I spent in Cincinnati," she points out. "I made a focused effort to make brand manager while at Procter & Gamble before moving out. The track record I developed there works for me in both substance and perception and has helped me in everything I've done here. It's not enough just to be bicultural and bilingual. If you want to see excellent opportunities, you have to bring on-board concrete business skills."

Allan Kwan also made a conscious decision early on to work in the U.S. and Canada before moving to Greater China. In addition to an MBA from Wharton business school, he spent nine years at Northern Telecom in manufacturing engineering, product services, new product development, operations, marketing, and business planning roles. "Out here, it's more chaotic. There are less resources. If you don't have solid, well-rounded skills, you won't make it into higher management levels," he says.

In 1992, Northern Telecom sent Allan to Hong Kong as their director of wireless marketing to oversee the launch of new products in the region. After two years, he joined Motorola in Beijing, as the director of sales and distribution for their Greater China paging systems division, responsible for US$700 million in annual revenues and managing an organization of over one hundred staff. He was 36 years old at the time. Today, Allan is the operation's general manager and one of Motorola's youngest vice presidents ever to be appointed.

Allan points to his ability to translate local knowledge and information in a way that U.S. headquarters can understand as one of his greatest strength. "Because of my bilingual background, I was always sure I could do business in this region," he says. "But by working in North America first, I know how the home office thinks, their expectations, and how to deal with them."

Allan advises young professionals not to be too concerned over when to move to Asia. "There is no perfect timing," he says. "It's more a matter of when you feel you're ready. China's growth isn't one or two years, or even five to ten. It will be continuous."

Another benefit of gaining U.S. experience first is the clearer perspective it gives on the skills you develop. I've met several candidates who came to the region right after college. They've spent their entire career in Greater China, where they've worked in unstructured, entrepreneurial operations and dealt with difficult, complicated business situations. They've functioned with little support or prior training to help them perform their job. After a few years, they have difficulty determining and measuring what it is they know or don't know. As a result, they carry a high degree of professional insecurity. Working in the States first develops your understanding of where you stand in comparison to others. Knowing this helps you move forward in your career in a more confident manner.

9) Should I Quit My Job In The U.S. And Just Come Out To Look For Work?

Although it's difficult to recommend such an extreme course of action to anyone, I know of numerous cases where people have taken the plunge and left their job in the U.S. to come and find a position in Greater China. Although not everyone's situation is suited for such a bold move, it does work out for many. Those who have successfully made the jump out generally fall into two categories.

The first type were taking a fairly safe, calculated risk. They had already made an initial job search trip to meet employers and to speak with others working in the region. During their trip, they were able to assess the job market and their chances for finding employment. They concluded that opportunities were available. Landing a position was only a matter of time once they could put a concentrated, prolonged effort into their search. Many gave themselves two months or so to find something. Most did. Those that didn't, extended their projection. They usually had one or more substantial job leads that needed just a little more time to be realized.

The second type were just entirely committed to the idea of working in Greater China. Developing their career elsewhere was not an option. As a result, they did not feel there was any big risk or sacrifice in moving out. They took a long-term perspective and saw each day here as another day they could develop their career in the region.

In both cases, there is one key similarity. All parties knew people here that they could stay with. These were relatives, friends, or even friends of friends with extra space to share. For professionals used to working and pulling in a salary, unemployment can be a psychological and financial strain. Having a stable place to return to every night and minimizing expenses are two significant issues that are good to have under control while you're job searching.

Quitting your job and moving to the region is not a decision anyone can make for you. You have to weigh your own personal situation, abilities, motivation, and objectives. There are no guarantees, but with the right preparation and perspective, it's highly likely that such a move can work out successfully.

10) How Difficult Is It To Get A Work Visa?

Hong Kong

To work in Hong Kong, you must obtain a work visa issued by the Immigration Department. The immigration policy allows foreigners to work in Hong Kong if they possess special skills, knowledge, or experience that are not readily available in Hong Kong, or if they are in a position to add substantial value to Hong Kong's economy.

Although the process is a little difficult, an employment visa is obtainable after you arrive. For those with previous work experience of two years or more, obtaining a work visa is primarily a paper process that requires time to complete. You must be sponsored by a company, which must justify to the Immigration Department why they have chosen to hire you over a local. It typically takes two to three months to successfully obtain a work visa.

US citizens are allowed to stay in Hong Kong without a visa for up to 30 days. Since the visa process usually takes over one month, many job seekers take one-day trips to Shenzhen or Macau near the end of their 30-day period and then return to Hong Kong for another 30 days. As you might guess, the Immigration authorities may soon suspect your exit and entry ploy from your passport full of 30-day entry and exit stamps.

It's also possible to extend your stay. Valid justification, however, must be provided to the Immigration Department (i.e. need more time to visit friends/family, take care of a family member, etc.).

Mainland China

Obtaining a visa to work in China is also fairly straightforward and is typically not an issue for foreigners working there. The mainland government collects a good deal of tax revenues from expatriates working in the country. As a result, they don't attempt to make the application process difficult. It mainly involves filling out paperwork. Visas can even be obtained in a single day.

There are several options when considering the visa issue for China. A type L, or travel (*luyou*), visa allows you single entry travel in China for up to one month. Many people doing business in China go for a type F, or business (*fangwen*) visa, which allows you multiple entries for up to six months. For a resident, or type D, visa, more time and sponsorship from your company or an official Chinese organization is required. If you're working in China, your company will help you apply for the appropriate visa you require.

Taiwan

Although not as straightforward as in Hong Kong, obtaining a work permit in Taiwan is not so difficult if you have three or more years of previous work experience. Most multinationals, including advertising agencies, consumer product companies, and market research firms, are registered with the Ministry of Economic Affairs (MOEA), which only requires two years of general work experience abroad. Those registered with the Ministry of Finance (MOF), however, such as banks and other financial institutions, have stricter hiring policies for non-Taiwanese citizens.

Many Chinese Americans and returnees go so far as to obtain dual citizenship because of special clauses in the law that permit such legal status. It's an alternative to getting around the work permit issue. Generally speaking though, obtaining a work visa is an uphill battle. I've heard the effort required compared to applying to an MBA program. Expect the process to take at least one to three months, a couple of thousand dollars, and significant documentation if you're a non-Taiwan citizen trying to receive a work permit.

Chapter 13 Once You're Out Here

Doing Things The Local Way

It's Not The United States

The "American way" to get things done doesn't work in Greater China the way it does in the U.S. For instance, in China you can't just push things through like you may be used to doing. You might try, but you're likely to end up frustrated and unsuccessful. Many end up learning this lesson the hard way. Instead, you need to exercise flexibility and patience, as well as have an understanding of the situations you're dealing with. Ultimately, the more you can step out and localize yourself, the more likely your success.

Your ability to adjust familiar western habits and practices will affect your ability to manage effectively and get results. Ron Chow works as a sales manager for a U.S. electronics company in Hong Kong. When he first came to Hong Kong in 1994, he noticed he was always the first to shoot out answers during meetings attended by the local staff in his company. "Because I was the one always speaking up, I thought nobody else knew what was going on. It was very American of me," he recalls. "What took me a while to realize was that Chinese people don't like to shine like a light bulb. So in meetings, they rarely express their opinions. Once you got them one on one though, they were much more open to talking about things. Here I was making a judgment about them, and it was actually me who was not with the program. I was making a fool out of myself and not even knowing it."

One Chinese American also found it difficult to adjust his western business style to the local corporate culture of his software company's Taipei operation. He returned from Boston to become its managing director two years ago. "I'm trying to introduce a lot of new business concepts to the local management team," he explains. "Because my managers are not as vocal and willing to debate issues as what I'm use to, it takes me longer to determine if they're buying into the approaches. As a result, I spend most of my time just on communications to gain acceptance, develop understanding, and raise the comfort level of new ideas."

Some find it a challenge to understand the specifics of each culture and country and how to respond appropriately to the corresponding business tactics. For example, in certain countries, business practices may call for you to entertain with clients. This may include nights out drinking or even going to night clubs and piano bars. To refuse may jeopardize a business relationship or hinder a project or deal altogether. As someone from the West trying to get the job done and be effective out here, you may have to get use to a new value system.

Making A Connection

Doing business successfully in China, in particular, requires more than just having a strong knowledge of Chinese culture and customs. What also counts is a willingness and interest to get to know the people. To resolve issues and win confidence, you have to understand how they think and why they might think a certain way. Ultimately, this impacts your ability to communicate the right messages and respond to situations in the most appropriate way. Gaining an understanding of what's important to them begins with removing your biases and preconceived views towards local Chinese. If you can do this at a subconscious level, then you'll be able to mingle easier and in a way people will respond to.

For Chinese Americans, the capabilties are there to build close links with the Mainland Chinese. Unfortunately, many don't take the initiative to do it. "I see many overseas Chinese, including Chinese Americans, who speak excellent Mandarin and know Chinese customs," says Hector Wong, managing director of North Asia for St. Jude Medical, a U.S. medical products company. "When they do business in China, however, they aren't able to get results. In my opinion, it's because they differentiate themselves as foreigners and fail to make a connection with the Mainland Chinese as someone who is also a Chinese. That really hurts their ability to establish tighter relationships."

Hector uses the term "the brotherhood way" to describe how he approaches business and developing relationships in China. "Mainland Chinese are very patriotic. Even in business dealings, you have to show an interest in providing a benefit to them. They respond to that. If you can demonstrate your sincerity and build the trust, then you'll be treated as one of them or as part of their brotherhood. It then becomes easier to work together and accomplish things. But if you're just out to get something from them, they can feel that too. They may deal with you in the short term, but it'll be uncertain whether you'll win their favor when it counts the most."

Personal Travelogue

During my initial few months in Taipei with Wang Laboratories, I spent several weeks working on a proposal for a major government client. This was one of my first projects and I was eager to show my value to the local operations, particularly to the sales force and rest of the marketing team. I prepared cost comparisons and business process studies to justify why our computer system was the obvious solution to go with. After finishing, I showed my Taiwanese colleague my impressive report. I marveled at the spreadsheets, workflow diagrams, and bulleted points I had put together.

My colleague nodded and smiled in his typical manner as I provided him with a concise summary of each key point in my analysis. Although he always gave me his undivided attention, his enthusiasm and intensity rarely matched my own. Seldom did he have any comments to add to my work. After finishing my presentation, I asked him what he thought. He paused for a second, looking a bit perplexed. There was no response. Suddenly, his face lit up, as if suddenly struck with a revolutionary idea. With complete earnestness, he looked at me and said: "Have you thought about taking them out to lunch?"

I was stunned. "Lunch, huh? Why didn't I think of that?" I sarcastically thought to myself. "You've got to be kidding. I am a finely tuned, well-trained MBA! Give me a break."

The next day, I presented to the client my study as planned. Although they appeared to like my analysis, they did not end up contracting us for the project I proposed.

Today, I'd do it differently. There's a saying in Chinese, "do business with your head, but use your heart." Asians place a heavier emphasis on mixing social with business. You may have the right professional experience, but without the local sensitivity, understanding, and relationships, it doesn't mean much.

My colleague was right. I needed to put a greater effort into building a personal connection with the client. Particularly, in that situation, where I was an outsider. I needed to let the client understand and know me better, and vice versa. No wonder my colleague used to do so well without ever performing any pre-sales work or feasibility studies. I'm sure back then he must have been thinking to himself: "MBA, SchMBA."

Never Underestimate Karaoke

The first time I went to a karaoke club with colleagues, I was quite uncomfortable and embarrassed. Ironically, as the supposedly outgoing one from America, I was reserved while my co-workers were singing away and having a ball. Since then, I've gone out and sang the night away on many occasions. I've had some great bonding moments singing with both friends and people I hardly knew.

Karaoke is a large part of the social scene in Asia. I know of few locals who don't enjoy spending an evening out singing with friends. It's a relaxed and informal setting for meeting people and, yes, even doing business. It doesn't hurt to have a repertoire of three or four English favorites in your karaoke song bag. If you can belt out standards like *Yesterday* by The Beatles, *My Way* by Frank Sinatra (or you may prefer the Elvis version), *Country Road* by John Denver, or *Top Of The World* by the Carpenters, then you'll be a hit at just about any karaoke songfest. And if you can sing at least one song in Chinese, your audience will bombard you with unrequited adulation, clamors for additional requests, and maybe even a marriage proposal or two. My one Chinese standard, guaranteed to please, is, *Ke Neng Ni Bu Dong Wo De Xin*, or *Perhaps You Don't Understand My Heart*. It slays them every time.

You Know You're A Greater China Veteran When ...

- You feel more comfortable pricing things in the local Chinese rather than U.S. currency.
- You are no longer embarrassed to admit that you enjoy karaoke.
- It doesn't phase you any more to pay US$12 for a hamburger.
- You require a second Rolodex to hold all your business cards.
- Your passport becomes thicker than your wallet.
- You leave the office at 6pm and you feel that you're knocking off early.
- You know of the different electricity voltage requirements for Hong Kong, Mainland China, and Taiwan.
- You say lines like, "could you please open the lights," and think that you're using proper English.
- The clothes in your closet from Giordano begin to outnumber the clothes you have from The Gap.
- Tourists approach you for directions, and you actually give them successfully.
- You choose the dried, peppered cuttlefish instead of the M&M's from the snack counter when you go to see a movie.
- You look forward to watching repeats of *Mr. Belvedere* and *The Golden Girls* on StarTV.
- You can order a Chinese meal without having to look and point at what people at other tables are eating.

My all-time favorite karaoke experience happened in Taipei. A friend wanted me to meet the general manager of his company. One Saturday evening, the friend called to let me know that the general manager was going to be at a Cash Box (a well-known Taiwan karaoke chain) later that night. He said it would be a casual gathering and a good chance to introduce myself. He suggested I join the group with him.

When I got there, the room was already in full swing. Both drinks and songs were flowing freely. Eventually, I got a chance to sit next to the general manager. He was having a good time, but was polite in asking me about my business. He listened intently as I gave a short-order pitch on my company. When I finished, he began telling me about his operations and their hiring needs. Suddenly, the song *Night Fever* came up on the karoake screen and began piping in through the speakers. This was his song.

In mid-sentence he grabbed the microphone off the table, jumped to his feet, and began belting out the Bee Gees classic with passion and verve. I was dumbfounded. I looked around to find myself sitting next to and staring at an empty space. Our business conversation had evaporated in an instant. But within a split second, I jumped up too and began singing along with him. When he realized that I also knew the words (I'm ashamed to admit it), an instant connection was made. We both let it all hang out, finishing the song swaying shoulder to shoulder, like two army buddies out on the town. Before the evening ended, we set up a time to meet at his office later that week. We went on to place a candidate in his company.

The Right Attitude

When Greater China hands talk about what can make a difference between success or failure here, many single out one intangible quality in particular. It concerns having the right attitude. Hiring managers often stress this as a key success factor, especially for positions requiring frequent interaction with local colleagues and clients. Some are even wary of Chinese Americans who may carry an air of superiority, just because they are educated abroad and speak fluent English.

As a Chinese American in Asia, you're going to be especially scrutinized. Having an Asian face can be both a blessing and a curse. If you present yourself well, your Chinese background can be a tremendous asset. It can solicit a greater level of trust, comfort, and openness among the local parties you encounter. Project yourself in the wrong manner, however, and criticism will be given for insensitivity or arrogance. In many ways Chinese Americans must do things twice as correctly over their non-Asian counterparts. Whereas non-Asians are given more margin for error to make cultural mistakes, the feeling towards us is that we should know better.

"Attitude is always number one with me when I hire someone," emphasizes Allan Kwan, who has hired several Chinese Americans for his Motorola Paging Systems' China operations. "I need the Asian and western skill sets they offer. I believe in their value, but I only want ones who have exceptional attitudes."

"Attitude is always number one with me when I hire someone ... I need the Asian and western skill sets they offer. I believe in their value, but I only want ones who have exceptional attitudes."

Allan shares an experience he had in hiring three Chinese American staff. When they came on board, he emphasized to them that they would be closely judged by local staff, given their substantially higher compensation packages. At their junior management levels, however, they wouldn't have the aura or protection of an impressive title to differentiate them from locals who might be earning one-tenth their salaries. "I told them right off the bat that their number one priority was to demonstrate their value above anything else. You have to outwork your local counterparts and bring on a different dimension of thinking and performance. You must also make yourself available to peers and get to know them."

"What happened? During our first company outing, the three clustered together and separated themselves from everyone else. This reflected their conduct in the office as well. There was little effort made to associate with their co-workers on their part. As a result, they never ended up fitting in."

"In China, you have to be aggressive. At the same time, you must display a diplomacy and an empathy. Relationships matter in business here. It's important to take on your local counterparts as peers or equals. If you don't, they'll just say, 'screw you.' Eventually, these three failed because they couldn't gain the trust and support of those they needed help from most."

Personal Travelogue

During my Wang Laboratories days, I was sent out as the marketing specialist to support the sales staff in the Taipei office. And that's what I fully intended to do. I wasn't deterred by my poor Mandarin to stop me from performing my job before local customers. I told myself I needed to be persistent and thick-skinned. So with my 1500-word vocabulary, I constructed and practiced a 90-minute technical marketing presentation about Wang's product lines, corporate strategy, and customer service excellence.

For my first presentation, I was sent down to Kaohsiung in southern Taiwan to speak before a room full of nearly 100 local information technology managers. Most were either government employees or worked for large Taiwan companies. They attended my seminar in their company work uniforms.

I recalled how I used to always see non-native, English-speaking Asians give presentations in their halted English. Their delivery was reserved and uncomfortable. That wasn't going to be the case for me. After all, I was professionally trained in presentation skills.

I proceeded to deliver my Mandarin presentation to my audience in an animated and confident manner. I used eye contact, voice intonation, and body language to effectively communicate my point. I walked back and forth with energy and conviction. I was a regular Tom Voo informercial, preaching the glories of Wang computers.

In my mind, I was speaking fluent Mandarin. I sounded smooth and coherent, the way I would sound in English. "At Wang Computers, we have the best technology that can fit your business needs." But with a limited vocabulary and a few textbook sentence structures at my disposal, what they were actually hearing was more like: "No matter your company's needs, Wang have good computers."

And because of my inability to express certain points as creatively as I would in English, some phrases I would repeat up to a dozen times. I can only imagine what that was like to hear. "Yes, Wang computers are very good and very cheap ... very cheap and good ... extremely good, and not a lot of money."

One thing I have to say though, I never saw anyone in the audience not paying attention. Their eyes were glued on me. I believe they were just completely stunned at what they were seeing before them. A dichotomy of a seemingly intelligent, adult man giving a high-level technical, business presentation, only speaking like an eight year old child. And doing it with such enthusiasm. In the end, they were very receptive. I believe they sensed my sincere desire to communicate with them on their terms.

Working For A Multinational vs. A Local Company

Multinational Firms

As I'm sure you've noticed, the career opportunities I emphasize revolve around multinational firms. It's not that Asian firms don't hold good opportunities as well. There are local firms which are significant, even dominant players in their industries. Career tracks within multinationals are favored by most professionals, however, for several reasons.

Forcing The Action

Multinationals function with a much greater sense of urgency over local firms. With a relatively short history in Greater China and without the long-standing relationships that many local companies have, multinationals must be more aggressive and offer compelling products and services in order to win business and market share. Their rapid rate of growth in the region creates tremendous advancement opportunities for their employees.

American firms in Hong Kong employ 10% of the workforce, approximately 250,000 people — Information Services Department in Hong Kong

Appreciation of Skills

Although multinationals are developing greater local business capabilities, fundamentally, they still possess western-oriented corporate cultures and management styles. Most multinational managers have been educated and trained abroad. They have the same undergraduate and MBA degrees, as well as corporate experiences possessed by the western-trained professionals they supervise. As a result, they have a good understanding of your thought process, business orientation, and capabilities. This is not always the case in local companies, where many managers may not have the same degree of international training and exposure.

Value Added

Your ability to operate at a local business level has tremendous benefit to multinationals who tend to have fewer staff with this capability relative to Asian firms. Add to this your ability to communicate local information and business developments to corporate headquarters and western managers and the result is someone who is extremely valuable to a foreign company operating in the region.

Corporate Fit

Although I worked for a multinational firm when I came to Asia, I found myself in a local company environment at Wang Laboratories' in Taiwan. I was the operation's only overseas hire. From the general manager on down, the entire company consisted of native Taiwanese. As a result, the Taiwan operations possessed a corporate culture and style of doing business that was also extremely local. Internally, the management style was consensus-oriented. Externally, conducting business was relationship oriented.

I have to admit, it was a difficult environment for me, particularly since I arrived at Wang soon after completing my business school program. I was anxious to apply all that MBA stuff I had learned, such as team building, business modeling, strategic planning, cost/benefit analysis, and a consultative problem solving approach. Those practices, however, were generally out of synch with the business practices going on around me. The problem wasn't the company's. The operations was very successful. The problem was the difficulty I had in doing my job following the operation's local business style and approach. Although I learned a great deal in that environment, I never felt that I was as effective as I could have been in a slightly more international situation.

Better Pay

In Greater China the salary levels within multinational firms are typically higher than within local firms. In Asia, U.S. and European companies tend to pay the most, while Chinese companies the least.

Performance Driven Culture

Asian companies tend to have more traditional hierarchical structures that heavily favor longevity and company standing among employees. As a result, young and hungry staff are often made to wait their turn. Local managers who have been in the same company for twenty years aren't anxious to see someone advance to their level in half the time or less. In comparison, multinational firms are new to the region. Management teams are strikingly young. For multinationals, career advancement comes down to performance and producing results.

Local Companies

Despite the career development and financial benefits that multinationals offer, career opportunities within local companies are beginning to draw those who have typically sought positions in western firms. Local firms are realizing that in order to compete in both local and international markets, they have to develop higher caliber management, services, and expertise. To do this, they are starting to go after the same talent that multinationals attract.

The Road Less Traveled

While their friends work for well-known multinational firms, some candidates go against the norm and opt for the local track. Within a local firm, your western training can bring you more responsibility and greater latitude to handle situations beyond what local staff may be afforded.

After working in New York for four years, Amy Chu moved to Hong Kong in 1995 and found a position as a senior account manager for Occasions, a local public relations and events marketing firm. She reported directly to the executive director and managed a staff of six account managers and executives. "Management valued the positive 'can do' approach I brought to situations," says Amy. "I was able to offer different ideas and viewpoints on management issues, service, and how we should conduct our business. They would ask for my opinion, even if my exposure to local scenarios was more limited than others."

Amy also felt she had more freedom to address issues that her local colleagues backed off from. Although being different drew attention, it helped make her voice heard. After all, it was rationalized that she was someone who's not conformed to conventional constraints. Soon after joining Occasions, Amy served an unofficial role as the right-hand person to the executive director. Eighteen months later, she was asked by the managing partner to build up and head a new affiliated marketing and public relations business for the company.

There are also excellent opportunities within local firms that do international business. In these situations, management may put you at the forefront of business dealings to show western clients that you are a part of their local team. The result is a chance to stand out and have a substantial impact. Lilian Yip joined Kingsway Toy Company just over one year ago, directly after graduating from UC San Diego. Kingsway is a Hong Kong manufacturer that makes soft baby toys and stuffed animals for U.S. toy companies such as Gund and Kids II. "Our company is currently expanding and venturing into new deals with U.S. firms," says Lilian. "Because of my comfort level dealing within an international environment, I'm part of our efforts to develop business with our western clients."

Within her first year at Kingsway, Lilian traveled to the U.S. with top management on three trips aimed at soliciting business. Her role was not a minor one. She was brought along to communicate to new clients the company's local capabilities and resources.

It's not only the local company that may value you, but the western clients you deal with as well. Lilian notices the sense of security and clarity of communications she provides to her company's U.S. clients. "They feel more confident knowing they're dealing with someone who thinks in a similar way as them. When an important issue needs to be resolved, they'll often ask to speak with me to get their point across faster or just to make sure their point gets across, period."

Lilian and Amy both acknowledge the need to assess and face every situation they encounter with more care. They operate in family-oriented corporate structures and business styles that involve nuances in office politics and decision making. Each situation involves subtle issues not normally encountered in multinational settings. "It's a big adjustment adapting to a dramatically different corporate terrain," states Amy. "Whereas you can freely express your opinions in a western company, in a local firm you may have to accept the local view of handling certain business issues, or find a round-about way to communicate your point without coming across as a western-educated know-it-all."

Lilian also finds she has to put extra thought into how she projects herself and how she is perceived. Colleagues are constantly figuring out at what level they can interact with her in Cantonese and as a fellow Chinese. "Whether I'm perceived as a westerner or a Chinese definitely affects how I'm treated and what I may be asked to do," Lilian explains. "Therefore, it's important having a boss who will work with you and who understands your capabilities."

Overall, Amy and Lilian feel their local company experience gives their career development a faster, stronger track than if they were working for a multinational firm. Not only is their spoken Cantonese attaining native fluency (both spoke conversationally before arriving to Hong Kong), they are learning regional business practices. Working with a truly local customer base also exposes Amy to many aspects of Hong Kong society and allows her to build valuable contacts, areas not usually as accessible working in multinational firms. Given the increasing localization of Asia business, she believes that attaining these skills, experiences, and relationships are an excellent long-term bet. For Lilian, the responsibilities and chances she's seen are far beyond what she could have anticipated at this stage in her career.

Working Women In Asia

As it is for men, opportunities in Asia to excel for women exist in all industries. Successful female managing directors and senior executives can be found in financial institutions, security brokerages, consumer products firms, advertising and public relations agencies, and even local companies. Women are particularly prominent within marketing roles and client services fields. In general, women's issues aren't a big topic in Asia. There's less sensitivity and political correctness than in U.S. regarding women in the workforce.

Successful women in the region appear to have one thing in common. They don't let the issue of gender inhibit their opportunities. They spend less time thinking about discrimination issues and more on how to be exceptional at what they do. As mentioned before, Asia is a place that rewards performers. The axiom, "if you're good, you'll succeed" applies to everyone here.

This isn't to say that Asia is the easiest place for women to work. A male dominant mentality and manner of socialization does exist in Greater China countries. For example, within many front-end positions that encompass sales or business development, there is sometimes a need to dine, entertain, or go out drinking with clients. There is also a widespread deference in the society towards men. However, beyond acknowledging these situations and circumstances, most successful women find a way around them, or choose to ignore them and move on.

"For me, it's been somewhat of an advantage being a woman out here," says Fay Chen, senior product manager for Kimberly Clark in Taipei. "I find that many Chinese men have a hard time being straightforward with their thoughts and viewpoints. They have more difficulty expressing themselves, perhaps because of complicated and underlying face issues they must deal with in situations where they might stand out. But for me, it's not at all difficult to say what's on my mind. In a multinational environment, management likes to hear from employees who have ideas and opinions. That's to my advantage. As long as you have the confidence and know what you're talking about, it's not a problem being heard."

Karen Tsao worked in Shanghai for IBM China for three years as a project manager handling major banking and securities sector accounts. One year ago she moved to Hong Kong for a position in the financial software industry. "I would describe the attitude towards women working in the mainland as even more open and equal to that in Hong Kong or Taiwan," says Karen, a Taiwan-born Chinese American. "If there has been one positive from communism, it's that men and women have worked side by side at almost every level for decades and the 'comrade' mentality seems to transcend gender. For example, you'll find many women in high-ranking positions at municipal government levels. In my experience, I've found women are treated with fairness and equality in business situations."

Women in Asia also have greater latitude to take charge of their careers if they choose. Most working women have the option in Asia to hire affordable domestic help. Amahs from the Philippines or China are commonly employed at reasonable salaries. If that isn't an option, then many have in-laws or parents to help baby-sit. Many women in Taiwan don't seem to have a problem with having someone else take care of their babies, unlike in the U.S. One friend returned to work full-time three months after having her baby. The baby spent Sunday night through Friday in Ilan County (one and a half hours outside Taipei) with her mother, while she and her husband worked in Taipei. This type of situation is not so uncommon out here.

Overall, the professional environment for western women in Asia is not thought to be any more difficult than in the U.S. "If there are barriers, it's more so for local women," says Amy Chu. "They're more bound by traditional roles and expectations by society than someone like myself. As someone from the States, it's not as unusual for me to be outspoken and aggressive."

Chapter 14 The Realities To Face (Or Why Some Don't Make It)

So far, life in Greater China sounds pretty good, huh? No doubt, it can be. But there are aspects of living and working here that are tougher to deal with than you might think. Not everyone who comes out ends up a so-called "success story." There are many who struggle or who are even disappointed with the experience, even though they arrived seemingly prepared.

Before coming to Taipei, I thought I was completely ready, both mentally and emotionally. It was a move I had sought for several years. I had an open mind and humble attitude. I wasn't seeking any kind of preferential treatment. I anticipated the necessity to adapt to new situations and expected to work hard. Yet, many things still surprised me. Such realities aren't as apparent until after you've been here a while.

I'm Not Kidding! People Really Work Hard!

People here don't necessarily plan to work so hard. They just do. The pressure to perform can be relentless. "Everything happens so fast. You're almost afraid to jump off the treadmill," laments an investment banker in Hong Kong. "It's easy to let the pace control you and to lose perspective of your identity and values." As a result, people burn out.

Another reason for the tendency to work so hard is because recreational activities are not nearly as available as in the U.S. They're considerably more difficult to arrange and expensive. Take living in China. Two years ago I went to visit a friend in Shanghai, my first trip there in several years. I arrived on a Friday afternoon. That evening we went out to enjoy the city's renowned night life and stayed out quite late. After waking up Saturday morning, we went to the hotel where his office was located to have breakfast at the coffee shop. Later, we worked out in the hotel fitness center.

"There's always more that can be done. Because what you're doing is exciting and rewarding, there's a tendency to turn more and more to work."

When we finished, it was still early afternoon. We decided to walk around the city for a while. We checked out the No. 5 department store. Afterwards, we browsed the No.3 department store. We decided to skip the No.2 one (wanted to save something for Sunday) and went back to my friend's place to rest up (still a big Saturday night before us). That evening we did the town again until early morning.

On Sunday, we woke up again to have breakfast at the hotel coffee shop. By noon we were pondering what to do the rest of the day. Unable to think of anything else, we went to my friend's office and spent the whole afternoon working!

Okay, it could be that my friend and I are a bit socially inept, but our situation was not such an unusual scenario. What else are you going to do in China? We didn't have a car. Getting on a tennis court or golf course was not possible without advanced reservations. The nearby theaters were playing outdated movies (*Rambo*, I believe). And there were about ten thousand people wherever we could think of going.

As in our case, you often find yourself without compelling alternative ways to spend your time. You figure, the main reason you're here is to take advantage of the business developments and opportunities taking place. You may as well put your effort into the most worthwhile thing you can think of at the moment — your career. "There's always more that can be done," my friend said "Because what you're doing is exciting and rewarding, there's always an inclination to turn towards work."

To cope with the stress and pressure of the job, many use their vacation time to travel around the region for short rest and relaxation (R&R) getaways. Local scuba diving and beach resorts in Bali, Koh Samui, Phuket, and Cebu, to name a few, are frequented destinations.

Getting Used As Cannon Fodder

Cannon fodder is the term for discarded shrapnel packed into a cannon. The shrapnel is fired in the general direction of a target, with a hope that it will strike something. It's also a metaphor for eager, young professionals recruited by companies to help them break into the China market. The application of the term to a professional situation in Asia comes from a young Chinese American working in Hong Kong.

Coming out of college, Greg Li was optimistic about his career prospects in China. He majored in Asian studies at Cornell and studied Mandarin in Beijing and Nanjing during his junior year. When he moved to Hong Kong in 1992, he was fully prepared to pay his dues. The local plastics manufacturing company who hired him had a similar line of thinking, with more than enough tasks to let him prove himself. After a few brief weeks in Hong Kong, they sent him to Shenzhen, a special economic zone in China, where he was told to "analyze factory production and potential mainland business."

Greg was hopelessly over his head. To begin with, the company lacked management support and staffing resources. Greg knew next to nothing about factory operations and had no one to guide him. On top of all that, he could barely communicate with the Cantonese-speaking workers who could not speak English or Mandarin. From day one, his frustration and confusion were continual. Most disconcerting, he had no idea what his role was. He had to carve out for himself both his responsibilities and understanding of how to do things.

After persevering for a year, Greg came across a well-known U.S. real estate company just getting started in China. Like most multinationals with big plans for the mainland market, this one was salivating over its huge potential. They also happened to be looking for someone bright, hardworking, and willing, who was familiar with China and could speak Mandarin. Again, Greg fit the bill. Flattered by the confidence the company managers placed in him, he seized their offer.

Again, however, he was sent into China with minimal training, little supervision, and the vaguest of instructions. It became quickly apparent there was also no well thought out business plan in place. Although, he was not opposed to working hard and knocking on doors, he rarely knew if what he was doing was on the right track. Cannon fodder was what he felt like. "My company kept 'firing' me into China hoping I would produce some results," Greg says. "Each time, I'd end up crashing to the ground. They'd load me up and fire me off again to see what kind of information or opportunity I might hit upon."

From Greg's point of view, he was an expendable body. "With each cannon fodder job I landed in, I saw my career prospects dimming," he recalls. "Those were self-defeating situations that only utilized my survival skills, but never provided me with the tools to actually perform. I knew I needed some real corporate training and functional expertise if I were to succeed."

Greg has advice for young professionals coming to Asia. "Back then, I was easily impressed by job titles and the excitement of being sent to China. Every opportunity seemed like a once-in-a-lifetime one to me. Now, I insist on clearly defined job responsibilities and company objectives. I ask for what kind of support I'll receive. Management must show commitment to the role they want me to play. Without it, you'll be set up for failure. I also take a more honest, realistic account of my own abilities, whether I can perform to expectations. I know I won't have the luxury of a training period, that rarely exists in Asia."

Greg is currently part of a team setting up the China operations for a large U.S. re-insurance company based in Hong Kong. He's confident this job presents real potential, as opposed to hyped possibilities. As an indication of the improved outlook of his situation, the first thing the company did when Greg joined was send him to the U.S. on a four-month management training program.

Fresh graduates are most susceptible to cannon fodder recruitment and can get mired in such no-win situations. Greg feels fortunate he was able to jump off the cannon fodder track and onto a real career track. Not everyone is as fortunate. The key is to recognize these dead-end jobs and avoid them.

Quality Of Life Issues

I truly enjoy my life in Asia. But I'm the first to admit my lifestyle here is far from ideal. I miss many things about living in the States. This became highly apparent the first time someone asked me what I missed about the U.S. It was surprising how many things came to mind.

I began with hot pastrami sandwiches, barbecue ribs and chicken, meatloaf, and just about any form of home-style cooking. I missed browsing through grocery stores and choosing from too many breakfast cereals and brands of ice cream to remember. I missed participating in sports. It's not only that I'm unable to do something I really enjoy, but being much less active here athletically, I'm not as healthy as I was when I lived in the States. I wonder what the effect of the continuous work, travel, and physical inactivity might be having on my body in the long run. That concerns me.

I even missed things basic to my life in the U.S., such as driving a car, watching television, and outdoor barbecues. Out here, I don't own a car. I don't even own a television — there's no time for it. Even if I had one, watching it is not the same as in the States. There aren't the late night talk shows, sporting events, and weekly sitcoms I enjoy. In my seven-plus years in Asia, I've probably gone to a half dozen barbecues. Most people don't live in a place where it's convenient or spacious enough to lounge around outside with a group of friends.

Perhaps these aspects I've mentioned sound like trivial things to forego when compared to the personal, cultural, and career gains that can be attained. When accumulated over an extended period of time, however, your overall quality of life does get affected. Life in Greater China is not as convenient or unhurried as in the U.S., nor is it as diverse or well-rounded. The demanding pace and constant pressures you face, combined with the reduced outlets for relaxation, can translate into a difficult existence for many. In the end, it can wear you down both physically and emotionally.

Transience

I lived in Taipei for four years before moving to Hong Kong. Because Taipei is where I first started out here, I consider it my home in Asia. While there, I was actively involved in the business community and got to know a good many people. I even formed a non-profit organization called Chinese American Professionals in Taiwan (CAPT). At its peak in 1993, CAPT claimed over 300 members.

> ***"It seems like I'm constantly on a 'meet new people campaign.' In the two years I've been here, I've already gone through three different groups of friends."***

Although I live in Hong Kong now, I go to Taipei at least once a month. With each successive visit though, I feel increasingly like an outsider. It's only been three years since I moved away, yet I hardly know anyone there anymore! Many have moved on like me. They're back in the U.S. or relocated to other Asian destinations like Hong Kong or China. Moving around is a common occurrence for people in Asia. If you live here, it's something you have to get used to.

Judi Moi is a born and raised New Yorker. In New York City, she was used to having a tight-knit circle of friends whom she saw regularly. When she graduated from college and moved to Hong Kong in 1995, she discovered the social life here to be a revolving door. "It seems like I'm constantly on a 'meet new people campaign,'" she says. "In my two years here, I've already gone through three groups of friends."

People are always leaving, particularly those who reach their two to three-year mark here. Some return home for good. Some go back to graduate school, to return to Asia another day. Others move on because of more attractive opportunities elsewhere in the region. "Compounding the difficulty in developing strong friendships is that this place is a hotbed of workaholics," says Judi. "Heavy business traveling and busy schedules are the norm. Socializing takes a back seat. Although you meet a lot of people, you don't necessarily get to know them well." Judi's solution to the eventual disappointment of seeing friends depart is to get to know more local residents or expats who view Hong Kong as their permanent home.

Are You Chinese Or American?

Although her upbringing in San Francisco was very Americanized, Deborah Liu always felt very Asian. In fact, she felt more Chinese than American while growing up in the U.S. She spoke some Mandarin and took several trips to China at an early age. For most of her life, she envisioned the mainland as the place where she would feel most at home. At age 28, she finally got a chance to move to Hong Kong, landing a position as a brand manager with Clorox. She eagerly anticipated the chance to get more in touch with her Chinese heritage.

It's tough having a Chinese face and not being completely fluent in Mandarin, ... It's entirely up to you to fit in."

After spending a lot of time in China during her first six months though, an interesting revelation came to Deborah. Instead of feeling more Chinese, what she discovered was how American she was. In fact, she ended up feeling more American than she ever did before. "In many ways, it was far more difficult living in China than anything I had experienced in the States," she says. "I realized just how western my behavior and thinking was. And it's tough having a Chinese face and not being completely fluent in Mandarin. You don't get much help from the local Chinese. It's entirely up to you to fit in."

For Chinese Americans, Greater China can be a difficult place psychologically. If you're in Taiwan or Mainland China, and are not a native Mandarin speaker, you'll attract attention as soon as you open your mouth. Expectations of your language skills are much higher than for non-Asians. Local Chinese are not entirely understanding of your efforts. To them, the simple matter is that you are Chinese and should, therefore, be able to speak Chinese. They don't hesitate to openly ask, "Why is your Mandarin so bad?"

Frankly, it's difficult to shrug off that type of directness at times. It can wear on you. As an American-born Chinese, I grew up in an English-speaking household. What little Mandarin I knew, I learned as an adult. I came to Asia with the sincere intention to develop my Mandarin abilities and better understand Chinese people and culture. When I arrived in Taipei, I was aware that my Mandarin was poor. I was conscientious and earnest in my efforts to improve it though. A language as difficult as Mandarin requires you to constantly practice it. I'd speak whenever I had the chance. It isn't always easy. Sometimes, it's just intimidating. As a result, there are times when the last thing I want to hear is someone criticize my Mandarin.

Although the upsides are apparent, coming back to the region for Asian-born returnees can also have its drawbacks. Ken Mui found it difficult to fit back into the local social scene after returning to Hong Kong, even though he grew up here and spoke native Cantonese. "I felt like a stranger in my own home," he recalls.

Ken moved to the U.S. at 17. He returned to Hong Kong 15 years later, working for General Electric. "I thought I'd be able to resume old friendships and easily get reacquainted with a place I was once familiar with. But my recollections of Hong Kong were idealistic and simple. The place has changed quite a bit, and so have I. I found myself out of touch with the cosmopolitan characteristics and capitalistic attitudes that now represent the place."

Harry Hui, regional managing director for Warner Chappell in Hong Kong believes there comes a point where Chinese Americans must decide whether they are here as a Chinese or as an American. He's made a conscious effort to adopt a more local lifestyle and social circle. "I feel natural doing business and socializing with local Chinese people. Given their growing presence and influence in all areas of business, the local integration helps in my ability to pursue goals I have in the region."

Double Standard

I used to work with a Caucasian friend from Connecticut. He arrived in Taipei in 1983, seven years earlier than myself. As partners in a business, we frequently visited local clients together, where we'd begin meetings conversing in Mandarin. My friend's Mandarin was not bad, perhaps even slightly better than mine. (Actually, I'm being very Chinese. I have to say I always felt I spoke better than him).

Whenever local clients heard his Mandarin for the first time, he would receive effusive praise over his fluency. On the other hand, I would immediately get reprimanded for speaking so poorly. It was like a conspiracy! I was never given credit for also going out of my way to learn a language non-native to me. Talk about eating humble pie. I would get my fill every time in those situations.

For Chinese Americans in Greater China, our differences and deficiencies are often pointed out by those people we make great efforts to be accepted by. If you're sensitive, or if you carry ideals about how completely you might fit in, you may be severely disappointed. Many locals you encounter may not understand or acknowledge your efforts in Asia, even after you've taken the time to share them in detail. It, therefore, becomes important to establish your identity and understand your reasons for being here. That way, you'll be less affected by pointed comments that may be unfair.

A Fish Out Of Water

Asia is by far the most challenging place I've ever lived. In fact, I've never before felt so inept and clueless, so often in my life. During my first year in Taipei, I would encounter one situation after another where I had little idea what was going on. By the end of each day, I was exhausted. My whole life had become incredibly more demanding. Professionally, I was doing the same job I did in the U.S., but in a second language I was not yet proficient in. Just figuring out how to apply my western skills and business approach to local situations was mentally draining.

That was only in the office. After work I was always wandering around in a daze. I couldn't read most signs or get around easily. I had difficulty doing basic things, such as mailing letters, ordering food, or buying movie tickets. Too often, I could barely understand what people were saying. When out with native Mandarin speakers, my entire focus was simply on trying to follow conversations. After a full day of translating in my head every sentence I heard from Chinese to English and then from English to Chinese, it's no wonder I was so wiped out every night.

Don't get me wrong, having the chance to face these types of challenges was exactly why I came to Asia in the first place. It was difficult and tiring, but the progress I made was also exciting and deeply satisfying. One benefit from functioning in a second culture and second language is that, if you're able to do it, you'll rarely feel intimidated by other challenges in life. Whenever I would struggle through my marketing presentations in Mandarin, I'd remind myself that if I ever went back to the U.S., doing the same job would be a snap.

Steve Eng, a manager at a direct investment firm in Hong Kong believes that working in Greater China has helped him develop a competitive edge. "Since I started doing business in China, I've developed more of a 'can do,' resourceful attitude," says Steve. "When it comes down to almost any task, I know I can get the job done. After the situations I've participated in over the last three years, there aren't many challenges I wouldn't be up for."

Job Hopping

I was reviewing the resume of a candidate applying for a corporate finance position in Hong Kong. He was 28 years old and seeking his fourth job in five years. His resume looked horrible. However, his frequent movement is not uncommon among people working in the region. It's easy to find yourself job hopping. For those with a good educational background and fundamental business skills, there's always another opportunity that pays higher. And there are always other jobs that sound more exciting and glamorous given the rate of expansion by multinationals. The result of such movement, however, can be damaging in the long run. For this candidate, he had quickly reached a point where his stability, commitment, and career objectives were all in question.

Sam Su is the vice president for North Asia of Tricon Restaurants International. He is the head of the region and country manager for China. At the time he took charge of China operations, there were four Kentucky Fried Chicken restaurants in China. Now, seven years later, he oversees over 200 locations.

Sam's advice on developing a career is straightforward. "Build solid, fundamental business skills. Be well-rounded and expand your comfort zone of abilities. I see too many young professionals go from one position to the next for incremental salary increases every year or two. It's short-sighted. Think about what the resume of a CEO looks like. They get to where they are by showing they can build a business and get substantial results. That takes at least three to five years to do in most situations. You shouldn't make career decisions based on what you can get now. You need to remember that your career is 30 or 40 years long. What does a few thousand dollars mean today compared to what you could make one day as a senior executive for a major company? Most important is to consider how much you can grow in each opportunity and to always prove yourself before moving on."

When the economic picture is bright, job hopping can appear to be a fast, easy way to escalate both your job title and salary. During periods of growth, it can seem like a shrewd approach to developing your career. But you shouldn't count on unending prosperity. Although the region's long-term economic signs are positive overall, inevitably there are downturns where the job market becomes tight. In such hard times, the situation for job hoppers becomes the most unstable. Their inflated salaries stand out as overpriced against the experience they provide. Their marketability becomes tenuous. That's when patience and perseverance stand out as desirable characteristics to have.

Chapter 15 The Financial Payoff

Throughout this book you've read about outstanding career opportunities and chances for advancement. There have also been several statements about the significantly better financial rewards for individuals working in Greater China in comparison to the U.S. But what exactly does "significantly better financial rewards" mean? Perhaps you may be a bit skeptical over just how good the financial picture is for those working in Greater China.

To be honest, when I began interviewing people for this book and would bring up the issue of financial gains, even I was shocked at some of the responses I heard. I'd ask people to compare their financial situation here to how they believed it would be in the U.S. "Much better out here," was the immediate response I almost always got. In nearly every case, no matter what they believed they could be making in the States, they clearly knew they were earning and saving considerably more in Greater China. This was despite the region's higher cost of living. In many cases, people claimed to make out two, three, even five times better than what they would be earning in the U.S. Some joked that they couldn't afford to leave. As one person said: "I'm getting paid a whole lot more than what I'd get in the U.S. It makes me kind of reluctant to go back."

Actually, the reasons for such outstanding financial payoffs stem from some basic, but compelling factors.

Larger Salary Increases — Where salary increases in the U.S. might average 4-8 percent a year because of a flatter economy, the growth of multinationals in the region is supporting salary increases that are typically double digit. Regular salary increases of even 20 percent or higher are not unheard of.

Quicker Promotional Tracks — Promotions that correspond to substantial salary jumps also happen much faster in Greater China. The middle to upper-middle management bottlenecks found in the U.S. do not exist in the region. If you're on the fast track in the U.S. you may get promoted every three years. Because of the shortage of quality managers, it's not unusual for promotions in Greater China to occur every 18 months or so.

Positions They Would Not Have In The States — The aggressive expansion of multinationals allows many people to move into business development roles that they were unable to break into in the U.S. Related to such front-line positions are performance or incentive components, even stock options, that were never seen while in operational or support positions back in the States.

Significantly Higher Net Income — When comparing financial compensation between the U.S. and Greater China, you need to look at net income. What counts is the money you put in your pocket after factoring in taxes, housing allowance, living expenses, and other benefits. In Greater China, this net amount is much greater.

To begin with, U.S. citizens working abroad are exempt from paying U.S. taxes on the first US$70,000 they earn. In addition, tax rates in Greater China are significantly lower. For example, Hong Kong's tax rate is a flat 15%. In a straightforward example, if you're earning US$50,000 in Hong Kong versus California, the combination of U.S. tax exemption and lower Hong Kong tax rate amounts to an additional US$10,000 in your bank account (assuming a 35 percent total tax rate for U.S. federal and state tax, and therefore a 20 percent savings on US$50,000). *(See Appendix VIII for Greater China Tax References.)*

In the mainland, some multinationals may even cover the China tax for foreign employees. This means that practically your entire salary goes directly into your bank account.

Case Studies

If you're still wary about the attractive financial payoffs in the region, this will help. The following are case studies based on three Chinese Americans who have worked in Greater China for several years. Each person was asked to compare their current financial situation to the financial scenario they might face if had they remained in the U.S. I have intentionally selected middle management level cases which are not considered extraordinary, but are reflective of the situations Chinese Americans are realizing in the region. *None of these candidates are on U.S. expat packages.* They are compensated in accordance with their responsibilities and performance.

Candidate A

While in the U.S., Candidate A was on a steady career track in product development for a major computer company. After five years in this line of work, she attained the level of product manager. Before moving to Hong Kong, she spent three years pursuing a front-line, marketing position that would give her greater direct interface with customers and responsibilities for developing and managing business. She obtained an MBA while working full-time in order to pursue this goal. Unfortunately, even after receiving her business degree, the candidate was unable to attain the opportunity she sought within her company. Her situation changed after she moved to Hong Kong.

Four years later, she is the regional marketing manager for a U.S. software products and services company in Hong Kong. "The marketing and business management track I'm on now was not one I was seeing in the States," she says. "Out here, I've found much better chances to develop my career in that direction." She is 32 years old.

		U.S.	Hong Kong	
Base salary	*(projected, after 9 yrs in prod dvlpmt)*	$80,000	$90,000	*(actual)*
Performance bonus from business/sales growth			$22,500	*(candidate received a 25% bonus for 1997)*
Hong Kong tax			($16,875)	*(15% flat tax rate, $112,500 x 15%)*
California state/ U.S. federal tax	*(about 36%/10% or 46%)*	($36,800)	($6,800)	*($70,000 U.S. tax exemption, $42,500 x 16%*)*
House/monthly rent	*($1,250/mth x 12 mths)*	($15,000)	($30,000)	*($2,500/mth x 12 mths)*
	Net	**$28,200**	**$58,825**	

* *Overseas employees pay U.S. taxes only on the amount above US$70,000. In addition, only the differential is paid beyond what has already been paid in Hong Kong taxes (i.e. .31 – .15 = .16). Finally, no state taxes are paid on income earned outside the U.S.*

** *All numbers reflect US$ amounts*

Candidate B

Candidate B worked in the U.S. for five years in retail sales. Looking to leverage his Mandarin fluency, he moved to Taiwan in 1991, where he worked in sales and marketing roles for five years in two major consumer goods companies. In 1996, he accepted an offer in Shanghai as a marketing manager covering northern China for a large fast-moving consumer products multinational.

"I was doing well in the U.S., but I couldn't see where that success was leading. I felt like just another super sales person in the company," he reveals. "Out here, I feel the potential to rise into a general manager role is much more achievable for me." Candidate B is 33 years old.

He does not receive a U.S. expat package, but receives what is known as a third country national (TCN) package, a compensation package designed for local hires expatriated to another country in the region. In a typical TCN package, the company offers a U.S. comparable base salary, hardship allowance and/or cost of living adjustment, and housing. The company may also often equalize or cover China taxes for the employee.

		U.S.	China	
Base salary	*(projected, includes sales performance bonus)*	$100,000	$100,000	*(actual)*
Hardship allowance/ Cost of living adjustment			$20,000	*(20% of base salary)*
China tax			$0	*(company covers China tax)*
California state/ U.S. federal tax	*(about 36%/10% or 46%)*	($46,000)	($15,500)	*($70,000 U.S. tax exemption, $50,000 x .31)*
House/monthly rent	*($1250/mth x 12 mths)*	($15,000)	$0	*(housing paid by company)*
	Net	**$39,000**	**$104,500**	

Candidate C

Candidate C began his career as an auditor with a Big Six accounting firm in the U.S. After four years, he reached the level of audit manager. In early 1994, he moved to Hong Kong and landed a corporate finance position in a regional bank. Today, he is a vice president in corporate finance for a European bank. "I don't believe what

I'm doing now would have been available to me in the States, where it's a difficult switch to make from auditing," he admits. "When I came here, my timing was good and my Chinese language skills really made a difference." Candidate C is 30 years old.

		U.S.	Hong Kong	
Base salary	*(projected, after 8 yrs on a partner track)*	$85,000	$100,000	*(actual)*
End-of-year bonus			$60,000	*(candidate received a $60,000 year-end bonus for 1997)*
Hong Kong tax			($24,000)	*(15% flat tax rate, $160,000 x 15%)*
California state/ U.S. federal tax	*(about 36%/10% or 46%)*	($39,100)	($18,900)	*($70,000 U.S. tax exemption, $90,000 x .21*)*
House/monthly rent	*($1,250/mth x 12 mths)*	($15,000)	($30,000)	*($2,500/mth x 12 mths)*
	Net	**$30,900**	**$87,100**	

* *Given a U.S. federal tax rate of 36%, the candidate would pay U.S. taxes at a rate of, .36 – .15 = .21.*

Local Compensation — As Good Or Better Than The U.S.

I've mentioned in several places that multinationals are moving away from expatriate packages for most positions. How then are people here doing so well financially? Most companies are no longer paying premium packages to hire staff in Asia. Instead, they have gone over to what is termed a "localized package." This essentially translates to mean internationally competitive salaries with an amount added for cost of living adjustment or housing subsidy.

The term "local package" or "local terms" is misleading. These "local" salaries are competitive, and in most cases better than salaries in other international markets. According to the World Executive's Digest for April 1997, Hong Kong's managers have surpassed Tokyo's as the highest paid in Asia. In terms of purchasing power, they have outstripped those of any other country in the world. Companies are aware of how expensive it is to live in the region. Adjustments for housing and cost of living are typically factored into a total salary figure.

The key to looking at compensation in Greater China is to remember that financial rewards come to those who can show performance. If your company is not willing to compensate you for your value, then there are other firms that will. Greater China's headhunting industry is an active and aggressive one. Good people become known and are actively pursued. We always tell newcomers to Greater China to look for a fair compensation level, one that does not significantly compromise the lifestyle you're accustomed to. With this perspective in mind, the salary issue should not be a major factor when you first come out *(see Appendix IX for Greater China Salary Compensation Ranges).*

Part V

The Wrap Up

Chapter 16 The Long-Term Opportunity: Bridging The East And The West

The first time I realized how well-suited Chinese Americans are for serving as a bridge between the U.S. and Greater China was during a trip to Los Angeles in 1993. This was during the days before Wang & Li, when I was working in a small technology consulting firm. I had just finished my second year in Taipei and hadn't been back to the States in nearly a year.

The return trip was a personal visit, but I happened to have a meeting with the international vice president and the general manager of a growing telecommunications company in Los Angeles. They were thinking about marketing and distributing products in Taiwan. They had never been to Taipei though and knew little about the country's telecommunications infrastructure, state of technology, or presence of other telecom firms. The encounter was an unexpected eye opener.

In my second year in Taipei, I still struggled to master Mandarin and fit into the local business culture. Although I had made significant progress, I felt deficient in both what I knew and what I could do. In many ways, it still felt like I was swimming upstream.

During that meeting, however, my IQ seemed to jump 100 points. Suddenly, I was transformed from a Greater China outsider to Marco Polo, Asia expert. Everything I had to say was revealing and insightful to my audience. I was able to tell them which multinationals were already in Taiwan, what their presence and mode of operations was (i.e. joint venture, wholly-owned subsidiary, distributor relationship), and who the major local players were. I could even tell them the regulatory bodies they had to deal with in order to do business there.

During that meeting, my IQ seemed to jump 100 points. Suddenly, I was transformed from a Greater China outsider to Marco Polo, Asia expert. Everything I had to say was revealing and insightful to my audience.

The best part about the meeting was that I didn't do any research beforehand. What I told them were just things I knew from living and working in Taipei. The daily knowledge I had accumulated and took for granted suddenly became pearls of wisdom. What I didn't know, I knew where and how to find the answers. I felt like a genius.

Three things became apparent to me at that time. The first was that there was a tremendous lack of information and knowledge about Greater China among companies and individuals in the U.S. The region is still a black hole for most. For U.S. parties, the obstacles for doing business in the region are basic, but significant ones. What resources are available? What expertise already exists? How does one access them?

The second was that the marketing of Greater China and its capabilities to the United States is practically nonexistent. Despite the regional expertise, services, and information that are available, they are effectively communicated abroad by few individuals or companies.

Think about it. If you want to do business in Greater China, whom could you think to contact and work with? Perhaps some major multinationals that you'd assume would have Asia operations. For instance, if you were looking for consulting support to help you enter a new market in the region, firms like McKinsey & Company, Booz Allen & Hamilton, or AT Kearney may come to mind.

These firms are all unquestionably proven and highly respected. But what is their actual regional expertise? What is their local knowledge in your industry? Do they have the connections to channels and resources that can open doors to local markets? And beyond their capabilities, can every company or party wanting to do business in Asia afford the fees that these large consulting firms charge for an engagement?

In fact, there are many other highly competent consulting services available in Greater China that are equally, if not more knowledgeable about local markets and business. These are firms whose businesses are rooted and solely focused in Asia. Their expertise and professional practices are equivalent to those offered by multinationals, since the people in these companies are themselves originally from those same multinational firms. They've moved on to begin their own business or to be a part of a smaller organization.

Identifying these alternative resources is unlikely, however, because their existence outside of Asia is virtually unknown. The consulting industry example can be easily repeated for other services and industries. Whom would you seek out for regional investment advice, marketing expertise, business development support, or partnering resources? It's a common problem faced by U.S. companies wanting to do business in the region.

The last realization made clear from that meeting was that the two U.S. managers I met felt very comfortable dealing with me. I spoke their language, could key into their issues, and understood their thinking. I could even speak with them about baseball, movies, politics, and a wide range of other common topics. Most importantly, I could tell them what they wanted to know about the business environment they were targeting. To them, I was a Greater China insider.

Bridging The Gap

North America has a tremendous array of products, services, technologies, and skills it would like to introduce to Asia. Greater China is now able to afford these things to help raise its overall standard of living and quality of life. The challenge is the difficulty for parties from both sides to find and cooperate with each other. There is a deficiency and critical need for individuals and services that can deliver regional expertise and market access to U.S. businesses. A unique opportunity presents itself. In response, Chinese Americans are well-positioned to bridge the gap.

Not every company seeking to do business in Asia is a Fortune 1000 company in size. There are many successful, established firms with annual revenues in the tens to hundreds of million dollars, who need local expertise and services to help them build their business in the region. These firms are open to working through more affordable, alternative resources than what large multinationals offer.

Pacific Advantage is one such resource, an information technology services firm based in Hong Kong that assists U.S. technology firms wanting to enter the region. Pacific Advantage was started by Wayne Merrick and Hali Tsang in 1994. Both Wayne and Hali left behind their twelve-year corporate jobs to go out on their own. Their plan was to play an agent role to introduce U.S. companies to regional product distributors and resellers, and to provide marketing, sales, and support consultancy services within the relationship. Their main assets when they began were a Rolodex of business cards of regional contacts and a knowledge of technology needs in Asia.

Today, Pacific Advantage has exclusive product distribution relationships with ten U.S. companies who produce a range of wireless LAN (local area networks), wireless radio, computer hardware and software, and Internet products. Their clients, like NovaSoft Systems, Sync Research, and Acadia, each have annual revenues ranging from US$10–50 million. All successfully sell their products in North America and Europe.

Now, these companies are hungry to enter the Asia Pacific region. Yet, they know little about how to penetrate the market or operate here. That's where Pacific Advantage comes in. They provide a cost effective, low risk, results-oriented approach for companies to gain a foothold in Asia. Ultimately, Pacific Advantage helps its U.S. clients set up distribution channels and local partnerships spanning from China and Japan to India and Australia.

Despite minimal marketing effort, Pacific Advantage is actively sought by numerous information technology companies pursuing the Asia market. Their capabilities and services have spread through the word-of-mouth references of clients. With each new client they take on today, they consider more than 10 proposals that try to persuade Pacific Advantage to work with them.

An International Leadership Role

In Greater China, Chinese Americans are in an opportune position to apply our backgrounds and abilities to their full potential and to attain professional success and meaningful personal goals while doing so. But beyond what we can accomplish as

Norman Chen: Back to the Future

Personal History: *Born in Minnesota. Raised in Maryland. Living in Asia since April 1992.*

Parents: *Mom and Dad originally from Mainland China, and then Taiwan.*

Education: *B.S. in Biology from Massachusetts Institute of Technology. M.B.A. from Stanford University.*

Languages: *Native English speaker. Parents spoke Mandarin at home while he was growing up.*

Normen Chen during a vacation in Kyoto, Japan (August 1996)

"Back To The Future" is how Norman Chen describes the idea he came up with three years ago to set up a network of U.S.-quality, specialized medical centers in Asia. "Essentially, the U.S. healthcare industry is 10 to 15 years ahead of Asia's healthcare industry," explains Norman. "By knowing how medical centers have operated successfully in the States, in a sense I've seen the potential and future of healthcare in Asia. If you can just transfer the existing, proven western technology and management know-how, then high-quality medical centers in the region can also be set up and run effectively and economically."

Norman's business concept grew out of his years in healthcare, which originally began in the U.S. After completing his MBA in 1991, Norman took a position as a business development manager for a leading hospital supply company in the U.S. When his company began expanding more aggressively in Asia, he was appointed as the regional marketing manager for the Asia Pacific region. "Even in that first position, one of my key roles was being the information link between the Asia operations and U.S. headquarters," Norman recalls.

Two years later, Norman became a sales director in Guangzhou where he was responsible for business in Mainland China and Hong Kong. Although he had no previous sales experience, he was given a chance to manage a 15-person sales force. He did this successfully for another two years. Over a Thanksgiving dinner gathering with friends, he met someone who was working for a venture capital firm. The person happened to be looking for a direct investment manager specializing in healthcare. One conversation led to another. A few months later, Norman was asked to join the firm.

The chance to bring his medical center idea to life came about soon afterwards. While looking at venture capital proposals during his first year, he put his concept into a business proposal and presented it to the other partners. They liked it. So did four other "blue-chip" investors, including a leading chain of medical centers in the U.S. Together, they invested in Norman's new company — ARC Limited — which is now building and managing centers in Taiwan, the Philippines and other Asian countries. "Because we know what's happened in the U.S. market, we are able to position ARC as a leader in quality and cost management in Asia."

Norman also credits his Chinese American background for his ability to bring together both sides. "I'm not a medical doctor, and I've never directly managed a healthcare clinic before," admits Norman. "What I've done is utilize my bicultural background and experience to identify an opportunity, develop the concept, and package it together in a feasible way. I'm also able to leverage my U.S. healthcare contacts, knowledge of Asia's healthcare markets, and ability to get things done between the two sides. In a sense, I'm providing the glue to the whole puzzle."

individuals, what are the possibilities that can be achieved as a community during this special time?

Chinese Americans have always tried to play a larger, more influential role within America's domestic scene. An ongoing effort has been made to integrate, overcome barriers, and strive for status and recognition. Although the achievements of Chinese Americans in the States have been significant, what has the overall impact been on the politics, economic development, and social trends of the U.S.?

With sights firmly set on competing in the United States, I believe many Chinese Americans overlook the chance to participate on a playing field where the rules and conditions are in our favor and where the ball is in our court. In Greater China, the opportunity exists for Chinese Americans to bypass the U.S. scene and play a leadership role within a larger international one. There is a window open where Chinese Americans can have an impact at a worldwide level, as facilitators between the East and the West.

Occupying the Middle Ground

A tighter, increasingly interdependent relationship continues to develop between North America and Greater China. "We could be the missing link to help bring China to the world ... or the world to China," proclaims a Chinese American entrepreneur stationed in Shanghai. "Our role can be potentially as diverse and large as we want it to be." I believe this statement holds a great deal of truth.

There is a critical middle ground that needs to be bridged in many areas. Companies, businessmen, educators, artists, and everyday people from both sides are all trying to better understand and cooperate with each other. Currently, few parties possess the skills, experience, and knowledge to manage the increasingly diverse interests between Greater China and the United States. There is a void that exists. As long as there is an interface of products, services, technology, and management between the East and the West, this niche will continue to present itself, and even grow.

There is a unique opportunity for Chinese Americans as a community to occupy that middle ground. It's a natural place for us to contribute a great deal of value. The result of our participation in this highly visible and critical place is the chance to distinguish ourselves and catapult our presence and influence into areas of society we have always sought to participate more actively and visibly in.

Epilogue

Each person's experience in Greater China is a highly personal and life-long lasting one. When people ask me why I enjoy living here, I have a difficult time pinpointing a single reason. One is, I've been able to develop a second language that I feel is important for me to know. I'm thrilled that I can now communicate with about a billion more people than when I first arrived. Each day I'm here, I'm also challenged to grow and learn new things about Chinese people and Chinese culture.

But perhaps the most gratifying reason relates directly to my family and Chinese heritage. For my grandparents, parents, aunts, and uncles, their lives were relatively pre-determined as soon as they immigrated to America from China. As new arrivals, their objective was clear-cut. Their sole option was to work hard and make a better life for themselves and their families. They accomplished this with flying colors.

For my siblings and me, we've had it much easier. We've had more choices and greater opportunities. Yet, despite our good fortune, I often felt at a loss over what I was doing with my life. Although it was never overtly impressed upon me, I've always felt the presence of my family's achievements in both Asia and the United States. I used to always wonder what my upbringing, education, and persona were meant to be applied towards? This was a tough question to answer.

Since coming to Greater China, I feel a much deeper sense of purpose. In an odd way, through my presence here, I feel I bring back with me much of what my grandparents and parents would want to share if they could participate in Greater China's resurgence. It's rewarding to be a part of a place where I feel my efforts can make a difference, whatever those efforts may be. And I feel good knowing that I'm applying myself in a place that my family is connected to and proud of as well. Although such feelings may fall dangerously close to being classified under "the warm and fuzzies," they are as meaningful as any I have about anything.

In interviewing people for this book, I came across one inspiring story after another. It is gratifying to see many other Chinese Americans find their own fulfillment through their presence and involvement in Greater China. I believe that the potential of the Chinese American community in the region is enormous. For Chinese Americans everywhere, I hope the successes seen out here are something they can support and feel proud of.

Appendix I Greater China Holiday Schedules*

1998 Hong Kong Holidays	
New Year's Day	1/1
Lunar New Year's Day	1/28-30
Day after Ching Ming Festival	4/6
Easter Holiday	4/10-13
SAR Establishment Day	7/1
Sino-Japanese War Victory Day	8/17
National Day Holiday	10/1-2
Day after Mid-Autumn Festival	10/6
Chung Yeung Festival	10/28
Christmas Day	12/25-26

1998 Mainland China Holidays	
New Year's Day	1/1
Lunar New Year's Day	1/28-30
International Working Women's Day	3/8
International Labor Day	5/1
Youth Day	5/4
Children's Day	6/1
Anniversary of the Founding of the Communist Party of China	7/1
Anniversary of the Founding of the PLA	8/1
National Day	10/1-2

1998 Taiwan Holiday	
New Year's Day	1/1-2
Eve of Lunar New Year	1/27
Lunar New Year	1/28
Day of Peace	2/28
Youth Day	3/29
Teacher's Day	9/28
National Day	10/5
Dr. Sun Yat-Sen's Birthday	11/12
Constitution Day	12/25

* *The exact date for some holidays may vary from year to year.*

** *Please check with your contacts in the region for final verification of holiday days.*

Appendix II Pager and Mobile Phone Services

Hong Kong

Star Telecom

G/F, 414 Kwun Tong Road, Star Telecom Tower, Kwun Tong, Kowloon
Tel: (852) 7116 8111

Pager Services and Rates:
Standard Services: HK$250/month

Secretary Services (professional answering): HK$290/month

Auto Paging (connection within in one minute): HK$320/month

HK$10, plus the service charges that you choose. HK$418 deposit. HK$75 license fee. Must pay two months of service charges in advance. HK$325 to buy the pager (includes the service charges and licenses fee).

Hutchison

2/F, 147 Johnston Road, Wanchai
Tel: (852) 2919 2134

Mobile Phone Rental Services:
Package A: 1st week GSM mobile phone and HK$500 SIM card rental: HK$780 per week

Package B: 1st week GSM mobile phone and HK$500 SIM card rental and HK$100 Hello phonecard: HK$830 per week

Package C: Package A + Package B and HK$88 Netcard, valid for 10 hours of local Internet access (includes PNETS charges): HK$880/week

HK$3,000 mobile phone rental deposit. HK$4/ minute for local calls. Mobile phone rental extension is K$280/week. No re-fill SIM Card services. You must purchase a new one.

Taipei

QIQI Communications Co.

Zhongxiao East Road, Section 4, Lane 223, #36, 2nd Floor, Taipei
Tel: (886) (02) 2775 3333
Fax: (886) (02) 2741 7421

Pager Services and Rates:
Standard Services: NT$200/day
NT$3,000 pager deposit required.

Mobile Phone Rental Services:
Domestic Rental
Daily rates: NT$800/day and NT$40/minute
Monthly rates: NT$500/day and NT$25/minute

International Rental
Daily rates: NT$800/day and NT$150/minute
Monthly rates: NT$500/day and NT$100/minute

NT$20,000 mobile phone rental deposit required (credit card imprint will be returned/ destroyed upon mobile phone return). Free delivery to renter's location.

Beijing/Shanghai

Phone Rent

Beijing: (Tel) 86 10 6422 9334/5
Shanghai: (Tel) 86 21 6249 2828

Pager Rental Rates:
Package A (with English message takers): RMB60/day; RMB250/week; RMB500month

Package B (Integrated Voice + Fax Mailboxes): RMB25/day (1–7 days); RMB16/day (8–30 days); RMB8/day (1 month or more)

RMB800 pager deposit required. No charges for usage. For 10% more on the rental fee, the user gets 24-hour access to an English help-line, information, translation, and booking services.

Mobile Phone Rates:

Rental Period	Mobile phone/day (RMB)	SIM card/day (RMB)
1-3 days	280	190
4-7 days	250	170
8-14 days	210	140
15-30 days	150	100
>1 month	120	80
>2 months	105	70
>4 months	80	55
>8 months	55	40
>12 months	40	30
Deposit	4,000	2,000

All amounts are exclusive of traffic costs (air-time) for the calls you make and receive. Traffic costs are charged to your credit card and will include 20.5% tax and service charges. Delivery/collection: Beijing or Shanghai/RMB60 each way, Shanghai Pudong area/RMB90 each way. Delivery/collection is free of charge for rental period more than seven days. Hong Kong drop off charge is RMB150.

Appendix III Helpful Greater China Associations And Resources

Hong Kong

American Chamber of Commerce in Hong Kong

Room 1904, Bank of America Tower,
12 Harcourt Road, Central
Tel: (852) 2526 0165
Fax: (852) 2810 1289
Website: http://www.amcham.org.hk
Contact: Jennifer Li - Executive Assistant
Events: Happy hour event, last Thursday of every month at JJ's at the Grand Hyatt in Wanchai
Directory: Mailing price to members HK$830/ non-members HK$1,530

Canadian Chamber of Commerce in Hong Kong

1602 Sin Hua Bank Building, 2-8 Wellington Street, Central
Tel: (852) 2110 8700
Fax: (852) 2110 8701
Website: http://www.cancham.com.hk
Contact: Mr. Andrew Work - Membership Director
Events: Happy hour event, 1st Friday of every month at Mr. Rhino Restaurant in Central
Directory: To be available after March 1998.

Organization of Chinese Americans (OCA)

GPO Box 9472, Hong Kong
Tel: (852) 2583 6577
Fax: (852) 2877 5288
Contact: Mike Wu - President
Events: 2nd & 4th Friday of every month at Winners Sport Bar at Lan Kwai Fong

Taiwan

American Chamber of Commerce in Taipei

Suite 1012, Chia Hsin Building Annex, 96 Chung Shan North Road, Taipei 104, Taiwan, Republic of China
Tel: (886) (02) 2581 7089
Fax: (886) (02) 2542 3376
Website: http://www.amcham.com.tw
Contact: Justine Liu - Manager of Member
Directory: US$35 for members, US$53 for non-members

Chinese American Professionals in Taiwan

3rd Floor, Hsin Yi Road, Section 3, Taipei
Website: http://www.capt.org.tw
Contact: Christine Hsu - Chairman
Events: Monthly happy hour event (check website for locations and times)

The Canadian Society in Taiwan

13/F, 365 Fu-Hsing North Road, Taipei
Tel: (886) (02) 2514 9477
Fax: (886) (02) 2712 7244
Website: http://www.ctot.org.tw
Contact: Lee Ting - Executive Director
Events: Social night/No regular place and date. Depends on the in-charge of Society.

Community Services Center

(Serving the expatriate community of Taiwan)
Chung Shan North Road, Section 6, Lane 290, # 25, Taipei
Tel: (886) (02) 2836 8134
Fax: (886) (02) 2835 2530
Contact: Jane Sispeosom

* *All information confirmed as of February 1, 1998.*

Mainland China

American Chamber of Commerce in Beijing

Great Wall Sheraton Hotel, #352, Zhao Yi District, Dong San Huan North Road, Beijing
Tel: (86) (10) 6500 5566 x 2378
Fax: (86) (10) 6501 8273
Website: Launch at Mid-February
Contact: Susan Allison - Assistant Director
Events: Happy hour event, 1st Thursday of every month at San Francisco Brewing Company
Directory: No charges for members, US$100 for non-members

American Chamber of Commerce in Shanghai

4/F Portman Hotel, 1376 Nanying Xi Lu, Shanghai, China 200040
Tel: (86) (21) 6279 7119
Fax: (86) (21) 6279 8802
Website: http://www.amcham.online.sh.cn
Contact: Julie Chang Holt - Program Manager
Events: Information meeting, 1st Tuesday of every month at US Commercial Centre. Membership mixer on last Wednesday of every month
Directory: US$35 for members & non-members

American Business Association in Guangzhou (ABAG)

c/o Mr. Ed King/Proctor & Gamble, Guangzhou
Tel: (86) (20) 778 2888 x 5034
Fax: (86) (20) 777 0688

United States

U.S. Chamber of Commerce

1615 H Street, N.W., Washington D.C. 20062-200
Tel: (1) (202) 463 5464
Fax: (1) (202) 463 3114
Website: http://www.uschamber.com
Contact: Melissa Doumitt - Publication Coordinator
Directory: Membership directories for all international AmChams can be purchased directly from the U.S. Chamber.

Appendix IV Helpful Greater China Job Search Websites

Internet News Resources	
Apple Daily Online (Hong Kong - Chinese)	http://www.appledaily.com
Central News Agency (Taiwan - Chinese/English)	http://www.taipei.org/teco/cicc/news
China News Services (China - Chinese/English)	http://www.chinanews.com
China Times Inter@ctive (Taiwan - Chinese)	http://www.chinatimes.com.tw
Commercial Times (Taiwan - Chinese)	http://www.infotimes.com
Commonwealth Magazine (Taiwan - Chinese)	http://www.cw.com.tw
Far Eastern Economic Review Interactive (Asia - English)	http://www.feer.com
Hongkong Standard (Hong Kong - English)	http://www.hkstandard.com
Inside China Today (China - English)	http://www.insidechina.com
Lianhe Zaobao (China - Chinese)	http://www.asia1.com.sg/zaobao
Ming Pao Electronic News (Hong Kong - Chinese)	http://www.mingpao.com/newspaper
Singtao Daily (Hong Kong - Chinese)	http://www.singtao.com
South China Morning Post (Hong Kong - English)	http://www.scmp.com

Greater China Job Listings Sites	
Sinanet Job Bank	http://ww5.sinanet.com/jobs
Escape Artist	http://www.escapeartist.com/jobs7/asia.htm
Career Mosaic Hong Kong	http://www.careermosaic.com.hk
JobAsia	http://www.jobasia.com
Asia-Net	http://www.asia-net.com
Asian Mall - Top Jobs in Asia	http://www.asianmall.com/jobs
JobChina.net	http://www.jobchina.net
China Cyber City Tech	http://www.ccctech.com/career/

Recruiting Firm Sites	
Wang & Li Asia Resources	http://www.wang-li.com
China Executive Search	http://www.china-executives.com
Pacific Bridge	http://www.pacificbridge.com
Executive Access	http://www.hk.net/~eal
Job Access Limited	http://www.jobaccess.com
Recruit Online	http://www.recruitonline.com

Company Research Sites	
Hoover's Online	http://www.hoovers.com
Companies Online	http://www.companiesonline.com
EDGAR Online	http://www.edgar-online.com

Networking Organization Sites

American Chamber of Commerce in Taipei	http://www.amcham.com.tw
American Chamber of Commerce in Hong Kong	http://www.amcham.org.hk
Chinese American Professionals in Taiwan	http://www.capt.org.tw

Asian/Asian-American Content Internet Sites

Channel A	http://www.channela.com
ABCFlash	http://www.abcflash.com
Dynetek Infoworld	http://www.info168.com
AsiaOne	http://www.asia1.com
Chinese Cyber City	http://www.ccchome.com

Others Sites Worth Visiting

Expatriate Resources Abroad	http://www.escapeartist.com/expatriate7
Taxes for Expats	http://www.escapeartist.com/expatriate6
International Moving Information	http://www.escapeartist.com/moving
Embassy Pages	http://www.escapeartist.com/embassy1
Currency Converter	http://www.xe.net/currency
Interactive Map of Asia	http://city.net/regions/asia/maps
Asian Stock Exchanges	http://www.asianmall.com/arc/stock

Hip Greater China Spots On The Net

WebHK in the Corner (a news & lifestyle guide to Hong Kong)	http://www.corner.com
Shanghai-ed.com (a guide to life & business in "China's greatest city")	http://www.shanghai-ed.com
Beijing Scene (a guide to living & doing business in Beijing)	http://www.beijingscen.com

* *Website addresses confirmed as of February 1, 1998.*

Appendix V A Four Cities Comparison

	Hong Kong	Taipei
Most Suited For ...	• Those who like to work hard, play hard • Those seeking a highly westernized Chinese society • Those seeking dynamic and challenging business environment/regional opportunities	• Those who like to work hard, play hard • Those seeking a submerged, traditional Chinese culture/ society, blended with increasing western influences • Those seeking a steadily evolving business environment
Economic Stats ... • *Urban Population* • *Per Capita GNP* • *GDS (% of GNP)* • *Int'l Reserves* • *US$ Exchange R*	 • 6.1 million • US$21,556 • 4.7% • US$57.31 billion • US$1 = HK$7.7	 • 5.3 million • US$12,439 • 6.6% • US$85.18 billion • US$1 = NTD32.4
Predominant Languages Used ...	• Cantonese • English • Mandarin	• Mandarin • English • Taiwanese
Living Environment ...	• Weather is like Taipei's, though breezier • Residents tend to be more status conscious and materialistic than their regional neighbors • Crowded, cosmopolitan, and efficiently run • Locals/foreigners don't often mix	• Cool/cold winters. Humid summers • Residents known to be down-to-earth/friendly. Relative to HK-ers, perhaps not as worldly • Crowded, polluted and heavily trafficked city • Locals/foreigners more integrated than in Hong Kong
Quality of Life ...	• Keeps pace with western countries • Cosmopolitan. Many things run orderly and efficiently • Fast-paced, dynamic, and high pressure business environment • Diverse/international culture and people • Foreign community large, but relatively tight	• Good, but still lags behind HK • Chinese/local flavor, but internationalizing • Disorderly, but things somehow get done • Hardworking business culture. More homogeneous population • Small/close-knit foreign community. Many Mandarin-studyers/English teachers

Shanghai	Singapore
• Those who work hard • Those seeking submersion in a 'pure' Chinese culture that is quickly internationalizing • Those seeking changing and always-challenging business environment/ opportunities	• Those who can stand the heat • Those seeking a highly Westernized/ international society & culture • Those seeking exciting Southeast Asia-oriented business environment/ opportunities
• 14.1 million • US$1,990 • 8% • US$82.7 billion • US$1 = RMB8.3	• 3.0 million • S$36,719 • 7.0% • US$70.28 billion • US$1 = S$1.6
• Mandarin • Shanghainese	• English — "Official" language • Mandarin — "Official" Chinese language
• Cold winters. Hot, but not-too-humid summers • Residents are reputed to be aggressive & smart, particularly in business • Local/foreign communities are not integrated • A double standard exists for foreigners, who are given special treatment	• Subtropical/balmy, with temps in the high 80s year round • Residents are friendly and helpful • Crowded, cosmopolitan and efficiently operated • International environment, with a good integration of the Chinese, Malay, Indian and foreign communities
• Improving • Most cosmopolitan/international city in China, but still distinctly Chinese • Infrastructure/living conditions improving rapidly • Nightlife limited, but growing • Culture and people more homogenous in nature • Foreign community fairly small, but growing	• Keeps pace w/western standards • Cosmopolitan/slightly more international than Hong Kong • Everything runs orderly and efficiently • Dynamic/high pressure business environment • Diverse/international city. Though has no one dominant culture, heavily influenced by Chinese, Malay and Indian cultures • Large, fragmented expat community

	Hong Kong	Taipei
Activities ... • *Athletics*	• Confined indoors for lack of large open spaces in the city • Indoor/outdoor facilities available, but can be pricey	• Traffic limits running/cycling • Ultimate frisbee/softball/volleyball teams to join • Clubs are available, but pricey
• *Nightlife*	• Bustling — dance clubs, bars, KTVs, but gets very expensive • Foreign social scene centers around Lan Kwai Fong/Wan Chai	• Bustling — dance clubs, beer/ jazz pubs, pool halls, KTVs, bowling alleys — expensive
• *Organizations/ Associations*	• Professional/social groups cater to wide range of interests	• Growing, but still limited • Caters to older expats
• *Art & Culture*	• Activities and facilities widely available and suit all interests	• Extensive Chinese art collections. Growing art/culture scene
Housing ...	• 2–3 bedrooms, 25% smaller than US sizes, for US$2,000–4,000 • Many share apartments for US$700–1000 each	• 2–3 bedrooms (of reasonable size) within US$1,500–2,300 • Many share apartments for US$400–600 each
Food ...	• Great variety. Restaurants among best in the world for local and international selections	• Local food is excellent and reasonably priced. Diverse foreign fare, but expensive
Degree of Westernization ... *(on a 1 to 10 scale — 10 being equivalent to life in the US)*	**9:** • Has remained "the West" in Asia for a long time. • Many live a fully sheltered/ western lifestyle	**7:** • Society still very Chinese • Westernization hasn't overrun the society
Cost of Living ... *(Based on figures from Corporate Resources Group survey (1997) with NYC =100)*	**153:** EXPENSIVE • Nightlife/western restaurant eating is very expensive • HK-ers reputed to lead high-spending lifestyles	**116:** EXPENSIVE • Nightlife/western restaurant eating can be very expensive • Best bargain a local call using a public phone (3 min = NT$1)
Getting Around ...	• Very easy: Buses, taxis, mass transit convenent/inexpensive • During rush hour, gridlock can make walking more preferable • Cars not necessary or practical	• Easy: Convenient if you can speak/read Chinese • Limited mass transit service • Moderately priced/plentiful taxis • Traffic bad at rush hour

Shanghai	Singapore
• Tennis courts available at hotels or clubs • Few health clubs. Those available are expensive • Golfing inconvenient	• Scuba diving/watersports popular. Heat often prohibits other outdoor activities • Club facilities available, but can be very pricey
• Limited — but western bars, pubs, and restaurants increasing • Yes, there's even a Tony Roma's! • Your chances to be a KTV king/queen!	• Bustling — clubs/bars are popular (and expensive) nightime entertainment • Boat quay, an outdoor eating and drinking area, attracts lively after-work crowd
• Professional groups cater to business community	• Professional groups cater to largely older, senior expatriate groups
• Art and cultural activities limited, but historical places of interest abound	• Activities are widely available. Government encourages appreciation of the arts
• Foreign housing supply has increased, dropping prices over the past year • 1 bedroom apartments start at UD$1,500 • Housing much cheaper in suburbs	• 2–3 bedrooms for upwards of US$2,800 • Studios available beginning at US$2,500 • Many foreigners receive some housing allowance from employers
• Local food good and cheap • Western selection limited, expensive	• Numerous restaurants to choose from • Foods from SE Asia, North Asia and the West to suit any palate
3: • Society still very Chinese/Shanghainese • Small/fragmented western community	**9:** • Its British colony origins, diverse base of citizens, & large expat population make it an international/westernized Asian place
136: EXPENSIVE • Nightlife and western restaurant eating can be very expensive • Smart people keep costs down by avoiding government regulations	**127:** EXPENSIVE • Nightlife and western restaurants expensive • Alcohol is very pricey • Shopping (a national past-time, given the number of stores) can also get expensive
• Easy: Taxis are a real bargain • Walking and cycling usually faster than cars within the city • Buses packed and slow. Should be avoided	• Very easy. Excellent/inexpensive mass transit • Taxis can be hard to get. Added charge to restricted zones or at rush hour • Cars prohibitively expensive

Appendix VI Greater China Mandarin Language Programs

Among those who have studied Mandarin in Asia, the majority opinion is that the language programs and quality of the teaching in Taipei is better than in China. Taipei instruction tends to be more western style, while teaching in China relies more on rote memorization. Teachers in China also have a reputation for being less motivated. The upside to studying in China is the cultural experience of living in the mainland. Many who begin in a language program in China eventually find it more productive to hire a tutor for more focused and disciplined private sessions.

Mainland China

Beijing Foreign Language and Cultural University (formerly Beijing Language Institute)

Contact Information: *Office Address:* The Admission Office for Foreign Students, Beijing Language and Cultural University, 15 Xueyuan Road, Haidian District, Beijing, 100083. Tel: (8610) 6205 1463 x 2059. Fax: (8610) 6205 1461.
Upsides: A much larger program than Bei Da. Easier to get into and offers greater scheduling flexibility. Offers both short and long programs. The enrollment process allows you to sign-up for a language class after your arrival in Beijing. Considered one of the two most popular places to study Mandarin in China (along with Bei Da).
Downsides: Offers fewer levels, only 4-5 to Bei Da's 19. Program's location, on the outskirts of Beijing proper, makes it difficult to access the city's business/expat community.

Beijing University (Bei Da)

Upsides: Considered the most prestigious Mandarin language program in China. Its name can serve as an attention-getter on your resume.
Downsides: Considered difficult to get into because of its formal application process. Limited enrollment and quite expensive. Enrollment must occur before you arrive to Beijing. Your application must be submitted through an intermediate agent/program (i.e. Council on International Education Exchange (CIEE) or UC Study Abroad Program).
Comments: Separate dormitories for foreign and Chinese students make interaction with native Mandarin speakers difficult and creates a tendency to speak English with the other foreign students. When encounters with Chinese students arise, they're intent on practicing English with you. Program's location (close to BLCU's) removes it from Beijing's business community.

Taiwan

The Mandarin Training Center at Taiwan Normal University (Shi Da)

Contact Information: *Office Address:* 6F, Po-Ai Building, #127-2, Ho-Ping E. Road, Sec. 1, Taipei. *Mailing Address:* #162, Ho-Ping E. Road, Sec. 1, Taipei. Tel: (886) (02) 2321-8405. Fax: (886) (02) 2341-8431.
Upsides: Considered the most popular program in Taipei. According to recent statistics, approximately half the people studying Mandarin in the city attend Shi Da. Teachers are certified and go through prior training. Offers an excellent social environment. Accredited by the Ministry of Education (MOE) and, therefore, offers resident visas and later Alien Resident Certificates (ARC) free of charge after four months of classes (good until you terminate enrollment).

Downsides: The program's large size does not allow it to tailor to individual needs. Not as flexible as TLI.

Comments: For many, the best way to start studying Mandarin because of the discipline it offers over privately-run programs. A relatively rigorous program. Group classes at lower rates (around NT$150/hour per person) tend to attract fresh college graduates. Most classes are 5-6 people, but can get as large as 7–10. Has a detailed registration process.

Taipei Language Institute (TLI)

Contact Information: 4F, 50 Roosevelt Rd., Sec.3, Taipei. Tel: (886) (02) 2367-8228/2367-2112. Fax: (886) (02) 2363-4857.

Upsides: For those who require focused learning, TLI is the most efficient and effective way to go. Popular with working professionals because of its one-on-one tutoring or small group instruction, flexible scheduling (i.e. offers early morning and late night classes, or you can set your own private lesson schedule), and custom-tailored classes. Programs are tailored to individual needs and learning speed (i.e. if you speak already, you can just concentrate on reading and writing). They'll teach according to the books and material you choose. You can study at your own pace, which may be faster than normal classes. If you miss a class, you can make it up later. Several branch locations around Taipei.

Downsides: Not recommended for those just starting out (much less structured than Shi-Da). Discipline and focus are up to the individual. You may also miss out on interaction opportunities with other students. A private language school, not accredited by MOE. Therefore, TLI does not offer resident visas and ARC, only semester-by-semester tourist visas*.

Comments: TLI teachers are trained and pass standards set by the institution. Many Japanese and Korean businessmen study there, as do American journalists. One-on-one classes are around NT$350/hour, or around NT$150-250/hour for semi-private classes. TLI has a website.

* *Tourist visa holders must apply for a visa extension every two months. The first time no questions are asked, but for a second extension you must submit proof of class attendance since your arrival in Taiwan. There are no third extensions. You must leave and re-enter the country after six months if you wish to stay longer.*

Stanford Program at Taiwan University (Tai Da)

Contact Information: *Office Address:* Language Building, Taiwan University campus. *Mailing Address:* P.O. Box 13-204, Taipei. Tel: (886) (02) 2363-9123. Fax: (886) (02) 2362-6926.

Upsides: Considered one of the best programs in the world.

Downsides: Subject matters tend to be "academic" and not necessarily applicable to the every day life. A certain percentage of students drop out each year from the intense demands of the program.

Comments: A rigorous, full-time, one year program divided into a fall, spring, and summer semesters. Most in the program are graduate students. Requires taking a placement test beforehand. Three students per class, four times a day. Around US$3,000/semester. Full-year resident visas and ARCs are provided for students. Recently, funding from Stanford University has shifted from Taiwan University to Beijing. The program's name has been changed to Tai-Da Inter-University Board (IUB).

* *All information confirmed as of February 1, 1998.*

Appendix VII Price Comparison On Common Supermarket Items

	Shanghai	Hong Kong	Taipei
Corn Flakes - 340 grams	RMB 44.30	HK$19.90	NT$107
Kellog's Mueslix	RMB 64.8	HK$33.40	NT$142
Lay's Chips	RMB 29.9	HK$15.80	NT$82
Doritos (7oz)	RMB 26.90	HK$17.50	NT$100
Peperidge Farm Milano Cookies	RMB 34.1	HK$16.80	NT$95
Peperidge Farm Goldfish - 6oz	RMB 28.90	HK$14.90	NT$95
Cambell's Soup	RMB 15.6-18.4	HK$6.50-8.50	NT$35-39
Heinekin (single can)	RMB 8.9	HK$7.70	NT$39
Taster's Choice, Original Blend - 175grams	RMB 140.5	HK$75.50	NT$195
Skippy Peanut Butter (Creamy) - 18oz	RMB 43.10	HK$23.20	NT$99
Haagen-Dazs - 474cc	RMB 60.00	HK$59.00	NT$190
M&M's, plain or peanut - 158.8 grams	RMB 17.60	HK$17.50	NT$48
Vidal Sassoon Shampoo - 400ml	RMB 68.50	HK$35.50	NT$129
Head & Shoulders - 400ml	RMB 41.10	HK$29.90	NT$140

* *Items priced at Wellcome supermarkets as of February 1, 1998.*

Appendix VIII Greater China Tax References

HONG KONG

Tax Filing Date: May 31
Tax Authority: Inland Revenue Department
Rate of Taxation: Hong Kong tax is calculated in one of two methods, whichever assigns the smaller liability

Progressive Tax Table for Resident Individuals:

Taxable Annual Income in HK$	Rate %	Tax on Lower Limit in HK $
0 - 20,000	2	—
20,001 - 40,000	9	400
40,001 - 60,000	17	2,200
60,000 and above	25	5,600

Flat Salaries Tax for Residents: 15% of net taxable income before deductibles

Individuals residing less than 60 days in Hong Kong in a calendar year for short-term employment are exempt from tax on their Hong Kong-source employment income.

TAIWAN

Tax Filing Date: March 31
Tax Authority: National Tax Administration
Rate of Taxation: Progressive Tax Structure

Tax Table for Resident Individuals:

Taxable Annual Income in NT$	Rate %	Tax on Lower Limit in NT$
0 - 330,000	6	0
330,001 - 890,000	12	23,100
890,001 - 1,780,000	21	94,3001
780,001 - 3,340,000	30	254,500
3,340,000 and above	40	588,500

Non-resident individuals (those residing less than 183 days in Taiwan in a calendar year) are taxed at a flat rate of 20% on Taiwan-source income.

MAINLAND CHINA

Tax Filing Date: Monthly
Tax Authority: National Taxation Bureau
Rate of Taxation: Progressive Tax Structure

Tax Table for Resident Individuals:

Taxable Annual Income in RMB	Rate %	Tax on Lower Limit in RMB
0 - 500	5	0
501 - 2,000	10	25
2,001 - 5,000	15	175
5,001 - 20,000	20	625
20,001 - 40,000	25	3,625
40,001 - 60,000	30	8,625
60,001 - 80,000	35	14,625
80,001 - 100,000	40	21,625
100,000 and above	45	29,625

U.S. Taxpayers: Things to Know

Everyone Must File

Leaving behind US life doesn't mean leaving behind US taxes. In addition to being subject to the tax regulations of the country in which you work, US Citizens and Residents are required to file an annual federal income tax return with the IRS. Failure to file may result in difficulties in renewing your passport or residency permit.

Foreign Earned Income Exclusion

US Citizens and Residents are entitled to a Foreign Earned Income Exclusion of up to US$70,000. To qualify for the Foreign Earned Income Exclusion, one must satisfy at least one of the following three conditions:

- Physical Presence Test – Reside outside of the U.S. for 330 days out of 12-month period and have a foreign tax home.
- Bona Fide Resident Test – Keep a tax home outside of the US for an uninterrupted period including an entire tax year.
- Tax Home Test – Must have a tax home in a foreign country which is generally your primary place of employment.

Filing Deadlines & Extensions

You qualify for an automatic extension of two months, until June 15th, to file and pay your federal income taxes if, on April 15th, you are living outside the US and Puerto Rico AND your main place of business is outside of the US and Puerto Rico.

IRS On-Line

Download all IRS booklets and forms, access recent tax changes, and ask specific questions on-line via the IRS' World Wide Web home page at "http://www.irs.ustreas.gov".

IRS' Asia Regional Office Contact Info

Internal Revenue Service
United States Embassy, Tokyo
10-5 Akasaka, 1-Chome, Minato-ku, Tokyo 107 Japan
Tel: +81-3-3224-5466 Fax: +81-3-3224-5274

A Comparative Income Tax Analysis

Currency Unit: US$
Individual Income Taxes**
Net Income After Taxes***

Net After Taxes	US/California		Taiwan		Hong Kong	
	Marginal Tax Rate	*Salary Base*	*Marginal Tax Rate*	*Salary Base*	*Marginal Tax Rate*** **	*Salary Base*
$25,000	28%/8%	$31,000	13%	$27,500	15%	$28,750
$50,000	31%/9.3%	$72,000	30%	$61,000	15%	$61,625
$100,000	36%/10%	$160,000	40%	$130,000	15%	$115,000
$150,000	36%/11%	$249,000	40%	$212,000	15%	$172,500

** *Tax figures are estimates only*
*** *US citizens are entitled to a foreign-earned income exclusion of maximum US$70,000*
**** *Based on total net income without allowances*

Appendix IX Greater China Salary Compensation Ranges*

	Taiwan	Hong Kong	Mainland China	Singapore
Finance				
Analyst (0-2 yrs)	$25,000-45,000	$35,000-50,000	$42,000-60,000	$32,000-45,000
Associate (2-5 yrs)	$45,000-80,000	$50,000-80,000	$60,000-96,000	$45,000-72,000
Fund Manager	$50,000-100,000	$90,000-120,000	$108,000-144,000	$90,000-120,000
Managing Directors	$90,000-200,000	$130,000-200,000	$156,000-240,000	$130,000-200,000
Information Technology				
Systems Engineer	$35,000-45,000	$38,000-51,000	$46,000-61,000	$35,000-46,000
Sales/Mktg Mgr	$50,000-100,000	$60,000-105,000	$72,000-126,000	$54,000-95,000
Managing Director	$96,000-200,000	$130,000-200,000	$156,000-240,000	$130,000-200,000
Consumer Products				
Marketing				
Asst Mgr (3+ yrs)	$30,000-45,000	$30,000-50,000	$36,000-60,000	$27,000-45,000
Manager (5+ yrs)	$45,000-80,000	$50,000-100,000	$45,000-100,000	
Advertising				
Account Executive	$18,000-30,000	$18,000-30,000	$22,000-36,000	$17,000-27,000
Account Manager	$34,000-48,000	$30,000-60,000	$45,000-72,000	$27,000-54,000
Account Director	$40,000-60,000	$60,000-100,000	$72,000-120,000	$54,000-100,000
Managing Director	$96,000-150,000	$100,000-150,000	$120,000-180,000	$100,000-150,000
Services				
Accounting				
Senior Auditor	$30,000-45,000	$40,000-60,000	$48,000-72,000	$36,000-54,000
Manager	$60,000-70,000	$60,000-90,000	$72,000-108,000	$54,000-81,000
Senior Manager	$70,000-80,000	$90,000-100,000	$110,000-120,000	$81,000-90,000
Consulting				
Consultant	$30,000-50,000	$40,000-60,000	$48,000-72,000	$40,000-60,000
Sr Consultant (4+ yrs)	$50,000-80,000	$90,000-120,000	$110,000-144,000	$90,000-120,000
Manager (7 yrs)	$80,000-100,000	$120,000-180,000	$144,000-216,000	$120,000-180,000

All figures in US dollars per annum.

* *Salary figures reflect the general salary conditions of a respective country. Ranges provided can be quite broad when factoring in commission & bonus structures, but do not include housing & other perks.*

Appendix X Hotels and Guest Houses

Hong Kong

Garden View International House

1 MacDonnell Road, Central
Tel: (852) 2877 3737
Single Room Rate: HK$616 + 10% service
Comments: 130 Rooms. Very nice, quality rooms. Located in a high-end residential area. 15-minute walk to Central district.

Booth Lodge

11 Wing Sing Lane, Yau Ma Tei, Kowloon
Tel: (852) 2771 9266
Single Room Rate: Summer – HK$620 + 10%
Comments: 53 Rooms. Simple, clean rooms. Affiliated with the Salvation Army. Breakfast included. Cozy restaurant. 15-minute MTR ride to Central district.

Harbour View International House

4 Harbour Road, Wan Chai
Tel: (852) 2802 0111
Single Room Rate: Summer HK$800 +10%
Comments: 320 Rooms. Nice, quality rooms. Next to the Hong Kong Convention Center, in the middle of the business district. A little less accessible to convenient transportation.

The Salisbury, YMCA

41 Salisbury Road, Tsim Sha Tsui, Kowloon
Tel: (852) 2369 2211
Single Room Rate: HK$880 + 10%
Comments: 380 Rooms. More like a four star hotel. Nice rooms. Right next to the MTR and shopping district. Very popular among western travelers. Book early.

Caritas Bianchi Lodge

4 Cliff Road, Yau Ma Tei, Kowloon
Tel: (852) 2388 1111
Single Room Rate: HK$450 + 10% (ask for discount dates)
Comments: 90 Rooms. Simple, clean rooms. 5-minute walk to MTR. Frequented by local business travelers.

Note: *Peak tourist season in Hong Kong is from August to December. Room rates during these months are especially high. For hotels, refer to reference section or the four city comparison.*

For airlines, peak season is from September to January for travel between NYC-HKG, NYC-TPE, SFO-HKG, and SFO-TPE. Call a travel agent in your local Chinatown district for the best packages and deals.

When you call the hotels, they'll always quote you their rack rates first. Make sure you ask for special seasonal rates, which can be up to 40–50% less than the rack rates.

Room rates quoted as of February 1, 1998.

Taipei

Hope City Hotel

Nos 275, Fuhsing S Road, Sec. 1, Taipei
Tel: (886) (02) 2703-9990
Fax: (886) (02) 2706-8547
Single Room Rate: NT$1,760, includes tax and breakfast
Comments: 60 Rooms

First Hotel

63, Nanking E. Road, Sec. 2, Taipei
Tel: (886) (02) 2541-8234
Fax: (886) (02) 2551-2277
Single Room Rate: NT$2,600, plus 10% service fee
Comments: 175 Rooms. A bit farther from central Taipei.

Volvo Hotel

Nos 9, Fuhsing S. Road, Sec. 2 Taipei
Tel: (886) (02) 2325-0722
Fax: (886) (02) 2702-8630
Single Room Rate: NT$1,980
Comments: 41 Rooms

The Hotel Dynasty

41, Fuhsing S. Road, Sec. 2, Taipei
Tel: (886) (02) 2708-1221
Fax: (886) (02) 2325-7265
Single Room Rate: NT$3,400, plus 10% service fee
Comments: 90 rooms. Convenient location to business districts and shopping areas. Two-minute walk from mass transit stop.

Sowa Hotel

156 Nanking E. Road, Sec. 4, Taipei
Tel: (886) (02) 2579-6162
Fax: (886) (02) 2577-9463
Single Room Rate: NT$2,250, includes tax
Comments: 78 Rooms. No restaurant. Convenient location to business districts and shopping areas.

Shanghai

Shanghai Education Hotel

3 Fenyang Road, Shanghai.
Tel: (86-21) 6466-0500
Fax: (86-21) 6466-3149
Single Room Rate: RMB$380
Comments: 32 Rooms. Small, simple local hotel, located next to Shanghai Music College. Frequented by students and budget travelers.

City Hotel Shanghai

Nos. 5-7 Shan Xi Road (South), Shanghai.
Tel: (86-21) 6255-1133
Fax: (86-21) 6255-0211
Single Room Rate: RMB$688, includes service fee
Comments: 264 Rooms. Local business hotel. Small, but nice rooms. Centrally located.

Shanghai Haigang Hotel

Nos. 89 Tai Xing Road, Shanghai
Tel: (86-21) 6255-3553
Fax: (86-21) 6255-0151
Single Room Rate: RMB$320, includes service fee
Comments: 88 Rooms. Small local business hotel. Simple, affordable rooms. Within two minutes walk of the Westgate Mall.

Beijing

Beijing International Hotel

Nos, 9 Jianguo Mennei Dajie, Beijing.
Tel: (86-10) 6512-6688
Fax: (86-10) 6522-8777
Single Room Rate: RMB$630, plus 15% service fee
Comments: 1,008 Rooms. Excellent international four star hotel. Modern facilities. Nice rooms.

Golden Era Hotel

No, 1 South Dongsanhuan Road, Beijing.
Tel: (86-10) 6778-2255
Fax: (86-10) 6775-3886
Single Room Rate: RMB$500, plus 10% service fee
Comments: 101 Rooms. Small, but clean hotel. Mostly frequented by budget travelers.

Asia Vision Hotel

75 Chong Nei Street, Dong Cheng District, Beijing.
Tel: (86-10) 6513-2288
Fax: (86-10) 6513-6809
Single Room Rate: RMB$830, plus 15% service fee
Comments: 400 Rooms. A clean and nice local hotel. Near the Beijing train station.

Chong Wen Men Hotel Beijing

Nos. 2 West Chong Wen Men Street, Beijing.
Tel: (86-10) 6512-2211
Fax: (86-10) 6512-2122
Single Room Rate: RMB$480, plus 10% service fee
Comments: 300 Rooms. Similar to the Golden Era Hotel, except more centrally located. Near the Beijing train station.

Bibliography

Ayala, Jim, and Richard Lai. *The McKinsey Quarterly.* 1996. Number 3

Chan, Yvonne. "Adviser opens doors to Asia." *South China Morning Post.* 18 March 1997.

Deal, Helen, and Jim Plouffe. "Change Is In The Air." Ninth Annual Executive Compensation Survey. *World Executive's Digest.* April 1997.

Der, Henry. "The Glass Ceiling: New Era of Civil Rights Activism?" Affirmative Action Policy. 1992

Einhorn, Bruce. "Schools: No Tiger." *Business Week.* 9 June 1997.

Engardio, Pete. "Why Multinationals Are So Gung Ho." *Business Week.* 9 June 1997.

Enright, Michael J. "Even more than before, it's worth betting on Hong Kong." *AsianBusiness.* 1997.

Enright, Michael, Edith Scott, and David Dodwell. *The Hong Kong Advantage.* Hong Kong: Oxford University Press (China) Ltd., 1997.

Gilley, Bruce. "Regional Politik." *Far Eastern Economic Review.* 29 May 1997.

Nisha, Gopalan. "Age of the expat ends as old China hands lose their touch." *South China Morning Post.* 6 April 1997.

Granitsas, Alkman, and Trish Saywell. "Managing Barely." *Far Eastern Economic Review.* 28 August 1997

Healy, Tim. "Mainland Lessons." *Asiaweek.* 14 February 1997.

Hibbard, Peter. *The Odyssey Illustrated Guide To Shanghai.* Third Addition. Hong Kong: The Guidebook Company Ltd, 1995.

Keating, John. Two Billion Armpits. Hong Kong: Hambalan Press, 1996.

Kuo, Debbie. "Telecom market to be fully open by 2001." *Central News Agency.* 8 May 1997.

Lau, Annie. "Hiring the professional way." *China Commercial News.* December 1996.

Leung, James. "Slaughtering the sacred cow." *Asian Business.* May 1997.

Linn, Eugene. "The Power of Money." *Far Eastern Economic Review.* 15 May 1997.

Lipper, Hal. "Employers Maneuver to Help Expats Survive China." *The Asian Wall Street Journal.* 16 September 1997.

Naisbitt, John. *Megatrends Asia.* New York: Touchtone, 1997.

Orr, Deborah. "Bank expansions stall." *South China Morning Post.* 6 October 1997.

Ramachandran, Devi. "Asia urged to think more creatively." *The China Post.* 15 June 1997.

Shinagawa, Larry. The Impact of Immigration on Demography.

Stevens, Andrew. "Expats' golden era at an end." *South China Morning Post.* 25 September 1994.

Tripathi, Salil. "Who Needs Stanford?" *Asia, Inc.* September 1996.

Tung, Lily. "A foot in the door." *Asian Business.* January 1997.

Valles, Eric. "Vendors jockey for position in booming wireless phone market." *China News.* 16 January 1997.

Yip, Alethea. "Careers on the Fast Track." *AsianWeek.* 7-13 March 1997.

"Local service sector grows, but behind HK." *The China News.* 1 May 1997.

"Shanghai takes shape." *The Economist.* 3 May 1997.

1997 Beijing Scene Guidebook. Beijing Scene Publishing, 1997.

Executive Summary. *The Glass Ceiling Commission.* January 1996.